Poverty Targeting in Asia

Edited by

John Weiss

*Research Director, Asian Development Bank Institute,
Tokyo, Japan*

A JOINT PUBLICATION OF THE ASIAN DEVELOPMENT BANK
INSTITUTE AND EDWARD ELGAR PUBLISHING

Edward Elgar

Cheltenham, UK • Northampton, MA, USA

Published by
Edward Elgar Publishing Limited
Glensanda House
Montpellier Parade
Cheltenham
Glos GL50 1UA
UK

Edward Elgar Publishing, Inc.
136 West Street
Suite 202
Northampton
Massachusetts 01060
USA

A catalogue record for this book
is available from the British Library

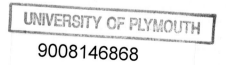
ISBN 1 84542 123 X (cased)

Printed and bound in Great Britain by MPG Books Ltd, Bodmin, Cornwall

Contents

Contributors

Arsenio Balisacan is Professor of Economics at the University of the Philippines-Diliman and Director of the Southeast Asian Regional Center for Graduate Study and Research in Agriculture, Manila.

Rosemarie Edillon is Executive Director of the Asia-Pacific Policy Center, Manila.

Elvira Kurmanalieva is a Research Associate at the Asian Development Bank Institute, Tokyo.

John Maxwell is a Fellow at the Research School of Pacific and Asian Studies, Australian National University, Canberra.

Heather Montgomery is a Research Fellow at the Asian Development Bank Institute, Tokyo.

Ari A. Perdana is a Researcher at the Center for Strategic and International Studies, Jakarta.

Isra Sarntisart is Professor of Economics at Chulalongkorn University, Thailand.

Pradeep Srivastava is Chief Economist at the National Council for Applied Economic Research, New Delhi.

Wang Sangui is a Senior Researcher and Professor at the Institute of Agricultural Economics, Chinese Academy of Agricultural Sciences, Beijing.

Peter Warr is John Crawford Professor of Agricultural Economics at the Research School of Pacific and Asian Studies, Australian National University, Canberra.

John Weiss is Director of Research at the Asian Development Bank Institute, Tokyo. He is on long-term leave from the University of Bradford, UK, where he is Professor of Development Economics.

Preface

As a subsidiary of the Asian Development Bank, the Asian Development Bank Institute (ADBI) is committed to a program of research and capacity building that supports the Bank's overarching goal of poverty reduction in Asia. As an important part of this work, in 2003 a series of studies were undertaken on the effectiveness of various measures aimed at channeling resources directly at the poor and vulnerable – so-called 'poverty targeting'. Five important countries were selected for study – India, Indonesia, the People's Republic of China, the Philippines and Thailand. The results of this work were discussed at an internal workshop in Tokyo in November 2003 and the final drafts were produced in mid-2004. Edited versions of these are presented here as country chapters.

In addition in 2003 ADBI commenced work on issues relating to micro-finance with a major conference on this topic held in Tokyo in December 2003. The final chapter of this volume was presented at that conference as a survey of knowledge on the impact of micro-finance institutions on poverty in Asia.

ADBI will be pursuing these topics in more depth in the future, but we are delighted at this stage to be able to publish our material internationally through this joint publication with Edward Elgar Publishing.

I wish to acknowledge the help of colleagues at ADBI in putting this volume together, particularly Reiko Nishiura, who tidied up all the files. The efforts of all our country authors are also gratefully acknowledged.

John Weiss
Director of Research,
Asian Development Bank Institute.

Abbreviations

AAY	*Antyodaya Anna Yojana*
ACC/SCN	Administrative Committee on Co-ordination/Sub-committee on Nutrition
ADBI	Asian Development Bank Institute
ALEK	*Alasan Ekonomi* (for economic reasons)
ASA	Associations for Social Advancement
BAPPENAS	*Badan Perencana Pembangunan Nasional* (National Development Planning Board)
BIDS	Bangladesh Institute of Development Studies
BKB	Bangladesh Krishi Bank
BKK	*Badan Kredit Kecamatan* (sub-district credit board)
BKKBN	*Badan Koordinasi Keluarga Berencana Nasional* (National Family Planning Co-ordinating Board)
BP3	*Badan Pembantu Penyelenggara Pendidikan* (Board of Education Assistance)
BPS	*Badan Pusat Statistik* (Central Bureau of Statistics)
BRAC	Bangladesh Rural Advancement Committee
BRDB	Bangladesh Rural Development Board
BRI	Bank Rakyat Indonesia
Bulog	*Badan Usaha Logistik* (National Logistics Board)
CAG	Comptroller and Auditor General of India
CARP	Comprehensive Agrarian Reform Program
CEO	Chief Executive Officer
CIDSS	Comprehensive and Integrated Delivery of Social Services
CIMU	Central Independent Monitoring Unit
CPI	Consumer Price Index
CSS	Centrally Sponsored Schemes
DDP	Desert Development Program
Desa	Village
DPAP	Drought Prone Areas Program
EAS	Employment Assurance Scheme
EGS	Employment Guarantee Scheme

ESCAP	Economic and Social Commission for Asia and the Pacific
FAO	Food and Agriculture Organization
GDP	Gross Domestic Product
GMA	*Gamot na Mabisa Abot-Kaya* (Affordable Medicine for All)
GOI	Government of India
IAY	*Indira Awas Yojana*
ICDS	Integrated Child Development Services Scheme
IDT	*Inpres Desa Tertinggal* (Presidential Decree on Neglected Villages)
IFAD	International Fund for Agricultural Development
IMF	International Monetary Fund
IMI	International Management Institute, Orissa
INPRES	*Instruksi Presiden* (Presidential Decree)
IRDP	Integrated Rural Development Program
IWDP	Integrated Wastelands Development Program
JGSY	*Jawahar Gram Samridhi Yojana*
JPKM	*Jaminan Pelayanan Kesehatan Masyarakat* (Community Health Care Guarantee Program)
JPS-BK	*Jaring Pengaman Sosial-Bidang Kesehatan* (Social Safety Net-Health Sector)
JRY	*Jawahar Rozgar Yojana*
Kabupaten	District
KALAHI	*Kapit-Bisig Laban sa Kahirapan*
KDP/PPK	Kecamatan Development Program/*Program Pembangunan Kecamatan*
Kecamatan	Sub-district
kg	kilograms
KPS	*Keluarga Pra-Sejahtera* (Pre-prosperous Family)
KS	*Keluarga Sejahtera* (Prosperous Family)
KURK	*Kredit Usaha Rakyat Kecil* (Credit for Activities of the Poor, East Java)
KVIC	Khadi and Village Industries Commission
LGPR	The Leading Group for Poverty Reduction
MAKER	Mathura Krishna Foundation for Economic and Social Opportunity and Human Resource Management
MBN	Minimum Basic Needs
MDG	Millennium Development Goals
MFI	Micro-finance Institution
NBS	National Bureau of Statistics, formerly State Statistics Bureau

NESDB	National Economic and Social Development Board
NFA	National Food Authority
NGO	Non-Governmental Organization
NOAPS	National Old Age Pension Scheme
NSAP	National Social Assistance Program
NSDP	National Slum Development Program
OECD	Organization for Economic Co-operation and Development
OPK	*Operasi Pasar Khusus* (Special Market Operations)
ORG	Operations Research Group
P2KP	*Program Penanggulangan Kemiskinan Perkotaan* (Urban Poverty Alleviation Program)
P3DT	*Pembangunan Prasarana Pendukung Desa Tertinggal* (Supporting Infrastructure Development for Neglected Villages)
PCF	People's Credit Fund
PDI	Planning and Development Initiatives, for Planning Commission, Government of India
PDM-DKE	*Pemberdayaan Daerah dalam Mengatasi Dampak Krisis Ekonomi* (Empowering the Regions to Overcome the Impact of the Economic Crisis)
PDS	Public Distribution System
PEO	Program Evaluation Organization, Planning Commission, Government of India
PG	Poverty Gap
PKDP	*Padat Karya Desa* Program (Labor-intensive Development Program)
Podes	*Potensi Desa* (Village Potential)
Pokmas	*Kelompok Masyarakat* (Community Groups)
PRC	People's Republic of China
PTCCS	Primary Thrift and Credit Co-operative Society
Puskesmas	*Pusat Kesehatan Masyarakat* (Community Health Center)
R&D	Research and Development
RAKUB	*Rajshahi Krishni Unnayan* Bank
Raskin	*Beras untuk Keluarga Miskin* (Rice for Poor Families)
REECS	Resources, Environment and Economics Center for Studies, Incorporated
REGP	Rural Employment Generation Programme
Repelita	*Rencana Pembangunan Lima Tahun* (Five-year Development Plan)
RMB	Yuan, Chinese currency

Rp	*Rupiah,* Indonesian currency
RPS	Retention Pricing Scheme
Rs	Rupees
SC	Scheduled Caste
SEWA	Self Employed Women's Association
SGP	Scholarships and Grants Program
SGRY	*Sampoorna Grameen Rozgar Yojana*
SGSY	*Swarn Jayanti Gram Swarozgar Yojana*
SMERU	Social Monitoring and Early Response Unit
SPG	Squared Poverty Gap
ST	Scheduled Tribe
SUSENAS	*Survey Sosial Ekonomi Nasional* (National Socio-Economic Survey)
TCE	Targeting Count Error
TCG	Targeting Count Gap
TIE	Targeting Income Error
TIG	Targeting Income Gap
TRDEP	Thana Resource Development and Employment Project
UNDP	United Nations Development Program
UNICEF	United Nations Children's Fund
USAID	United States Agency for International Development
VAM	Vulnerability Analysis and Mapping
VBA	Vietnam Bank of Agriculture
VBP	Vietnam Bank for the Poor
VIP	Village Infrastructure Project
WHO	World Health Organization
WNT	*West Nusa Tenggara*

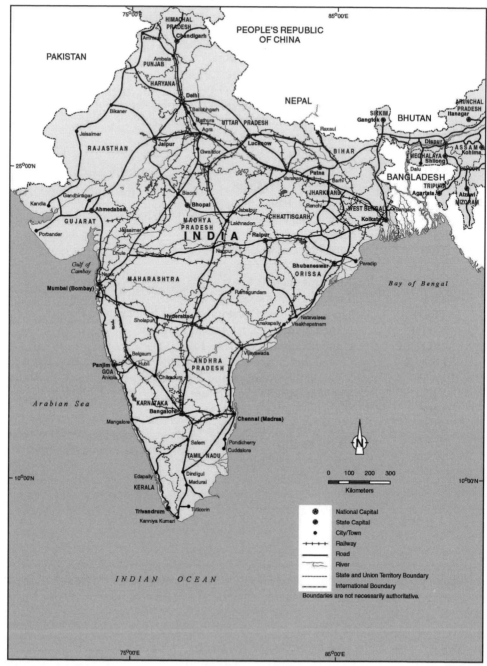

Map of India

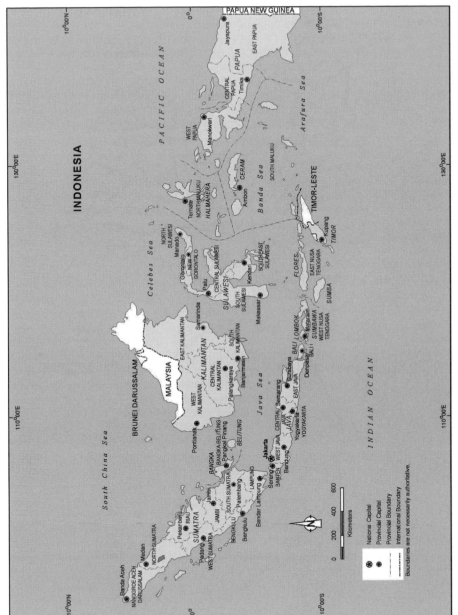

Map of Indonesia

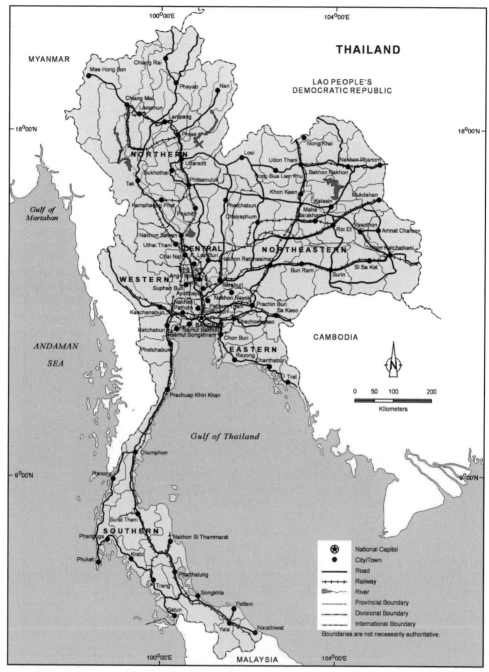

Map of Thailand

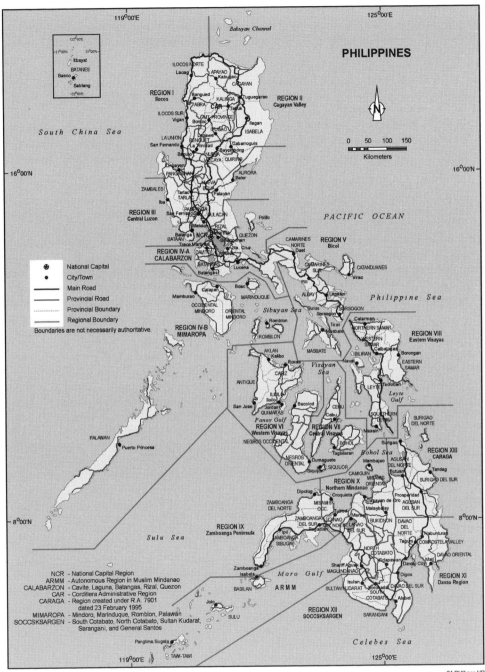

Map of the Philippines

xvii

1. Experiences with poverty targeting in Asia: an overview

John Weiss

INTRODUCTION

Poverty targeting can be thought of as the use of policy instruments to channel resources to a target group identified below an agreed national poverty line. In principle, these resources can be either for protectional (to maintain welfare in the face of adverse shocks) or promotional (to help raise welfare in the long term) purposes. Whilst debates concerning targeting versus universalistic approaches to social benefits have a very extensive history, they achieved prominence in the development context only in the later 1980s. At that time with government budgets in many countries under serious pressure, questions were raised concerning the effectiveness of broadly-based subsidy schemes that often benefited the poor far less than the better-off (the 'non-poor'). The World Development Report of 1990 (World Bank, 1990) summarized evidence on the degree of leakage from general subsidies and stressed the importance of a labor-intensive pattern of growth and the development of the human capital of the poor, combined with targeted social safety net measures, as the long-run solution to poverty. Broadly speaking this view has remained the conventional wisdom.[1]

This volume surveys the experiences with poverty targeting in a number of large economies in South Asia (India) and South East Asia (Thailand, Philippines and Indonesia) as well as in the People's Republic of China (PRC). In some of these countries poverty targeting has a relatively long history stemming from longstanding social welfare concerns (India and to some extent the Philippines and PRC), whilst elsewhere it originated principally in the late 1990s in response to the impact of the regional Financial Crisis (Thailand and Indonesia). The focus is principally on measures that provide subsidized food, employment, access to health and other social facilities and occasionally cash transfers. The use of micro-finance is considered separately in Chapter 7 of this volume.[2] The country studies that are chapters in this volume present information on these interventions in considerable detail. In India and Indonesia there is a very extensive 'grey cover' literature on the impact of targeted interventions, and the country studies survey these official or quasi-official evaluations. In the Philippines, PRC and Thailand there are fewer official evaluations of targeting measures available and the country authors draw heavily on their own work in assessing poverty impact. This opening chapter brings together the results from the selected country cases and also draws on the wider literature on poverty and development. To clarify some of the issues it begins with an introduction to the theory and practice of targeting.

THE THEORY AND CLASSIFICATION OF TARGETING

A basic distinction in the targeting literature is between two forms of error, that of undercoverage, that is the failure to reach some of the target group, and of leakage, that is where benefits accrue to those outside the target group. Following statistical terminology these are termed 'type 1' and 'type 2' errors, respectively. Practical application of targeting measures inevitably involves some trade-off between these two errors. For example to minimize undercoverage or type 1 error, more generous means of assessing eligibility may be used, whilst to minimize leakage or type 2 error, stricter criteria may be applied, and if these are not specified or applied correctly they may serve to exclude some of the target group. The social costs of the two types of error need to be compared and arguably the poorer a society, the more serious will be errors of omission or undercoverage relative to the costs of leakage (Cornia and Stewart, 1993).

Figure 1.1 illustrates the alternative possibilities with the areas labeled C and D corresponding to type 1 and type 2 errors, respectively. Another way of expressing this information is to identify the targeting ratio, that is the share of the non-poor (or non-target group) in benefits, relative to their share in total population. The closer this ratio gets to unity, the weaker will be the effectiveness of targeting.

In terms of theory, the comparison between a universalistic and a targeted approach has been analyzed by Besley and Kanbur (1991) and here we follow their presentation. If the poverty line is set at income level z and individuals have incomes of y then an ideal targeting solution would be transfer amounts of $z-y$ varying between individuals depending upon their initial income level. In this way all would be brought to the poverty line. The costs of transfers would have to be borne by those above the poverty line. Figure 1.2 illustrates this, showing initial income on the horizontal axis and income after the transfer on the vertical. For points on the 45-degree line

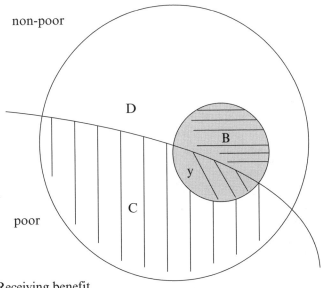

non-poor

poor

□ Receiving benefit
y   Target group receiving benefit
B   Non-target group receiving benefit
C   Target group not receiving benefit
D   Non-target group not receiving benefit

Note: Targeting ratio is share of non-poor in benefits divided by share of non-poor in total population, or B/(A+B) divided by (D + B)/(A + B + C +D).

Figure 1.1   Two types of error in poverty targeting

initial and post-transfer income are equal. Line 1 shows the post-transfer outcome in relation to initial income. Those below the poverty line z receive a total transfer equal to the shaded area and those above face a tax, as their post-transfer income is below their initial income. The fiscal cost will be the sum of $z - y$ for all in poverty initially. In contrast a universal approach transfers the same sum to everyone. If poverty is to be alleviated fully and the marginal poor person has zero income (because they rely on a share of the family income) the transfer will be z per person and this will entail a much higher fiscal cost, which will be z times the population.

Figure 1.3 illustrates this case with (as before) the shaded area giving the amount of transfer. Those with initial incomes below z gain the full transfer, whilst taxes are imposed on those above the poverty line, so their gain is z minus the additional tax they must pay; at income level y^* individuals will

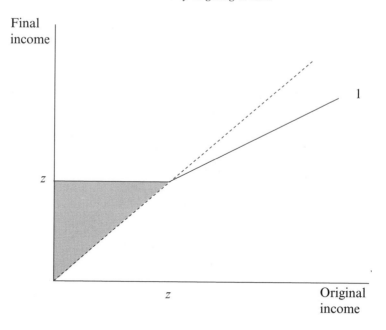

Figure 1.2   'Perfect targeting': the ideal solution

start to lose from the scheme as extra taxes will exceed z. There is leakage
to the non-poor at income levels between z and y^*. Such leakage is the 'type
2' statistical error in the poverty literature, but undercoverage (or type 1
error) will be zero, as all are brought up to the poverty line.

Given the relatively high leakage and the fiscal costs involved, universal
transfers may appear obviously unattractive. However in any real world
situation there are also difficulties with the 'ideal solution' of Figure 1.2.

- There are practical problems of lack of information concerning
  beneficiaries, so that the initial incomes (the y's) are not known
  accurately. Hence the need for indicators of poverty that should be
  correlated with income. We discuss below approximate ways used in the
  past in the country cases to identify the poor. Where not all of the poor
  can be identified and reached, there are potentially serious problems
  of omission from targeting schemes (the undercoverage rate), which
  by definition should be absent in universalistic approaches. Hence, as
  noted above, the social costs of errors 1 and 2 need to be compared.
- There can be costs to individuals of their participation in targeted
  programs – for example psychic costs arising from social stigma or cost
  in terms of time for travel or in the provision of information. In terms

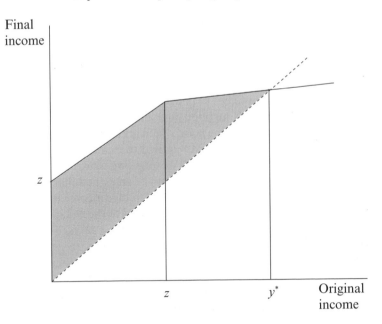

Figure 1.3   A universal scheme

of the ideal solution in Figure 1.2, if costs are c per person, then those
of the poor with an income above $z-c$ will choose not to participate
in a targeted program, so that those with an income between z and
$z-c$ will remain below the poverty line. Universal schemes may also
impose costs, and individuals may choose not to participate, but the
expectation is that such costs will be lower per dollar of benefit.

- Incentive effects can undermine the impact of a finely targeted program
since in the 'ideal solution' the marginal tax rate is 100 per cent for the
poor. This arises since any shortfall in income below the poverty line
is to be covered by a transfer, and if incomes rise the transfer will fall
to match this. Hence if marginal tax rates influence the poor in their
productive activity there is a serious problem of dependence.

- Finely targeted schemes imply high administrative costs for their
operation and in general there will be an expectation that the more
finely targeted these are (that is the lower is the degree of leakage)
the higher will be the ratio of administrative costs to benefits to the
poor. This has the important implication that the optimal degree of
targeting need not be to aim for the minimum degree of leakage since
the costs of such targeting need to be compared with the benefits. We
can illustrate this simply in Figure 1.4 where the horizontal axis shows

the degree of targeting – that is the share of benefits going to the poor
– from an intervention. This ranges from a low but positive figure
(T min), since the poor will gain something from any non-targeted
activity, to just below 100 per cent, since zero leakage to the non-poor
is implausible. The vertical axis gives monetary values of cost and
benefits per dollar received by the poor. Line A shows the relationship
between increasingly finely targeted interventions and administrative
costs per dollar of benefit to the poor, which is assumed to rise steeply.
There will be some minimum cost required to establish any scheme,
which is shown as C min. Unit costs of targeting must be compared
with B, which is the marginal social benefit of an extra dollar going to
the poor as compared with someone at the average income level. This
value must exist conceptually, provided benefits to the non-poor have
a positive social value (implying a trade-off between gains to different
groups). B is drawn as declining with the accuracy of targeting and
the intersection between the curves A and B gives the optimal degree
of targeting T^*.

• Finally in political economy terms since only the poor gain, in
comparison with a universalistic approach there may be no influential
political constituency arguing for targeted schemes. This raises the
potential paradox that programs with a high leakage may have strong

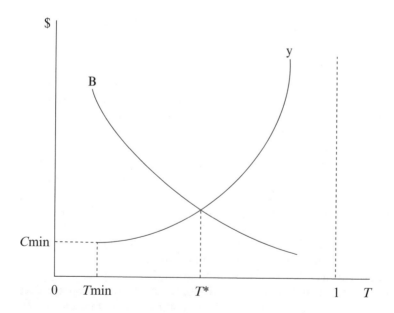

Figure 1.4   Optimal targeting

political support, due to gains by a politically influential middle class, which sustains a higher level of program expenditure than would be otherwise possible. It is thus conceivable that in absolute terms the poor may gain more from a universal scheme than from a more finely targeted one.

The strong implication of these points is that whilst concerns over leakage and budgetary costs may undermine the case for a universalistic solution, methods of targeting must balance costs, associated particularly with administration and incentives, against gains to the poor. The test for targeting measures therefore becomes one of cost effectiveness where the objective is to create income or income equivalent gains for as many of the poor as possible at the minimum cost.

The country cases shed considerable light on issues of leakage and undercoverage, but other aspects noted here remain unclear. For example, there is little evidence from the country cases surveyed on the quantitative importance of either costs to the poor from participation in targeting schemes or of incentive effects. Also estimates of benefits to the poor, in terms of income, consumption or welfare changes, relative to costs, are rarely available to allow precise comparisons between alternative targeting schemes. However in a few cases there are data on costs of transferring income to the poor, for example from employment creation schemes or food subsidies. In the absence of this type of data it is difficult to estimate the optimal degree of targeting. Finally, the studies do confirm the political economy problem of generating support for targeting. The relatively low amount of resources devoted to targeting schemes in all of the countries indicates a problem with generating an influential political constituency for these measures.

Classification of Targeting Measures

A wide variety of measures have been applied over the last two decades as a means of reaching the poor and these can be classified in different ways (World Bank, 2000: 85). The following four-fold classification is used commonly;

- *Targeting by activity*, such as primary health care and primary education, where it is established that the distribution of benefits tends to be progressive. It has become commonplace to argue that these types of activity should have priority over, for example, urban hospitals or higher education on the grounds of the lower uptake of the latter services by the poor. This has been termed 'broad targeting', as compared with narrower forms of targeting that attempt to identify the poor more precisely.

- *Targeting by indicator*, where alternatives to income, which may be expected to be correlated with poverty, are used to identify the poor. These can include lack of or size of ownership of land, form of dwelling, and type of household, for example number of children or gender of the head of the family.
- *Targeting by location*, where area of residence becomes the criterion for identifying the target group, as a particular form of indicator targeting. Poor area programs, where all residents are assumed to be poor, have become relatively common and for example were a central element in poverty reduction initiatives in PRC.
- *Targeting by self-selection or self targeting*, where programs are designed to be attractive only to the poor. An example is workfare, where payment is either in cash or in food, at equivalent wage rates that are below market-clearing levels and therefore only of interest to those with an opportunity cost below the market wage. Another self-selection procedure is the subsidization of low quality foodstuffs (like high-broken rice).

Measuring Poverty

The standard approach is to establish a poverty line, normally reflecting a minimum necessary standard of living (or that adequate for a minimum calorie intake), and to identify who falls below this line. Establishing the poverty line can be complex, and the Appendix to Chapter 4 discusses the experience in PRC, where there has been considerable discussion about the level and trend in the poverty line. Once such a line is available there are alternative ways of quantifying the degree of poverty. Of these the simplest and most widely cited is the 'headcount index', which gives the proportion of the population below the poverty line.

For our country cases Figures 1.5 to 1.9 show the official estimates of the poverty headcount (proportion of the population below the official national poverty line) for each country.[3] As they are based on different poverty lines the estimates are not directly comparable across countries. They show that poverty remains very high in India and the Philippines and by official figures is now very low in PRC (although as we have noted the accuracy of the official poverty line used in PRC is widely disputed) (Riskin et al., 2001). In all countries however there is a downward trend in poverty estimates and it is the role of targeting programs in this process that we examine.

However, more sophisticated indicators are also available and are drawn on in the country studies. These aim to assess the depth of poverty (that is

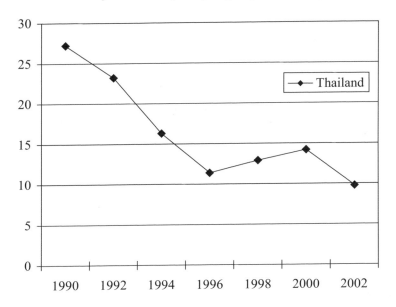

Figure 1.5   Poverty headcount (%): Thailand

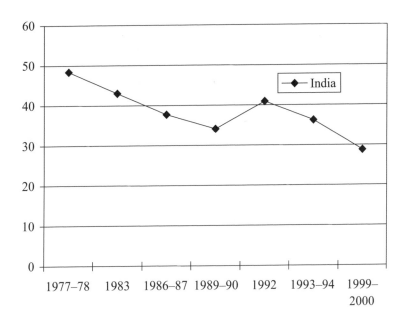

Figure 1.6   Poverty headcount (%): India

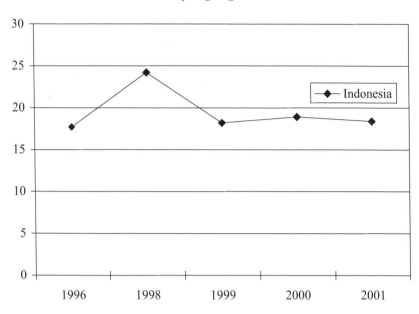

Figure 1.7   Poverty headcount (%): Indonesia

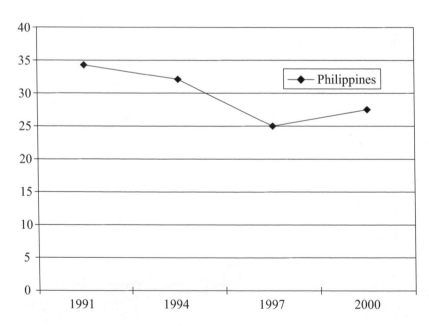

Figure 1.8   Poverty headcount (%): Philippines

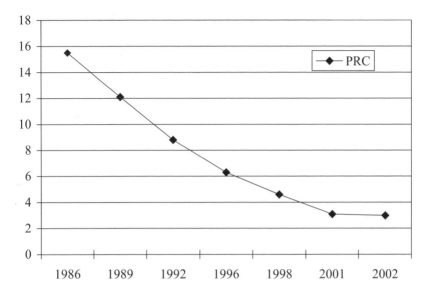

Figure 1.9   Poverty headcount (%): PRC

how far on average the poor are from the poverty line) and the severity of poverty (that is the distribution of income or consumption within the group of the poor). The depth of poverty is captured by the 'poverty gap' measure, which is the difference between the income (or consumption) of a poor individual, and the income (or consumption) poverty line as a proportion of the poverty line, aggregated for all of those in poverty and then divided by the total population. Hence a poverty gap of 0.2 should be interpreted to mean that averaged over the whole population the living standard of the poor is 20 per cent below the poverty line. Hence, assuming away targeting problems, the cost of removing poverty totally will be 20 per cent of the poverty line multiplied by the total population.[4]

A variant of the poverty gap that reflects distribution within the poor is the squared poverty gap, which is calculated in the same way, except for the important difference that the gap between the income of a poor individual and the poverty line as a proportion of the line is squared, so that the larger gaps are given a greater relative weight in the indicator.[5] Hence for a given average income of the poor, a worse distribution within the poor will result in a higher value of this indicator, capturing a greater severity of poverty. This indicator also has the convenient property that it is decomposable, so that it can be calculated for different subgroups in the population, and total poverty can be derived by weighting this poverty indicator for each subgroup by their population share.

As they offer different types of information, often all three indicators are calculated for individual countries and their trends over time tracked. However, the basic headcount indicator and the squared poverty gap can give quite different perspectives because of the latter's incorporation of a distributional dimension.

Errors of targeting can in principle arise for several reasons; inaccurate specification of who are in fact poor; poorly designed programs that do not reach the target group even if it is known accurately; and poor governance in the implementation of schemes so that benefits leak to the non-poor. Since targeting in its broad and narrow sense has been widely used over the past two decades there is now a relatively long record of experience that can be surveyed to attempt to establish generalizations about the effectiveness or otherwise of particular measures. Experiences in our five case-study countries suggest that errors have been significant and that in some cases these programs have had only a minor impact on poverty reduction.

The rest of this chapter is structured as follows. The second section looks at the scale of resources devoted to poverty-targeting measures in the different countries and how this has changed over time. The third section examines the criteria used in the different cases to identify who are 'the poor'. The fourth section looks at the type 1 and 2 errors associated with different forms of targeting, looking in particular at the effectiveness of the most common measures – location targeting, self-targeting, and broad targeting. These errors raise questions about governance and the capacity of states to mount effective targeting policies. The final section looks at poverty reduction in the countries covered and the role of targeted measures in the process.

HOW IMPORTANT HAVE POVERTY-TARGETING MEASURES BEEN IN MONETARY TERMS?

This question is important not just in assessing the overall impact of such expenditures on the poor, but also in terms of the potential trade-off between poverty alleviation and economic growth. In most countries, however, the scale of public poverty-focused expenditures has not been large enough to raise the issue of a potential or actual trade-off. India is the country with the longest record of poverty-focused interventions and of our cases the one where such expenditures appear to have taken the highest share of the budget of central and state or local governments. Estimation of total expenditure on poverty-targeted programs in India is difficult because of the variety of schemes and the range of financing whether at the central, state or district level. Excluding fertilizer subsidies, which are not explicitly targeted at poor farmers, Srivastava (Chapter 2 in this volume) estimates expenditure on the largest targeted programs to be about Rs 411 billion in 2001–02 (which is about 11 per cent of the central government expenditure and 2 per cent of GDP).[6] If fertilizer subsidies are treated as poverty-targeted interventions the proportions rise to 15 per cent and 3 per cent, respectively. Another estimate of the time trend of this expenditure suggests a rise of about 50 per cent in real terms over the 1990s with the main increase between 1992–93 and 1993–94 (Shariff et al., 2002).

In PRC since the mid 1980s, when the responsibility for poverty reduction initiatives was centralized in the Leading Group for Poverty Reduction of the State Council, three types of funds are categorized in official statistics as central government poverty reduction funds – subsidized loans, workfare programs and budgetary funds for poor counties. In 2002 these were RMB 29.1 billion showing a real average annual growth since 1986 of around 6 per cent. Most of this real increase came after 1996 and the real value of these funds almost trebled between 1996 and 2002 (Wang, Chapter 4 in this volume, Table 4.2). There are also poverty expenditures by local governments and government departments that might be as much as 25 per cent of the central government poverty expenditure (or around another RMB 7.5 billion). In combination, this estimate of RMB 37 billion is 5 per cent of the central government budget in 2002. Over the period 1986–2002 central government poverty expenditure has averaged 5 per cent of the budget and no more than 0.2 per cent of GDP (Wang, Chapter 4 in this volume, Table 4.2).

In Indonesia there have been a variety of targeted measures broadly covering employment creation, food subsidies, and education and health provision for the poor. The main program to pre-date the Financial Crisis of the late 1990s was a poor village credit scheme introduced in 1994 (the Inpres Desa Tertinggal or IDT), which had a budget of around $200 million annually over 1994–96 (Perdana and Maxwell, Chapter 3 in this volume). The IDT reached around 20 000 villages and was designed around a small-scale revolving fund as credits were to be repaid and relent in the targeted poor villages. Although it is difficult to obtain data on the costs of all schemes in 1998–99 at their peak, approximate estimates suggest that they might have taken around 9 per cent of the central government budget (Perdana and Maxwell, Chapter 3 in this volume, Table 3.5).

In Thailand government poverty reduction programs have focused on cash and in-kind (principally health facility) transfers to poor families, and interest-free loans for either productive activities or education. Over the 1990s these programs in total rose from 1.1 per cent (in 1993) to 4.6 per cent (in 2000) of central government expenditure (Warr and Sarntisart, Chapter 5 in this volume, Table 5.8). However, the education loans program is controversial and there is some dispute as to whether it is poverty-focused. If it is excluded, the increase in poverty-related expenditure is from 1.1 per cent to 3.3 per cent of total central government expenditure. Since 2000 the government definition of poverty-focused expenditure has been widened considerably with the result that now officially a significantly higher proportion of expenditures are seen as poverty programs. Under this wider definition these activities took 10 per cent of central government expenditure in 2000 rising to around 13 per cent in 2003 (Warr and Sarntisart, Chapter 5 in this volume, Table 5.11).

In the Philippines a range of anti-poverty programs have been applied with different approaches and nomenclature used by different administrations. Location targeting has been important in identifying where schemes would function. Funds are provided for a range of services identified by communities themselves. There is also a rice subsidy program for farmers and consumers implemented by the National Food Authority (NFA) and a scheme to provide a limited range of free drugs to the poor. Even including the food subsidy activities of the NFA total direct poverty-focused expenditure was not more than 1.5 per cent of total central government expenditure in the immediate pre-Crisis period in 1997–98 and no more than 0.3 per cent of GDP. In the years since then, government social sector expenditure on all categories has fallen as a proportion of GDP and real government health and education expenditure has fallen in per capita terms, although data on actual poverty targeted expenditure are not available (Balisacan and Edillon, Chapter 6 in this volume).

IDENTIFICATION OF THE POOR

Apart from self-targeting and the use of broad targeting, which focuses on particular categories of activities rather than their users, other forms of targeting, by definition, require inclusion and exclusion criteria, so that the poor can be separated from the non-poor. However, collecting accurate data on income or consumption is difficult. The use of modern 'poverty mapping' techniques, which combine data from household surveys (which allow a link between consumption levels and various household characteristics) with data from population censuses which collect detailed location-based data on households, is very recent for our country cases.[7] Hence in practice up to very recently all of the countries used approximate indicators for identifying the poor; for example various basic need measures or rough estimates of average income in a particular village or larger unit.

In India there was a serious effort in the 1990s at administrative identification of the poor as a means of targeting principally the food and other subsidies from the public distribution system. As income estimates were uncertain, other additional criteria included housing conditions, number of family earners, land access and ownership of livestock and consumer durables. State governments had the responsibility for identifying the poor, although the process was slow and incomplete and even where surveys were undertaken identification cards were not provided to a significant number of poor families.[8]

In Indonesia receipt of food subsidies was determined by the classification scheme of the National Family Planning Coordinating Board (BKKBN), which covers households nationally. This classified households into a number of categories on the basis of criteria including food consumption patterns, access to health care and possession of alternative sets of clothing. In response to the impact of the Crisis of 1998–99 additional economic criteria were added; the poorest category covered households that failed any one of the following;

- all family members are normally able to eat at least twice a day;
- all family members have different types of clothing for home, work or school;
- the largest section of the floor of the family home is not made of earth;
- sick children are able to receive modern medical attention and women have access to family planning services.

However, administration of the food subsidy program showed both a disappointingly high leakage rate to the non-poor and high undercoverage.[9]

Village-based programs were also an important part of targeted poverty measures in Indonesia. Here poor villages were designated using a scoring system covering social and economic characteristics, including infrastructure, housing and population. Classification of a village as poor ('neglected') was based on a combination of its position relative to the provincial average and a subjective assessment from a field inspection by local officials. By this twin approach, 31 per cent of villages in the country were classed as neglected in 1993. Within these villages village leaders appear to have had a major influence on how program funds were allocated (Perdana and Maxwell, Chapter 3 in this volume).

In PRC geographic targeting has been the key approach with (up to 2001) poor counties being the basic units for central government poverty reduction funds. Although originally when the poor county designation system was initiated in 1986 the aim was to base this on average per capita income of rural residents, this came to be superseded by other criteria, with counties in areas of Revolutionary bases and minority communities, as well as pastoral areas, receiving the 'poor' designation despite the fact that their income per capita was well above the initial norm.[10] The re-designation of counties in 1993 was again intended to apply an income criterion, based on an estimated national poverty line, and although many poor counties were added to the list, since few counties were dropped, many (266 out of 592) counties still did not conform to the income criterion (Wang, Chapter 4 in this volume). Within poor counties officials could have discretion in allocating poverty reduction funds.

In 2001 the focus shifted from 'poor county' to 'poor village' designation, so that in principle poor villages could receive poverty funding even if they were not located within a poor county. Poor village designation was carried out using a weighted poverty index generated by the scores under various indicators; grain production per person year; cash income per person year; percentage of poor quality houses; percentage of households with access to potable water, electricity and all-weather roads; percentage of women with long-term health problems; and percentage of children attending school. Weights for these indicators in different counties should be determined by groups of villagers in a participatory manner. Within a village, in the absence of firm income data, again a participatory approach is recommended to identify who are poor and therefore eligible for poverty reduction funds. County governments have responsibility for the implementation of the system.

In Thailand poverty estimates have traditionally been based on income and expenditure data from the Socio-Economic Survey of the National Economic and Social Development Board. Poverty is concentrated heavily in the rural areas particularly in the North East (with 60 per cent of the officially estimated poor in 2000). In principle regional targeting of poverty funds should have been important but as we discuss further below there is only a very weak correlation between provincial incomes and the allocation of central government expenditure. In addition, the education loans program in particular does not appear to have been carefully targeted, since education institutions themselves were left to decide who was a poor student (Warr and Sarntisart, Chapter 5 in this volume).

In the Philippines again location targeting was significant with priority provinces identified for most schemes; within these provinces the most depressed districts (barangays) were to be the main beneficiaries. For the Care for the Poor program, the flagship of the Estrada administration, there was a finer screening of the beneficiaries within priority provinces with attempts made to identify the poorest families in particular areas. Where feasible, poverty was defined in terms of unmet basic needs (in terms of shelter, health and education, for example). Where data were unavailable, local social workers were consulted in the identification of the poor. More recent initiatives of the Arroyo administration, which provide support to local communities, combine a location targeting approach with poverty mapping within provinces. Provinces were ranked by poverty incidence and approximately the poorest half were deemed eligible. Within provinces the poorest 25 per cent of municipalities are selected using a poverty map. All districts within the chosen municipalities can receive funds.[11]

ERRORS OF TARGETING – MISAPPROPRIATION

Apart from technical difficulties in identifying who the poor actually are, governance issues are raised in all the country cases to explain relatively high levels of leakage as funds intended for the poor are diverted to others. This is brought out in a number of evaluation reports on the various targeting schemes. Food and credit subsidy programs and employment creation schemes, in particular, offer considerable scope for malpractice. India may not be the worst of the country cases studied here, but various evaluation reports, both official and unofficial, have documented the problem clearly.

Apart from the early days of the Maharashtra Employment Guarantee Scheme, employment creation and food-for-work programs are judged to have fared poorly.[12] An assessment of the Employment Assurance Scheme (EAS) found that the rules were being broken (for example self-selection was undermined by the use of contractors who hired local labor, and the norm that 60 per cent of costs should be on labor was often ignored). Nationally it was estimated that only 15 per cent of expenditure on the scheme was going as benefits to workers, against a target of 60 per cent. Another well-studied scheme has been the Comprehensive Rural Employment Scheme formed by a merger of the EAS with another scheme. Here poor workers are to receive foodgrains as payment in kind for wages, as well as some money income. There is an estimate that due to malpractice amongst local government administrators and contractors no more than 25 per cent of the wage fund that the poor are entitled to actually reaches them (Nayak et al., 2002). Another study drawing on a village-level survey in Andhra Pradesh finds local elites controlling the implementation of the scheme at the village level, with beneficiaries (that is those who would obtain work and food) selected at local meetings. Contrary to the guidelines of the scheme the use of contractors was widespread. The contractors were often found to obtain profits illegally through a number of means including claiming the full rice quota for incomplete work, double-claiming to different government departments, submitting inflated costs and paying workers wholly in cash and reselling the rice on the open market (Deshingkar and Johnson, 2003). A self- employment scheme – the Golden Jubilee Rural Self Employment Program – was launched in 1999 as a means of consolidating other programs that encouraged self-employment. An important component of this program is a credit subsidy for beneficiaries. Official evaluations have revealed banks imposing illicit charges on borrowers of up to 20 per cent of the loan. An official audit of the scheme found that over 50 per cent of the funds were either diverted to other purposes (state governments putting the funds in special deposits), mis-utilized or misreported. Here, as with the employment programs discussed above, there was strong evidence of beneficiaries paying bribes to receive funds. It is informative that in the survey of Indian experience, the scheme that is found to be most closely targeted is the very modest National Old Age Pension Scheme, which targets destitute pensioners with a very small monthly pension. Evaluations have concluded that it reaches the needy with benefits, either in cash transferred directly at village meetings or through deposits in post office savings accounts. The small amounts and direct transfer are seen as helping avoid leakage (Srivastava, Chapter 2 in this volume). The point is that even in an environment of weak governance, modest but well thought-out schemes can work effectively.

The Indian cases of malpractice in poverty-focused expenditure may be far from the worst but they are the best documented. In Indonesia there have been many allegations of corruption and malpractice, but these are less firmly based on evidence. For example, the employment creation programs through labor-intensive infrastructure schemes, which were one of the key planks of the response to the impact of the Financial Crisis, were alleged to have been associated with considerable malpractice by local officials as expenditures designed to cover wages were diverted to materials and equipment, which could be sold locally (Perdana and Maxwell, Chapter 3 in this volume). As we have noted, food subsidy schemes everywhere provide an opportunity for diversion of goods for sale at commercial prices. This no doubt occurred in Indonesia, although the main complaint of evaluation reports on the rice subsidy scheme, for example, has been that village officials and community leaders chose not to target within their own village communities but rather distributed more or less equally between families regardless of apparent poverty status. This is put down principally to social pressure rather than corrupt practices. The consequence was, however, that on the basis of selective survey data roughly twice as many families were receiving subsidized rice as planned by the central government and hence average allocations per family were well below the target of 20 kg (Hastuti and Maxwell, 2003).

The Philippines is another case where malpractice is often alleged and a number of targeting schemes left considerable discretion for politically determined allocations. For example, in the 1990s under the Care for the Poor program to meet basic needs of the poor, two-thirds of funds were allocated on the decision of Congressmen, not on the decision of government implementing agencies (Balisacan et al., 2000).

Apart from motives of corruption, the institutional objectives of public officials can also create targeting errors. This appears to have been particularly important in the poor county employment creation and subsidized loan programs in PRC, where because of the financial constraints they faced, local officials had incentives to divert funds to projects capable of generating revenue rather than funding projects with the greatest direct poverty impact (Wang, Chapter 4 in this volume). Similarly with micro-credit schemes, the officials of the implementing banks were under pressure to lend to the more credit-worthy customers, who would not be the poorest households (Park and Ren, 2001).

Errors of Undercoverage and Leakage

Aside from malpractice, which has been relatively common, if not always well documented, in our country cases there are instances of what we can term technical errors of targeting. This can be demonstrated most readily for location targeting measures, since average income and consumption estimates are normally available at the level of provincial or local government units and these can be compared with national or provincial poverty lines and with the allocation of public expenditure. Most studies indicate that regional targeting has in practice been a relatively 'blunt instrument' for reaching the poor.

For Thailand, we have detailed evidence from Warr and Sarntisart (Chapter 5 in this volume), who examine the distribution of government expenditure between rich and poor provinces, although they have no information to allow an assessment of intra-province distribution. They correlate provincial public expenditure per capita under different broad categories with provincial per capita incomes, and find positive elasticities, so that in general expenditure per person and, by implication, benefit rises with income. Hence there is no evidence of progressive targeting across provinces by broad expenditure category. When the same exercise is repeated for the specifically poverty-focused expenditure no significant relationship with provincial income per capita is found for most categories. However, provincial size does appear to matter so that, in general on a per capita basis, smaller provinces are favored in poverty-targeted expenditure. Only in the case of one minor category (the 'Poor and Low-Income People' expenditure) is there a significant negative relationship between allocations per capita and provincial income. This category was only 6 per cent of total poverty expenditures over 2000–2002, and within it the clearest evidence of a progressive allocation was for grants for health care. Hence on a regional basis within Thailand, there is no evidence of a successful targeting at poorer provinces.

For PRC, Park et al. (2002) and Wang (Chapter 4 in this volume) assess what they term 'targeting gap errors' by examining the classification of counties as 'poor' in the light of their estimated income per capita relative to the poverty line.[13] What they term the 'targeting count gap' (TCG) can be interpreted as the percentage of counties that are mis-targeted and this can be disaggregated into the two types of error. Table 1.1 below shows the situation taking the official poverty line to estimate mis-targeting.

Table 1.1   PRC provinces: targeting count gap 1986 to 1995

Year	Type 1 error (undercoverage)	Type 2 error (leakage)	Total
1986	0.094	0.050	0.144
1987	0.082	0.065	0.146
1988	0.044	0.101	0.144
1989	0.056	0.096	0.152
1990	0.078	0.093	0.171
1991	0.058	0.101	0.158
1992	0.038	0.107	0.145
1993	0.002	0.225	0.227
1994	0.005	0.232	0.237
1995	0.004	0.218	0.222

Source: Park et al. (2002), Table 4.

The data have an intuitively clear interpretation showing that the effectiveness of targeting has decreased over time. Initially undercoverage was the major problem, but over time leakage became considerably more important, particularly after the re-designation of poor county status in 1993, when about 20 per cent of counties with incomes above the poverty line became mis-targeted. However even with perfect designation at the county level there would still be targeting errors due to the presence of the non-poor in poor counties and of the poor in non-poor counties. Estimates suggest that the share of the poor (at the official poverty line) living in non-poor counties rose from 29 per cent in 1992 to 38 per cent in 2001 (Wang, Chapter 4 in this volume).[14]

Further evidence of errors in regional targeting comes from the Philippines. Balisacan et al. (2000) identify the 25 most depressed provinces in the late 1990s ranked both by the incidence of poverty or by the poverty gap measure (the rankings are not identical). These are then compared with the priority provinces under the Social Reform Agenda of the Ramos administration. Out of the 26 priority provinces only 11 are in the ranking of most depressed by the poverty indicators. It is clear that formal poverty data were only one of a number of factors used by the government to determine priority status.

Similar recent assessments of regional targeting for Indonesia are unavailable, however survey work illustrates the error of omission in the national Neglected Village program 1994–96 (IDT). As noted above, this was a location-targeting program designed to channel small-scale credit to the poorest households targeted at over 20 000 'neglected' (that is poor) villages across the country. Using a pilot study of the IDT in 384 villages in 6 provinces Sumarto et al. (1997) demonstrate the weakness of targeting. They illustrate undercoverage by focusing on the provinces of Central Java and West Nusa Tenggara (WNT). In the former, 30 per cent of all villages are classed as neglected and covered by the program, but 46 per cent of the poor (insofar as these can be identified accurately) are in villages that are not covered. In WNT a much higher proportion of all villages are classed as neglected, but still over 40 per cent of the poor live in non-IDT villages and are not covered by the program.[15] In addition for Indonesia, the National Economic Survey (SUSENAS) provides detailed information, which has been used to assess who has benefited from the set of poverty-targeting measures introduced in the wake of the Financial Crisis (Perdana and Maxwell, Chapter 3 in this volume). Table 1.2 summarizes the results of the most detailed study based on this data.

The data are extremely detailed and reveal clearly that of the anti-poverty programs over the period only the subsidized ration scheme reached a significant proportion of those eligible (40 per cent). Subsidized rice reached over 50 per cent of households in the bottom quintile, but for all other schemes the proportion of the target group reached was below 20 per cent and often well below it. Hence undercoverage was clearly a problem. In terms of leakage this was most serious for the rice and nutrition programs, where gains to the richest 20 per cent were high and the ratio of non-poor beneficiaries to their share in total population was highest (nearly 1.0 for the nutrition program implying nearly zero targeting effectiveness), although these figures do not reveal the magnitude of gains per family, only whether they were in receipt of some benefits.

Table 1.2 Indonesia: Impact of anti-poverty programs August 1998–February 1999

Program	Potential recipients (million)	Coverage Poorest 20% (%)	Coverage Richest 20% (%)	Coverage all potential recipients (%)	Proportion of beneficiaries from non-poor	Targeting ratio[a] (%)
Subsidized rice[b]	50.4	52.6	24.3	40.1	0.74	0.92
Employment creation[b]	50.4	8.3	2.5	5.6	0.70	0.88
Primary scholarships[c]	29.7	5.8	2.0	4.0	0.71	0.89
Lower secondary scholarships[c]	10.4	12.2	4.9	8.4	0.71	0.89
Upper secondary scholarships[c]	6.4	5.4	2.0	3.7	0.71	0.90
Health cards[d]	27.6	10.6	3.1	6.3	0.67	0.83
Nutrition[e]	20.0	16.5	14.2	15.9	0.79	0.99

Notes:

[a] Targeting ratio is share of non-poor (defined as those above bottom quintile) in total beneficiaries to their share in total population, which is 0.80 by definition.

[b] Subsidized rice and employment creation programs potentially available to all households.

[c] Scholarships are potentially available to all individual pupils enrolled at the relevant levels.

[d] Health cards potentially available to all those individuals who were estimated to have visited a health care provider in the three months prior to the survey.

[e] Nutrition support potentially available to all individuals in the 'pregnant women and children under three years' category.

Source: Sumarto et al. (2001)

Self-targeting schemes were intended to overcome many of the problems faced by directed or narrow targeting. Nonetheless they have also proved disappointing in many cases. In India there has been considerable experience with food-for-work and employment creation programs designed to attract the poor by offering below market-clearing wage rates. Evaluations have revealed serious undercoverage. In the 1990s the Employment Assurance Scheme offered on average only 17 days of employment per person per year against a target of 100 days. Further, its village coverage was low with another evaluation finding no more than one third of eligible villages actually covered. This meant that in some states less than 10 per cent of the target group was reached. This, combined with the low number of days' work on offer under the scheme, rendered its overall impact on the welfare of the poor largely minimal. In this case part of the problem had to do with the slow release of central government funds to the states and part to lack of matching funding by the states themselves (Srivastava, Chapter 2 in this volume). In other schemes, however, the level of wages set for employment has been identified as a critical factor with relatively high and therefore attractive wages leading to a 'crowding out' of the poor. In India under the food-for-work scheme in a survey in Andhra Pradesh, Deshingkar and Johnson (2003) conclude that wages either in cash or in kind were set too low in prosperous villages thus attracting non-poor migrants, but too high in poorer villages leading to crowding out of the poor. A similar conclusion is reached for an Indonesian employment creation scheme (the Padat Karya). An evaluation of this, drawing again on the SUSENAS data, found that for the 1998–99 period, as many as 70 per cent of beneficiaries were from non-poor households (Perdana and Maxwell, Chapter 3 in this volume).

Self-targeting has also been implied by health and nutrition and many micro-credit schemes. For example, in Indonesia the poor are entitled to health cards giving them access to free medical treatment. The definition of the poor was based on the BKKBN classification scheme noted above. Insofar as the better off will prefer to pay for improved access to health care there is an element of self-targeting in such a measure. Initial assessments of the Health Card program in its first six months of operation, again using SUSENAS data, showed substantial undercoverage with only around 10 per cent of the poorest 20 per cent of households covered. A subsequent more detailed analysis suggested that even though coverage may have been low, the scheme did help to prevent a decline in use of health facilities by the poor in the wake of the Financial Crisis (Pradhan et al., 2002). More explicit self-targeting is involved in the Affordable Medicine for All (GMA) program in the Philippines which provides free drugs for a limited number of conditions at public hospitals and a limited number of distribution outlets, to which it is expected only the poor will choose to go for the drugs. There is no firm evidence on the undercoverage or leakage associated with this scheme (Balisacan and Edillon, Chapter 6 in this volume).

Micro-credit programs aimed at the poor have a substantial element of self-targeting insofar as they involve the potential embarrassment of clients being associated with poverty programs and the inconvenience of frequent group meetings. Micro-credit is seen by many in the development community as an important innovation in the fight against poverty (Morduch, 2000). There is now considerable evidence that micro-credit has had a positive impact on poverty reduction in a number of countries, although often it is not the 'core poor' who are the main recipients, but rather those close to or just above the poverty line. In terms of our case-study countries (and elsewhere) there is also evidence of some leakage from micro-credit programs (Weiss et al., Chapter 7 in this volume). However, this leakage appears to be much less than from conventional subsidized credit programs. For example, for PRC the subsidized loan program available for poor counties went principally to economic entities rather than poor households (although formally it was an obligation that recipient enterprises should have at least 50 per cent of their employees who were below the poverty line). Many of these loans went to Township and Village Enterprises in poor counties and the direct link with poverty reduction came to be questioned. The introduction of micro-credit schemes in PRC in 1997 was a direct response to this concern (Wang, Chapter 4 in this volume). In the Philippines an assessment of the main low interest credit program for the poor (the Tulong sa Tao program) of the Aquino administration concluded that targeting was vague and that only around one-third of beneficiaries were from low-income groups (let alone being amongst the core poor) (Balisacan et al., 2000). Similar assessments are given for such schemes in India. For example, an assessment of the Integrated Rural Development program, which was designed to provide subsidized credit to the poor for income-generating activities, found that in the states of Bihar and Jharkand, 24 per cent of beneficiaries were above the poverty line and a high proportion had incomes just below it (MAKER, 2003).

Finally, broad targeting based on types of expenditure that the poor will use disproportionately offers an alternative to the type of narrow targeted schemes discussed above. Assessing the impact of measures like health and education expenditure is normally done by 'benefit incidence analysis' (van de Walle, 1998a). A typical conclusion is that primary health care and primary education expenditure have a disproportionate positive effect on the poor, whilst expenditure on hospitals and higher education have a disproportionate positive effect on the better-off.[16] The net effect of aggregate health and education spending will vary therefore depending on how expenditure is allocated within the sector, but in general there is evidence that broad targeting within these sectors can reach the poor.

In terms of other evidence on the impact of broad categories of investment, a simulation exercise for the Philippines, using coefficients derived from a regression model of poverty, shows general road expenditures to have high economic returns, but to have a negative direct effect on the poor, although this is compensated by a positive impact from growth. Electrification emerges as the best option in terms of high economic returns and a relatively strong positive effect in reducing poverty (Balisacan and Edillon, Chapter 6 in this volume).

How Effective has Targeting Been?

Some errors of targeting and some misappropriation are inevitable in any economic environment and more can be expected in low-income countries. Further, the very modest level of resources directed at the schemes would also limit their impact, even given far lower targeting errors. However, the consistent picture that emerges from the available evidence is that while some schemes may have had a modest positive effect on the poor, in our case-study countries in general, trends in poverty reduction have been driven by macroeconomic developments – the rate and pattern of economic growth – rather than by targeted interventions.

There is a vast literature on the relationship between growth and poverty, which concludes there is virtually everywhere a clear negative relationship, although its strength varies between countries with different social, economic and political structures. This can be illustrated for our country cases. Warr (2000), for example, examines changes in poverty incidence (the headcount ratio based on official poverty estimates) across a set of countries including India, Indonesia and Thailand. He finds elasticities of poverty incidence (the proportionate change in the headcount ratio relative to the proportionate change in GDP per capita) of –0.9 for India, –2.0 for Thailand, and –0.7 for the Philippines.[17] For PRC a similar exercise finds an elasticity for poverty incidence of –0.8 (World Bank, 2001). Estimates are also available for the income poverty elasticity, that is the relation between growth (change in mean income) and the change in the income of the poor (normally taken as the bottom quintile). For the Philippines the income poverty elasticity (defined as the ratio of the latter to the former) is found to be relatively low at 0.54, whilst for Indonesia the comparable elasticity is 0.71 (Balisacan and Pernia, 2003; Balisacan et al., 2003). In both countries there is a clear tendency for the elasticity for different quintiles to rise as one moves up the income scale, although this is particularly marked in the Philippines. In other words, although the poor benefit from growth they do not benefit as much (both proportionately as well as absolutely) as the better-off.[18] Similar results with growth accompanied by a strongly worsening income distribution are found for PRC, with an implicit poverty elasticity of around 0.5 (Stern, 2001).[19]

These results imply that growth reduces the headcount index of poverty and raises the income of the poor, although often not by as much as it raises the income of better-off groups.[20] However, the issue remains of the impact of poverty-targeted programs discussed here, either in reinforcing the positive effects of growth or in protecting the poor at times of recession. As noted above, it would be unrealistic to expect a dramatic impact even in the presence of more accurate targeting, given the modest budgets allocated to these funds.[21]

Given the high leakage rates reported above and the administrative costs involved in reaching the poor, one would expect that these schemes involved relatively high costs of transfer per unit of benefit received by the poor. Estimates of the optimal degree of targeting, as discussed above, are rarely available. However, in a simulation exercise for the Philippines, Balisacan and Edillon (Chapter 6 in this volume) report that simple geographic targeting provides the maximum benefit to the poor for a given program cost, as compared with other schemes, once the administrative costs per applicant reach a modest figure (roughly 50 per cent of the daily minimum wage in Metro Manila). The implication is that, once administrative costs are allowed for, relatively simple forms of targeting dominate the alternatives.

Few rigorous cost effectiveness studies of alternative targeting schemes are available. For India a comparison of employment guarantee schemes and food subsidies suggests that at best the cost of transfer is nearly double the benefits received by the poor. Approximate estimates suggest that the cost of transferring a rupee to the poor through the Maharashtra Employment Guarantee Scheme in its early years (Rs 1.85 per rupee transferred) compared very favorably with both the later national employment scheme, the Jawahar Rozgar Yojana (Rs 2.28 per rupee transferred) and the food subsidy program under the Public Distribution System (Rs 6.68 per rupee transferred) (Dev and Evenson, 2003). Separate estimates for the impact of the Employment Assurance scheme in three states (West Bengal, Gujarat and Haryana) found the cost per job per day to be Rs 200–300, which is well in excess of wage rates, which were roughly in the range of Rs 35–50 (Srivastava, Chapter 2 in this volume).

The operations of the National Food Authority in the Philippines, particularly through its rice subsidy, have been the subject of several cost effectiveness assessments. For the early 1990s costs are again roughly twice the sum transferred to consumers (Subbarao et al., 1996). However, NFA rice is sold in special retail outlets in a form of self-targeting, and much will leak to the non-poor. Assuming a 50 per cent leakage rate, more recent cost effectiveness estimates for the NFA rice subsidy suggest that in 1997 it costs Pesos 4.2 per peso of benefit received by poor consumers and Pesos 2.5 per peso of benefit in 1998. Much of this mis-targeting will have been due to a regional misallocation with some of the poorer provinces being under-represented, relative to their share in poverty, in the receipt of NFA rice (Manasan, 2001).

In addition, however, it is important to remember that despite high leakage and high cost, some of these schemes may nonetheless have been influential in protecting the poor at times of adverse shocks. This is the judgement on some of the many schemes introduced in Indonesia at the time of the Crisis of the late 1990s, particularly in relation to health and education initiatives. For example, there is some evidence that the education scholarship program helped in keeping up school enrolment rates and reducing drop-out rates from poor families. Similarly the Health Card scheme to allow free access to public health facilities is credited with stabilizing the utilization rate of such facilities by the poor (Perdana and Maxwell, Chapter 3 in this volume). Cost and leakage may have been high, but some real benefits appear to have been created.

Apart from these analyses of the cost of transfers to the poor, a few detailed quantitative assessments of the longer-term income effects of this type of program are available. Of our case-study countries, the most work has been done for PRC. From a regression model Rozelle et al. (1998) find some positive income effects from direct lending to households in poor counties in Shaanxi 1986–91; however, funds allocated directly to enterprises in these counties do not appear to have any positive effect on growth. Zhang et al. (2002) look at Sichuan province and compare growth across program poor, non-program poor and non-poor counties. Allowing for a range of other factors they find that program status does appear to have a positive effect on growth. Hence, whilst non-poor counties grew more rapidly, the gap between poor and non-poor counties is lower when counties have a designated poor status and receive poverty funding commensurate with this designation. An even stronger result is provided by Park et al. (2002) using a regression model, which makes growth across counties a function of initial income, other initial characteristics (principally grain production), time invariant characteristics, including poor county status, and a number of time-varying factors. They find that designation as a poor county increases household per capita income, over that otherwise expected, by 2.2 per cent annually in the 1986–92 period and 0.9 per cent annually in 1992–95. When this rate of increase is compared with the amount of funding to poor counties this gives a rate of return of between 12 per cent and 16 per cent depending on the time period.[22] This evidence needs to be qualified, however. First, even accepting the regression specification as a means of establishing the counterfactual in the absence of designation as a poor county, the study makes no claims to know how the extra income within the counties concerned was distributed. There need be no inevitable assumption that the incomes of the poor grew by the same rate as average incomes in the poor counties. Second, the authors make clear that their results may be an over-estimate as they have not been able to include all costs of the targeting programs. Third, their returns must be compared with the opportunity cost of capital in China at this time, which was probably relatively high, given the rapid growth rate, and may have been at least 12 per cent or more (which implies that equivalent or higher returns could have been obtained on investment elsewhere in the economy).

A detailed examination of the impact of public spending on poverty in PRC, which gives a less positive assessment of the poverty loans program, is provided by Fan et al. (2002). Using a simultaneous equation model, that has now been applied to a number of countries, they assess the effect on poverty in terms of numbers pulled above the poverty line due to a given amount of different public expenditures. By far the highest poverty effect is due to education, followed by agricultural research and development (R&D). Poverty loans have a relatively very small (and statistically insignificant) impact per unit of expenditure. They have the smallest poverty effect of any category of expenditure included (only 13 per cent of that of education, 15 per cent of that of R&D, and roughly one-third of that of roads).[23] Similar studies have been done for India and Thailand using the same model, but only the India study includes poverty loans (covering rural and community development and employment programs) as a separate expenditure category (Fan et al., 1999). For the Indian case in terms of poverty impact the relative ranking of the poverty expenditure category is higher than for PRC (it is fourth behind roads, R&D and education).[24] However, per unit its impact is still well below that of these other categories of expenditures, being 17 per cent of that of roads, 30 per cent of R&D and 88 per cent of education. No doubt the targeting errors reported in this chapter are a major part of the explanation.

CONCLUSIONS

What can one conclude from all of this for targeting policy? One clear implication is that altering the pattern of growth towards sectors with strong employment effects is likely to have the greatest direct impact on poverty reduction. Nonetheless, the need to reach the poor directly and to minimize leakage from and undercoverage of poverty programs remains critical. Self-targeting initiatives have proved only a modest improvement in leakage terms and raise issues of undercoverage. Technical improvements, principally new poverty mapping techniques, offer a means of more sharply identifying who the poor are, but in the absence of strong governance over poverty schemes the risk of misuse of funds remains. Whilst the case for special promotion and protection policies for the poor remains strong, past errors associated with their implementation and design must not be forgotten. In the debates of the 1980s more universal schemes were strongly criticized for their high leakage and their budgetary implications. The more targeted measures of the 1990s, as we have seen, have cost more modest amounts relative to the size of government budgets, but their leakage rates have also been disappointingly high, as have their costs per unit of benefit to the poor, where these can be estimated. Poverty-targeting measures should remain an important component of poverty-reduction strategies, but improvements in both governance and the technical design of schemes are needed. This is likely to require a combination of greater focus on broad targeting (primary education and health care, for example) and selective, narrowly focused, support for the very poor. Broad targeting measures, such as expenditure on primary health care, have been shown to reach the poor disproportionately in a number of countries, and clearly have an important role. Such measures are not solutions to the short-term problem of providing protection to the poor, which is why measures like employment creation schemes and food subsidies have been employed, with the disappointing results that we have observed. However what works, and what does not, is likely to vary substantially between countries. In this spirit the following chapters discuss in depth the experiences in our case-study countries.

NOTES

1. More recent World Development Reports broadened the definition of poverty to include various non-income dimensions (World Bank, 2000) and stressed problems of delivering services to the poor (World Bank, 2004). The discussion of corruption and clientelist politics in the latter is relevant to the governance problem associated with targeting implementation.
2. Meyer (2002) gives a useful survey of the difficulties of assessing the impact of micro-finance programs on poverty reduction.
3. The only exception to the use of official estimates is in the case of India, where in Figure 1.6 the final year observation comes from the estimates of Deaton (2001).
4. We can write the poverty gap (PG) as

$$PG = \frac{1}{n} \sum_{i=1}^{p} \left[\frac{z - y_i}{z} \right]$$

where z is the poverty line, y_i is income of individual i, p is the number of poor and n is the total population.

5. Hence the squared poverty gap (SPG) is

$$SPG = \frac{1}{n} \sum_{i=1}^{p} \left(\frac{z - y_i}{z} \right)^2$$

The theory behind SPG is set out in Foster et al. (1984).

6. Schemes with budgets of below Rs 1 billion are excluded from this total.

7. For example, a poverty map has just been completed on a trial basis for three provinces in Indonesia (Suryahadi et al., 2003). There are doubts however as to whether this approach can apply at the village level. Hentschel et al. (2000) explain the poverty mapping approach and illustrate how it can improve on the use of simple basic indicators to identify the poor.

8. For evidence of undercoverage a World Bank survey in Uttar Pradesh, one of the poorest states, found that 56 per cent of the lowest income quintile did not get identification cards to enable them to access the public distribution system (Srivastava, Chapter 2 in this volume).

9. Perdana and Maxwell (Chapter 3 in this volume) report evidence that in the late 1990s those in the top four quintiles of household expenditure were three quarters of the recipients of subsidized rice and that only roughly half of the poor families under the official criteria were recipients (see Table 1.2).

10. In the late 1980s in only one third of the classified poor counties was income per capita actually below the original norm of RMB 150 set by the Leading Group for Poverty Reduction of the State Council (Wang, Chapter 4 in this volume).

11. The poverty-mapping model is in Balisacan et al. (2002).

12. This scheme received a great deal of attention internationally and was commented on very favorably in World Bank (1990). Its performance declined substantially after 1979 following a large increase in the wage offered, thus weakening the self-selection by the poor (Gaiha, 1996).

13. The targeting count gap (TCG) is defined as

$$TCG_t = 1/N \sum \{I_{it1}(P_{it} = 0, \ Y_{it} < Z_t) + I_{it2}(P_{it} = 1, \ Y_{it} > Z_t)\}$$

where N is the total number of counties, indexed by i, and t is a time period. I_{it1} is an indicator of undercoverage (type 1 error) and equals 1.0 if a county is not designated as poor ($P_{it} = 0$), but its income per capita (Y_{it}) is below the poverty line (Z_t). I_{it2} is an indicator of leakage (type 2 error) that equals 1.0 if a county is designated as poor ($P_{it} = 1$), but its income per capita is above the poverty line.

14. Weiss (2003) finds that the key factor influencing rural poverty reduction in PRC across provinces has been the growth of grain production and to a lesser extent the trend in farm-gate prices.

15. Perdana and Maxwell (Chapter 3 in this volume) enter the qualification that firstly these results may not be representative of the national picture and secondly that the IDT scheme was revised to address the undercoverage problem.

16. van de Walle (1998b) reports this result for Indonesian data from the late 1980s, although the bias is much greater for hospitals where gains to the top decile of the income strata in monetary terms are roughly seven times those to the bottom decile. World Bank (2004) Figure 2.5 reports estimates for Indonesia in 1989 and 1990 showing the gains to the poor (the bottom 20 per cent) from public spending to exceed the gains to the rich (the top 20 per cent) for primary health care and primary education expenditure, whilst the reverse holds for aggregate expenditure under both headings.

17. In the analysis, variation in growth explains about 40 per cent of the variation in poverty reduction between countries. It is well known that there can be major regional variations in the growth–poverty relation within countries. Datt and Ravallion (1998) provide an analysis across Indian states and find that poor initial conditions in terms of the rural

sector and weak human resource development lower the impact of a given rate of non-farm growth on poverty.

18. The authors hypothesize that the lower poverty elasticity in the Philippines as compared with Indonesia is due to the relatively more agriculture and labor-based growth pattern in the latter.

19. The Chinese data can be interpreted in different ways. As Stern (2001: 109) points out 'For poor people in most countries of the world, of course, an average income growth of 4 per cent annually [sic for the 1990s] would be a great improvement – but in China that rate was just one-third of the 12 per cent growth rate that the wealthiest enjoyed.'

20. Cross-country analysis such as Dollar and Kraay (2004) has tended to find that as an average relation the income poverty elasticity is around unity, implying that the poor's income rises by the same proportion as the average of the country concerned. The country cases discussed above do not support this result.

21. The exception here is micro-finance funds, which have become significant in some countries, particularly Indonesia of those covered here.

22. Using a different approach Jalan and Ravallion (1998) find a similar return to the poor area development program in Southwest China.

23. Given that the poverty loan variable is not statistically significant it is unclear whether much meaning can be placed on the impacts for poverty loans. However it should be noted that the structure of the model appears to ensure that other categories of expenditure will have a greater impact on poverty reduction than will poverty loans. This is because these loans only impact on poverty directly (in equation 1 of the system), whilst other expenditure categories enter indirectly through their effect on growth in productive sectors (equations 2 to 11).

24. Here the coefficient is statistically significant. The poverty expenditure enters into the equation for non-agricultural employment (equation 6) and the latter is one of the terms in the poverty equation (equation 1).

BIBLIOGRAPHY

Balisacan, A. and E. Pernia (2003), 'Poverty, inequality and growth in the Philippines', in E. Pernia and A. Deolalikar (eds), *Poverty, Growth and Institutions*, Hampshire, UK: Palgrave, Macmillan.

Balisacan, A., R. Edillon and G. Duncanes (2002), 'Poverty mapping and targeting for KALAHI-CIDSS', final report prepared for the Department of Social Work, Government of the Philippines.

Balisacan, A., E. Pernia and A. Asra (2003), 'Revisiting growth and poverty reduction in Indonesia: what do sub-national data show?', *Bulletin of Indonesian Economic Studies*, **39** (3).

Balisacan, A., R. Edillon, A. Brillantes and D. Canlas (2000), *Approaches to Targeting the Poor*, Quezon City, Philippines: NEDA and UNDP.

Besley, T. and R. Kanbur (1991), 'The principles of targeting', in V. Balasubramanyam and S. Lall (eds), *Current Issues in Development Economics*, Hampshire, UK: Macmillan.

Cornia, G. and F. Stewart (1993), 'Two types of targeting error', *Journal of International Development*, **5** (5).

Datt, G. and M. Ravallion (1998), 'Why have some Indian states done better than others at reducing rural poverty?', *Economica*, **65** (257), 17–38.

Deaton, A. (2001), 'Adjusted Indian poverty estimates for 1999–2000', mimeo Research Program in Development Studies, Princeton, NJ, USA.

Deshingkar, P. and C. Johnson (2003), 'State transfers and to the poor and back: the case of the food for work program in Andhra Pradesh', Overseas Development Institute, Working Paper 222, ODI, London.

Dev, M. and R. Evenson (2003), 'Rural development in India', paper and powerpoint presentation at conference on Indian Policy Reforms, June 2003, Stanford University.

Dollar, D. and A. Kraay (2004), 'Trade, growth and poverty', *Economic Journal*, **114** (493).

Fan, S., P. Hazell and S. Thorat (1999), 'Government spending, agricultural growth and poverty: an analysis of interlinkages in rural India', International Food Policy Research Institute, Research Report 110, IFPRI, Washington, DC.

Fan, S., L. Zhang and X. Zhang (2002), 'Growth, inequality and poverty in rural China: the role of public investments', International Food Policy Research Institute, Research Report 125, IFPRI, Washington, DC.

Foster, J., J. Greer and E. Thorbecke (1984), 'A class of decomposable poverty measures', *Econometrica*, **52** (3).

Gaiha, R. (1996), 'How dependent are the rural poor on the Employment Guarantee Scheme in India?', *Journal of Development Studies*, **32** (5).

Hastuti, A. and J. Maxwell (2003), 'Rice for poor families (RASKIN): did the 2002 program operate effectively? Evidence from Bengkulu and Karawang', SMERU Working Paper, June, SMERU Research Institute, Jakarta.

Hentschel, J., J. Olson Lanjouw, P. Lanjouw and J. Poggi (2000), 'Combining census and survey data to trace the spatial dimensions of poverty: a case study of Ecuador', *World Bank Economic Review*, **14** (1).

Jalan, J. and M. Ravallion (1998), 'Are there dynamic gains from a poor-area development program?', *Journal of Public Economics*, vol. 67, pp. 65–85.

MAKER (2003), 'An empirical study of poverty alleviation programs in Bihar', Mathura Khrishna Foundation for Economic and Social Opportunity and Human Resource Management (MAKER), report to Planning Commission available at www.planningcommission.nic.in/reports

Manasan, R. (2001), 'Social safety nets in the Philippines: analysis and prospects', in 'Strengthening Policies and Programs on Social Safety Net Issues: Recommendations and Selected Studies', Economic and Social Commission for Asia and the Pacific, Social Policy Paper no. 8, UN, New York.

Morduch, J. (2000), 'The Microfinance Schism', *World Development*, **28** (4).

Meyer, R.L. (2002), 'Track record of financial institutions in assisting the poor in Asia', Asian Development Bank Institute Research Paper 49, ADB Institute, December.

Nayak, R., N. Saxena and J. Farrington (2002), 'Reaching the poor: the influence of policy and administrative processes on the implementation of government poverty schemes in India', Overseas Development Institute, Working Paper 175, ODI, London.

Park, A. and C. Ren (2001), 'Microfinance with Chinese characteristics', *World Development*, **29** (1).

Park, A., S. Wang and G. Wu (2002), 'Regional poverty targeting in China', *Journal of Public Economics*, vol. 86, pp. 123–53.

Pradhan, M., F. Saadah and R. Sparrow (2002), 'Did the healthcard program ensure access to medical care for the poor during Indonesia's economic crisis?', Tinbergen Institute Discussion Paper, Amsterdam.

Riskin, C., R. Zhao and S. Li (2001), *China's Retreat From Equality*, New York: M.E. Sharpe.

Rozelle, S., A. Park, V. Benzinger and C. Ren (1998), 'Targeted poverty investments and economic growth in China', *World Development*, **26** (12).

Shariff, A., P. Ghosh and S. Mondal (2002), 'Indian public expenditures on social sector and poverty alleviation programs during the 1990s', Overseas Development Institute, Working Paper 175, ODI, London.

Stern, N. (2001), 'Reform, poverty reduction and the new agenda in China', mimeo, World Bank website available at www.worldbank.org.

Subbarao, K., A. Ahmed and T. Teklu (1996), 'Selected social safety net programs in the Philippines: targeting, cost effectiveness and options for reforms', World Bank Discussion Paper no. 317, World Bank, Washington, DC.

Sumarto, S., A. Suryahadi and W. Widyanti (2001), 'Designs and implementation of the Indonesian social safety net programs: evidence from the JPS module in the 1999 SUSENAS', SMERU Working Paper, March, SMERU Research Institute, Jakarta.

Sumarto, S., S. Usman and S. Mawardi (1997), 'Agriculture's role in poverty reduction: bringing farmers to the policy formulation process', Agriculture Sector Strategy Review, mimeo Ministry of Agriculture, Government of Indonesia, Jakarta.

Suryahadi, A., W. Widyanti, D. Perwira, S. Sumarto, C. Elber and M. Pradhan (2003), 'Developing a poverty map for Indonesia: an initiatory work in three provinces, part 1: technical report', SMERU Research Institute, Jakarta.

van de Walle, D. (1998a), 'Assessing the welfare impacts of public spending', *World Development*, **26** (3).

van de Walle, D. (1998b), 'Targeting revisited', *World Bank Research Observer*, **13** (2).

Warr, P. (2000), 'Poverty reduction and economic growth: the evidence from Asia', *Asian Development Review*, **18** (2).

Weiss, J. (2003), 'Poverty in Western China: exploring the policy options', ADBI Discussion Paper no. 1, available at www.adbi.org.

World Bank (1990), *World Development Report 1990*, Washington, DC: World Bank.

World Bank (2000), *World Development Report 2000/01*, Washington, DC: World Bank.

World Bank (2001), *China: Overcoming Rural Poverty*, Washington, DC: World Bank.

World Bank (2004), *World Development Report 2004*, Washington, DC: World Bank.

Zhang, L., J. Huang and S. Rozelle (2002), 'Growth or policy: which is winning China's war on poverty?', University of California, Department of Economics, Working Paper.

2. Poverty targeting in India

Pradeep Srivastava

INTRODUCTION

This chapter addresses two broad questions related to poverty alleviation in India: how much in aggregate does the government spend on poverty-targeted programs and how effective have these programs been in targeting the poor and in alleviating poverty?

The apparently straightforward query as to how much the country spends on poverty alleviation, and how the money is spent, has several complex answers. Like the proverbial elephant being explored by seven blind men, the answer depends on the slice put under the analytical lens. There are several reasons for this, starting from the fact that in intensely poor countries with pervasive poverty, it is arguably legitimate to characterize a vast spectrum, if not virtually most government intervention as poverty reducing. These can include in principle investments in social and human capital, physical infrastructure, or even regulatory reforms to enhance economic growth. A first twist of the lens to focus on more direct poverty alleviation shows a great number of programs and interventions that may be characterized as broad or activity-targeting interventions, relying on broadly defined targets wherein the benefit incidence is expected to be higher for the poor than for the relatively better off. These typically include government expenditures on social sectors such as health and education, particularly primary education and basic health services. A further narrowing of the lens leads to a focus on government interventions that, within the broad spectrum of activities to reduce poverty, explicitly seek to target the poor, and particularly the poorest of the poor, for impact.

Poverty alleviation in India displays the whole panoply of such interventions – from broadly targeted to narrowly focused – which are quite substantial in magnitude, but difficult to track comprehensively since there is little effort at transparency and consolidation. To begin with, there are large sums of public money spent on activity-targeted interventions including expenditures on social sectors and subsidies for other economic services including irrigation, fertilizers, food and power. According to the

Indian Constitution, a majority of social sector expenditures are in the domain of state governments, and total expenditures by states far exceed those by the central government. There are considerable variations across states in the amounts spent and in the implementation arrangements and efficiency of expenditure.

Expenditures on subsidies, though large quantitatively, are not always transparent. According to recent estimates by Srivastava et al. (2003), aggregate budgetary subsidies of the central and state governments combined equaled Rs 2357.5 billion in 1998–99. This amounted to almost 13.5 per cent of the GDP at market prices, and roughly 86 per cent of the combined revenue receipts of the center and the states. The share of the central government is about one-third of this amount, with the state governments accounting for the rest.

In addition to these broadly targeted expenditures in social sectors and subsidies, the government also funds Centrally Sponsored Schemes (CSS), which are implemented by state governments. Despite repeated calls for consolidating and rationalizing these schemes, CSS have continued to proliferate and in 2001 there were 360 schemes in operation. The CSS subsume most narrowly defined, direct poverty-targeted programs, but also include several that are less directly targeted though they are explicitly aimed towards improving the welfare of the poor. Selecting a core group of poverty-targeted programs from the CSS portfolio thus inevitably entails qualitative judgement in some cases. Detailed information on the schemes under CSS is not easily available, being scattered across the numerous ministries that implement these schemes. In addition, budget documents of the Government of India show total amounts transferred to states under Centrally Sponsored Schemes, but these amounts do not include larger flows transferred directly from the center to the districts, bypassing the state governments. These transfers in 2001–02 amounted to Rs 150 billion compared to Rs 100 billion shown in the budget documents under CSS (Saxena and Farrington, 2003).

To address the second question above, assessing the effectiveness of direct poverty-targeted programs, the chapter focuses on five schemes that are nationally implemented, large in size, and include all relevant categories, namely self-employment, food-for-work, pure income transfers, and infrastructure creation. These schemes rely on a variety of targeting mechanisms, including self-selection and indicators (such as geographical location, social category and age). To retain focus and keep the discussion manageable, the large broadly targeted expenditures on social sector and general subsidies are not dealt with in any detail.

Given India's immense poverty, where more than 800 million people exist on less than US $2 a day, it is important to ask whether poverty targeting is an important objective. Targeting is most useful if there is a well-defined target within the whole, but less so when the target is almost as large as the whole. This issue has been most vocally addressed in India in the context of food security through subsidizing food using the Public Distribution System (PDS). The public distribution system was provided universally until 1992, but has since then sought to more narrowly target the poorest among the poor, with relatively disappointing results in the sense of excluding large numbers of people that are nutritionally at risk. In assessing the effectiveness of poverty-targeting programs in India, this broader context is worth keeping in mind. At the same time, the immense poverty also reinforces the need to directly assist the poorest among the many poor.

Since most poverty-targeted programs in India are sponsored by the central government but implemented by state governments and lower levels of government at district level and below, it is necessary to provide a brief review of the federal fiscal architecture of the economy. This is done in the next section, along with an overview of trends in poverty and poverty-targeted programs in the country. Subsequently, in the third section, a brief discussion of targeting mechanisms is provided, including the 'Administrative Identification' system. The selected poverty-targeted programs are reviewed in the fourth section, followed by a discussion of financial sustainability and the conclusions.

TRENDS IN POVERTY IN INDIA AND THE POLICY RESPONSE

South Asia is home to the largest number of poor in the world, and India accounts for the largest percentage of the region's share. The long-term performance of the Indian economy with respect to poverty reduction has been mixed, with poverty actually increasing in the first two decades after India became independent in 1947. However, there has been a sustained reduction in poverty since the 1970s. Figure 2.1 shows trends in poverty incidence over four decades, measured by the headcount ratio (that is the proportion of the population below the national poverty line). Rural poverty declined from 55.7 per cent in 1974 to 37.4 per cent in 1991, while urban poverty fell from almost 48 per cent to 33.2 per cent during the same period, with the major proportion of this decline occurring between 1978 and 1987. Estimated poverty rates increased after the macroeconomic crisis in 1991, though these estimates were based on a relatively smaller sample.[1]

The latest estimates for poverty in India, for 1999–2000, are deliberately not included in Figure 2.1 since they are at the center of considerable controversy. According to these estimates, poverty in India had declined

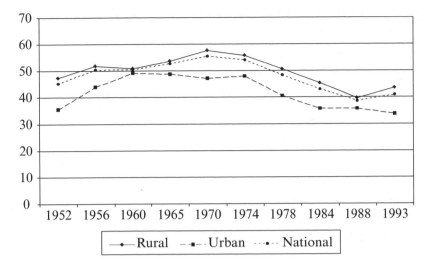

Figure 2.1   Rural and urban poverty in India, 1952–93

to 27 per cent in rural areas with a national figure of 26 per cent. However, the most recent household expenditure survey used a different methodology, resulting in a lack of comparability between the latest estimates and all earlier ones. The debate surrounding the latest poverty estimates in India is quite intense and wide-ranging, though largely arid at this stage given the fundamental lack of comparability between the latest estimates and those before. In a widely cited analysis, using official poverty lines of the Planning Commission, Deaton (2001) finds that poverty in India declined from 36.2 per cent in 1993–94 to 28.8 per cent in 1999–2000. Unfortunately, though, the actual status on poverty in India to date is ambiguous, with considerable skepticism attached to official figures.

Even with the latest questionable estimates, India remains the epicenter of poverty, both within South Asia and in the world, with as many as 259 million people below the national poverty line. In terms of the international poverty line of US $1 per day (measured at 1993 purchasing power parity exchange rates), there are 358 million poor in India. If instead we use the norm of US $2 per day, almost 80 per cent of India's vast population is below the poverty line (World Bank, 2003).

In terms of the non-income dimensions of poverty too, India continues to display intense poverty with relatively poor indicators of social and human development relevant to the millennium development goals (MDGs), such as infant and maternal mortality, literacy levels and gender inequalities (see Table 2.1). To the extent that poverty-targeted programs can ameliorate

Poverty targeting in Asia

Table 2.1   MDG related human development indicators in India

MDG 1. Goal 1: Eradicate extreme poverty and hunger; Goal 2: Achieve universal primary education	

1	Population living below $1 a day (%), 1990–2001	34.7
2	Share of poorest 20% in national income or consumption (%), 1990–2001	8.1
3	Children underweight for age (% under age 5), 1995–2001	47
4	Undernourished people (as % of total population)	
	1990–92	25
	1998–2000	24
5	Net primary enrollment ratio (%)	
	1990–91	–
	2000–01	–

MDG 2. Goal 3: Promote gender equality and empower women	

1	Ratio of girls to boys in primary education	
	1990–91	0.71
	2000–01	0.77
2	Ratio of literate females to males (age 15–24)	
	1990	0.74
	2001	0.82

MDG 3. Goal 4: Reduce child mortality; goal 5: Improve maternal health	

1	Under-5 mortality rate (per 1000 live births)	
	1990	123
	2001	93
2	Infant mortality rate (per 1000 live births)	
	1990	80
	2001	67
3	Maternal mortality ratio (per 100 000 live births), 1995	440

MDG 4. Goal 6: Combat HIV/AIDS, malaria and other diseases	

| 1 | Malaria cases (per 100 000 people), 2000 | 7 |
| 2 | Tuberculosis cases (per 100 000 people), 2001 | 199 |

MDG 6. Goal 7: Ensure environmental sustainability; water and sanitation	

1	Population with sustainable access to an improved water source, rural (%)	
	1990	61
	2000	79
2	Population with sustainable access to an improved water source, urban (%)	
	1990	88
	2000	95
3	Urban population with access to improved sanitation (%)	
	1990	44
	2000	61

Source: UNDP (2003).

these non-income dimensions of poverty, as is often their stated objective, these data only serve to highlight the importance and necessity of well functioning targeting in the country.

Poverty in India is overwhelmingly rural, with more than 70 per cent of the poor in rural areas. As might be expected, small and marginal farmers and landless rural labor are important contributors in aggregate poverty (see Table 2.2). Poverty is also disproportionately higher in population groups belonging to Scheduled Tribes and Scheduled Castes.

Table 2.2   Characteristics of the poor: Percentage of rural households below the poverty line, 1983, 1987–88, 1993–94

Livelihood Category	1983	1987–88	1993–94
1 Self-employed: agriculture	38.99	35.88	27.11
2 Self-employed: non-agriculture	42.89	36.11	29.13
3 Rural labor: agriculture	63.2	59.63	50.56
4 Rural labor: non-agriculture	44.13	43.66	34.62
5 Others	29.8	25.4	23.27
6 All households	46.8	42.25	34.7
7 Female-headed households	–	41.1	32.7

Source: Long and Srivastava (2002).

Poverty-Targeting Programs in India

As noted, the central government has large expenditures that, given the development status of the country and its poverty, could be related directly or indirectly to poverty reduction. In particular, substantial sums of public money are spent on broad targeting interventions, including expenditures on social sectors and subsidies for other economic services, such as irrigation, fertilizer, food and power. This important group of interventions is excluded from the main discussion despite their quantitative importance so as to enable a sharper focus on more narrowly defined, direct poverty-targeted interventions. The focus of the existing literature on social expenditures and subsidies in India is primarily their impact on public finances and their efficiency, both of which are less directly related to poverty reduction per se. In addition, as outlined below, broad or activity-targeted interventions in social sectors are constitutionally the responsibility of state governments, with the result that specific interventions show considerable variation across different states.

Fiscal context of targeting programs
The constitution of India ordains distinct responsibilities for the central
and state governments vis-à-vis expenditures and revenues for each level
of administration. The fiscal architecture of the federation is designed to
allocate responsibilities for revenue and expenditure between the center
and the states, as well as to devolve resources from the center equitably
to different regions of the large country. The structure, summarized in
Table 2.3, reflects attempts at providing vertical and horizontal balance by
emphasizing revenue collection at the center and expenditures at the state
level.[2] The central government collects all the major taxes and is obliged by

Table 2.3   Expenditure and revenue responsibilities of center and states

Central government expenditures	Central government taxes
Defense	Corporate tax
Railways, highways, airways, shipping	Import duties
Posts and Telecommunications	Property and wealth tax
Heavy and other strategic industries	Income tax surcharges
Strategic industries	Stock exchange stamp duties
External Affairs	
Foreign Trade	
State government expenditures	**State government taxes**
Irrigation	Personal income tax[*]
Power	Sales tax[**]
Education	Excise duties on alcohol
Health	and narcotics
Rural Development	Urban property tax
Roads	Mineral taxes
Public law and order	Stamp and registration duties
Culture	
Shared expenditure	**Shared taxes**
Population and family planning	Personal income tax[*]
	Excise duties (excluding alcohol
	and narcotics)
	Property and wealth tax
	Tax on railway tickets

Notes:
[*]   Except agriculture and professional self-employment.
[**]   India is planning to introduce Value Added Tax to substantially replace sales taxes.

Source: Hemming et al. (1997).

the constitution to share them with the states. In turn, states are responsible for expenditures in key areas, including sectors central to poverty alleviation such as health, education, rural development and irrigation sectors.[3]

With revenue raising concentrated at the center and expenditures assigned to states, the latter are compensated by statutory provisions for transfer of resources from the center through three channels that also seek to address horizontal equity in terms of regional distribution across states. These channels are the Finance Commission, the Planning Commission via support to the states' five-year plans, and via Ministries of the Government of India in the form of Centrally Sponsored Schemes (CSS). In 2001–02, annual transfers from the center to the states under the Finance Commission were approximately Rs 700 billion, while the corresponding figures for transfers through the Planning Commission and the CSS are Rs 400 billion and Rs 250 billion respectively.[4] Grants through these latter two channels are agreed through the Planning Commission and the Ministry of Finance.

The Finance Commission is a constitutional body appointed by the President of India every five years, whose main objective is to recommend devolution of tax revenues from the center to the states. It also recommends grants-in-aid to states that need additional assistance. Finance Commissions have been concerned primarily with the devolution of income and excise taxes, using these grants to address residual fiscal imbalances across the states. Transfers to states through the Finance Commission are essentially on the revenue account, and quite flexible in terms of their uses. Recommendations of the Finance Commission are generally adopted by the central government.

The Planning Commission, chaired by the Prime Minister, recommends financial support for states primarily to meet their capital expenditures, within the framework of the existing national five-year development plan and the states' five-year plans. Transfers through the Planning Commission are based upon socio-economic parameters including the proportion of population below the poverty line, tax effort of the states, and special problems facing specific states, but are not linked to the size of the states' development plans.

The Centrally Sponsored Schemes (CSS) are meant to supplement the resources of the state governments, who are responsible for the implementation of the schemes.[5] These are not statutory transfers but are determined each year by the Finance Ministry of the Government of India in consultation with the Planning Commission. Transfers under the CSS are relatively inflexible, bound by the provisions and guidelines attached to individual schemes, while the first two channels transfer resources as either grants or combinations of grants and loans. The CSS are the center of gravity of targeted poverty interventions in India with almost all the major targeting programs a large subset of these schemes.

The broad approach underlying the Government's poverty-targeted programs embodied in the CSS is three-pronged:

- Provision of assistance for creating an income-generating asset base for self-employment of the rural poor.
- Creation of opportunities for wage employment.
- Area development activities in disadvantaged and poor regions.

This strategy is supported by a cross-cutting theme of improving basic infrastructure and quality of life in rural areas, and by specific programs for social security for the poor and destitute through income transfers.

The CSS, including targeting programs, have a political genesis starting with the electoral strategy of Prime Minister Mrs Indira Gandhi in the late 1960s based on the populist slogan of *Garibi Hatao* (Eliminate Poverty). This strategy led to several initiatives such as nationalization of commercial banks and initiation of numerous poverty-targeted schemes sponsored by the central government and bypassing the state governments, many of which at that time were ruled by other political parties (Saxena and Farrington, 2003). This trend, once initiated, persisted even after the death of Prime Minister Gandhi, with the result that central government involvement has continually increased in subjects under the state governments, such as education, health, and poverty alleviation. Subjects such as population control and family planning, forests and education have been brought from the 'state list' to the 'concurrent list', under the jurisdiction of both central and state governments, through constitutional amendments. The central government has steadily increased the funding and number of CSS, with a dominant share of this funding going straight to district administration, bypassing the state government and placing the district bureaucracy somewhat directly under the central government. Severe deterioration in public finances of state governments, in part due to declining aggregate transfers to states from the center, has resulted in CSS as often being the only schemes in the social sector that are operational at the ground level, with states having little control over them. Poverty alleviation in India (as in many other countries) is clearly as much about politics as it is about the poor.

The political overtones of CSS allocations are as evident today as they were at the start of these schemes. Much like then, several states are ruled by political parties that are not part of the coalition in power at the center. Rao and Singh (2000) document evidence of considerable discretionary, non-economic considerations in transfers through CSS, with states that have greater bargaining power at the center receiving larger per capita transfers. In addition, many poor states are unable to provide matching transfers for the CSS, resulting in lower utilization of central transfers. Nonetheless, the CSS comprise the core of targeted poverty programs in the country, aside from broad-based poverty initiatives such as expenditures on primary health and primary education. Most specific programs targeted at poverty alleviation are a component of the CSS.

Proliferation of centrally sponsored schemes (CSS)

Despite severe fiscal imbalances in the country, manifested in continued high fiscal deficits through most of the 1990s, CSS have proliferated during the decade. In the terminal year of the ninth five-year plan (2001), there were 360 schemes in operation as CSS. The latest five-year plan has called for a convergence of similar schemes and the elimination of schemes that have outlived their utility, viewing the 'mushrooming growth' of CSS as a 'case of the state overreaching itself' (GOI, 2000). The Planning Commission recommended eliminating 48 schemes, merging 161 schemes into 53, and retaining the remaining 135 schemes, implying a continuation forward of a total of 135 schemes.

The large number of schemes under the CSS are a major source of ambiguity in assessing total government expenditures on targeting programs, since some of the schemes are directly targeted at poverty alleviation, while others have less direct yet substantial benefits for the poor in the medium and long term. The selection of specific schemes as poverty targeted will necessarily be qualitative, and vary according to sources. Figure 2.2 provides trends in total expenditure on targeting programs during the 1990s based on one such classification.

As can be seen, expenditures have increased substantially in nominal terms, by a factor of almost 500 per cent. However, due to relatively high inflation rates in the first half of the 1990s, the increase in real terms – in 1993–94 prices – has been relatively more modest. In particular, expenditures in real terms remained relatively static during the 1990s following an increase in 1993–94, and have only increased more recently in 2000.

For comparison, Table 2.4 provides estimates by the Planning Commission on poverty related schemes in 1999–2000. According to these estimates, total expenditure on poverty programs was Rs 342.6 billion, but if we exclude the subsidies on food and kerosene oil, the total is only Rs 170.2 billion. However, these data do not include transfers directly to the district governments by the center, which, as already noted, can be substantial (Rs 150 billion in 2002).

Although the estimates vary, they are quantitatively in the same order of magnitude. Nayak et al. (2002) estimated total expenditures on schemes

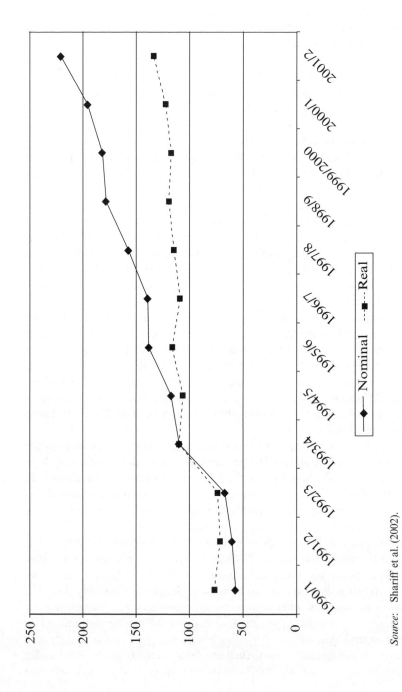

Source: Shariff et al. (2002).

Figure 2.2 Trends in central government expenditures on targeted programs (nominal and in 1993–94 prices)

under CSS at approximately Rs 250 billion in 2000, including direct transfers from the center to the districts. This amount was almost 3–4 times higher than all Official Development Assistance to India in 2000, which was US $1.49 billion or almost Rs 70 billion (at an exchange rate of Rs 47/US $1). Thus, notwithstanding a relatively static trend in real terms through much of the 1990s, expenditures by the Government of India on targeting programs are higher by significant orders of magnitude compared to all aid to the country. Not all CSS are narrowly defined poverty-targeted programs, since some of them may be more broadly targeted, focusing on irrigation or road development for example. At the same time, these amounts are also supplemented by expenditures made by state governments to share in costs of the schemes under CSS.

Table 2.4   Poverty programs in India, 1999–2000

Name of the Program/Ministry	Buduget allocation in 1999–2000 (Rs billion)
Rural Development Schemes	94.3
Food Subsidy	92.0
Subsidy on kerosene	80.4
Health & Family Welfare (only 70% of the outlay)	28.4
Social Justice & Empowerment Sector	12.1
Integrated Child Development Services	11.5
Midday meal	10.3
DPEP	7.6
Watershed development through agriculture	2.3
Tribal development	1.9
Swarnajayanti Shahari Rozgar Yojana (Urban Poverty)	1.8
Total	342.6

Source: GOI (2000), Chapter 31.

Table 2.5 shows trends in the relative composition of schemes under CSS over the last two decades in terms of broad heads of development. Evidently, the share of schemes under agriculture and rural development and social sectors has been rising consistently, exceeding 60 per cent in the previous decade, at the expense of schemes targeted at industry and minerals, energy and communications sectors. There was a marked increase in 2002–03, the first year of the tenth five-year plan, in the share of schemes directed at transport and in the share of 'others', which is due to several new schemes announced for impoverished northeastern states of the country. The

increased share of transport reflects a major expansion of road construction
in India funded by the center, but implemented by the states.

*Table 2.5   Distribution of central plan allocations through ministries, by
             heads of development*

	Sixth Plan 1980/81– 1985/86	Seventh Plan 1985/86– 1989/90	Eighth Plan 1992/93– 1996/97	Ninth Plan 1997/98– 2001/02	2002–03
Industry and Minerals,	51.0	44.0	25.3	16.9	13.0
Energy, Communications, Agriculture, Irrigation, Rural Development, Health and Family Welfare, Education, Water, Sanitation, Housing, Urban Development, SC's and ST's Welfare	33.0	40.6	62.5	61.3	55.3
Transport	14.1	14.1	9.3	17.3	21.3
Others	1.9	1.3	2.9	4.5	10.4
Total	100.0	100.0	100.0	100.0	100.0

Source: GOI (2000), cited in Saxena and Farrington (2003).

The large expenditures on poverty reduction through the CSS are
difficult to track for two reasons. First, they are routed through different
ministries of the central government of India with little centralization of
the relevant information. For example, although the aggregate budget
of the Government of India provides budgetary allocations on different
schemes, the information is scattered across accounts of different ministries
implementing the schemes. In addition, even within the relevant ministries,
the funds are allocated across numerous schemes, some large and some quite
miniscule.[6] As noted already, while the expenditures on the CSS in real terms
have not risen sharply, the schemes themselves have proliferated, resulting
in numerous instances of renaming schemes accompanied by merging and
restructuring of schemes that allocate specific components into other newly
created or renamed schemes. The result is erosion of transparency.

Table 2.6 presents an overview of direct poverty-targeted programs
in India, identifying major schemes under the CSS and the ministries
implementing the schemes. Only schemes with central funding exceeding
Rs 1 billion in 2001–02 are shown in the table. Clearly, several ministries of
the central government are involved in implementing targeting programs,

but, in terms of number of major schemes, the major entity involved is the Ministry of Rural Development. This is natural given that the vast majority of the poor in India live in rural areas. Allocations are much higher for schemes implemented by the Department of Public Distribution under the Ministry of Consumer Affairs, which provides subsidized food under the public distribution system targeted to those below the poverty line, and the Ministry of Fertilizers. However, fertilizer subsidies are distributed to the producers rather than directed to poor farmers, and their treatment as targeting measures is controversial.

TARGETING MEASURES USED IN ANTI-POVERTY PROGRAMS

There exist a large number of targeting programs in India of varying sizes, channeled through different ministries of the central government, and with different modalities of implementation. Some of these schemes are implemented by the state governments while others have a larger proportion of funds flowing directly from the center to district administrations. Obviously, a comprehensive review of each and every targeted activity would be neither feasible nor desirable. The discussion below therefore centers on a select subset of the targeting programs, based upon their relative quantitative importance, availability of information relating to their implementation monitoring and evaluation, and relevance to the objectives of the present analysis, based upon targeting design and effectiveness of the scheme. The schemes chosen include examples of pure income transfers, food-for-work, self-employment and infrastructure generation.

First, however, a brief discussion of targeting mechanisms in the Indian context is useful. A widely used categorization of targeting mechanisms that can be used to classify programs is given below (see also, Chapter 1, this volume).

- *Self-targeting*: Such schemes rely on differential incentives of agents in tackling the problem of asymmetric information between the principal (the government providing poverty relief) and the agents (households or individuals affected by the government schemes). The design of the schemes has the objective of making the scheme worth participating in only for those who are poor, not for others.
- *Activity targeting*: This relies on broad targeting, primarily through subsidized provision of goods and services, whose benefit incidence will be progressive, that is falling largely on those who are poor rather than better-off. Examples typically include primary education, provision

Table 2.6 *Major poverty targeted programs of the Government of India*

Ministry/Department	Schemes	Central funding 2001–02 (INR billions)	% of total expenditure	% of GDP
Ministry of Rural Development	1. Swarn Jayanti Gram Swarozgar Yojana (SGSY)	5.5	0.15	0.026
	2. Jawahar Gram Samridhi Yojana (JGSY)	18.8	0.52	0.090
	3. Employment Assurance Scheme (EAS)	18.8	0.52	0.090
	4. Sampoorna Grameen Rozgar Yojana (SGRY)	87.5	2.41	0.418
	5. Indira Awas Yojana (IAY)	16.9	0.47	0.081
	6. National Social Assistance Program (NSAP)	6.4	0.18	0.031
	7. Annapoorna Scheme	1.0	0.03	0.005
	8. Pradhan Mantri Gram Sadak Yojana	25.0	0.69	0.120
	9. Integrated Wastelands Development Program (IWDP)	4.3	0.12	0.021
	10. Drought Prone Areas Program (DPAP)	1.6	0.04	0.008
	11. Desert Development Program (DDP)	1.2	0.03	0.006
Ministry of Urban Development and Poverty Alleviation	1. National Slum Development Program (NSDP)	2.8	0.08	0.013
Department of Public Distribution, Ministry of Consumer Affairs	1. Targeted Public Distribution System (TPDS) and Antyodaya Anna Yojana (AAY)	176.1	4.86	0.842

Department of Education, Ministry of Human Resource Development	1. Non Formal Education (NFE)	4.0	0.11	0.019
	2. National Programme for Nutritional Support to Primary Education	9.3	0.26	0.044
	3. Operation Blackboard Scheme	5.2	0.14	0.025
	4. Sarva Shiksha Abhiyan	5.0	0.14	0.024
Department of Fertilizers	1. Retention Pricing Scheme (RPS)	73.7	2.03	0.352
	2. Concession Scheme for de-controlled fertilizers	45.2	1.25	0.216
Ministry of Agro and Rural Industries	1. Prime Minister's Rozgar Yojana	1.9	0.05	0.009
	2. Rural Employment Generation Programme (REGP)	1.2	0.03	0.006
	3. Khadi and Village Industries Commission (KVIC)	2.5	0.07	0.012
Ministry of Social Justice and Empowerment	1. Special Central Assistance To Special Component Plan For Scheduled Castes	4.5	0.12	0.022
Department of Women and Child Development, Ministry of Human Resource Development	1. Integrated Child Development services (ICDS) Scheme	12.2	0.34	0.058

Source: Various documents of Government of India. Percentages with respect to GDP and total government expenditure derived from National Accounts Statistics.

of primary health care and basic health services in rural areas, and broadly targeted subsidies for irrigation, power and fertilizers. As noted already, most of these broadly targeted interventions are not discussed in detail here.

- *Location targeting*: This is based on the geographical distribution of poverty, seeking to target interventions in geographic areas with high concentration of the poor.
- *Indicator targeting*: This relies on non-income indicators that are meant to be correlated with poverty. These can include lack of or size of ownership of land, form of dwelling, social status and gender of head of household.

Asymmetric information between the government, seeking to provide transfers to the poor, and individuals or households in the economy who can legitimately or otherwise seek these transfers, is the *raison d'être* of targeting. The underlying rationale of these targeting mechanisms is that administrative and other costs of identifying those who are poor are high, potentially reducing the resources that would be transferred to the poor under the scheme. Targeting mechanisms are a program-design innovation in response to the information asymmetry and the high costs of overcoming the information barrier.

However, this framework is implicitly less than comprehensive in approach, in the sense of focusing only on one scheme at a time. In a context where the principal (in a principal–agent context) has several schemes in operation, the administrative costs *per scheme* (of overcoming information asymmetry) can get diluted substantially, thereby vitiating the need for indirect targeting mechanisms for any specific scheme. Put alternatively, the issue of whether or not the administrative costs of identifying the poor are undertaken by the government usually does not depend on any specific scheme. In an inter-temporal context, where the government does not know what specific schemes it may want to implement in the near future, 'tagging the poor', which is known in the Indian context as 'administrative identification', may provide externalities in terms of greater choice of schemes and their design.

This is an important issue, as shown by the Indian experience where a large number of government poverty-targeted schemes rely on administrative identification to select beneficiaries. The most common criterion used in government schemes is that beneficiaries should be households classified as below the poverty line. Other criteria, such as focusing on Scheduled Castes or Tribes (which would represent indicator targeting in the Indian context) are overlaid onto poverty status. As mentioned above, it may be argued that with an aggregate annual budget on CSS schemes exceeding Rs 250 billion, it may be worthwhile for the government to undertake some form of poverty classification to better target the poor. Indeed, analytically it is perhaps more pertinent to ask why other targeting mechanisms should exist at all once the administrative identification process has been undertaken. For example, some schemes rely on self-selection (food-for-work and rural employment schemes), geographical location, and the use of social category like caste as indicators. Use of indirect targeting mechanisms in conjunction with administrative identification may reflect in part the recognition that classification of the poor may be imperfect due to various reasons. In particular, the process itself may suffer from high type one and type two errors, as discussed below, resulting in exclusion of many poor and inclusion of many non-poor. In addition, the frequency of identification is necessarily spread apart in time, which would make it impossible to differentiate between transient and chronic poverty, that is to differentiate the needy seeking food-for-work in the face of natural calamity from the longer term destitute.

Food Subsidies and Administrative Identification

Since most targeting programs currently in existence directly or indirectly rely on administrative classification of households into those above and below the poverty lines, it is useful to briefly explain how this identification is undertaken. The exercise is intimately related to government efforts to provide food security to the population through the Public Distribution System (PDS). The PDS is a major component of aggregate subsidies spent by the central government.

The PDS, in its earlier form, dates back almost fifty years and was a general entitlement scheme with universal coverage until 1992. It provided a rationed quantity of basic food (rice, wheat, sugar, edible oils) and some essential non-food items (kerosene oil and coal) at prices substantially below market prices. The central government was responsible for procuring, storing and transporting the PDS commodities up to central warehouses in each state or union territory, while the state government was responsible for distribution within the state.

While the universal coverage of PDS continued, the government introduced two major changes, the first in 1992, in the form of the Revamped PDS and, subsequently, in 1997 as the Targeted PDS, both innovations being targeted at poor households. The Revamped PDS relied on geographical targeting, being introduced with universal coverage in only 1775 blocks in poor areas – mainly tribal and hilly, drought-prone and remotely located areas. The Targeted PDS, on the other hand, was implemented in all areas, but was open only to those identified as below the poverty line. Along with the introduction of the Targeted PDS, the price differential between PDS shops and the open market was almost eliminated, effectively providing subsidized food only to families identified as below the poverty line.[7]

At the core of the Targeted PDS was division of the entire population into one of two categories, based on the poverty line defined by the Planning Commission of India for different states for 1993–94. Multiple criteria were adopted for classification of those households below the poverty line, which in addition to income also included qualitative parameters like household occupation, housing conditions, number of earners, land operated or owned, livestock, and ownership of durables such as a television, refrigerator, motor cycle, three wheeler, tractor, power tiller, or combined thresher. The responsibility for undertaking surveys and identifying the poor lay with the state government. However, the total number of below-the-poverty-line families in each state was capped somewhat arbitrarily at state-level estimates of the poor made by the Planning Commission using data for 1993–94, adjusted for growth in population in the interim. Hence the application of the new Targeted PDS system provided the opportunity to identify poor households and link these exclusively with a range of other targeted benefits.

Shortcomings of Administrative Identification

Despite introduction in 1997, surveys for the identification of poor families were not completed in 18 out of 31 states by 2000 (CAG, 2000). Even in states where identification was completed, identification cards were not provided to a significant number of poor families. Thus implementation of the exercise has been slow and inefficient.[8]

A major criticism of the targeting is also that it has wrongly excluded a large number of eligible families. There are several reasons for this, both conceptual and operational. Conceptually, the main issue has been the appropriateness of income poverty to define the poor, specifically the absolute poverty line used by the Planning Commission. It is argued that the official poverty line represents too low a level of absolute expenditure, which may exclude large sections of the population who experience low and variable incomes. If other criteria are used, such as nutrition, the number of households that can be deemed poor is much higher than ceiling figures estimated by the Planning Commission in 1993–94, (GOI, 2003).[9]

Operationally, as noted above, identification surveys have not been completed in 18 of 31 states and, across the country, 18 per cent of families identified as poor do not have identification cards. Even where surveys have been conducted, there still remain concerns on accuracy given the difficulties of measuring income. Since there are no regular official estimates of actual household incomes, implementation of administrative identification is subject to substantial practical and administrative problems. For example, an evaluation of the Targeted PDS in Uttar Pradesh – one of the poorest states in India – by the World Bank based on the Uttar Pradesh-Bihar Survey of Living Conditions (1997–98) found that 56 per cent of households in the lowest income quintile did not get identification cards. In the next quintile, 63 per cent of the households were without cards.

The actual income equivalent of the benefits received under the Targeted PDS has been found to be very modest. According to the review of CAG (2000), average income transferred per household per month to the below-poverty-line population was between Rs 22 and Rs 46 across different states. In Punjab, it was less than Rs 7. However, the government incurs substantial costs to achieve these unimpressive transfers. These costs include, aside from subsidizing the sale price of grains, the costs of transportation and storage and, even more significant, the minimum support prices paid to farmers (which are significantly higher than market prices). The total subsidy cost for the PDS system was Rs 410.8 billion during 1992–99, according to CAG (2000). The estimated cost of transferring 1 rupee of income to poor households under the Targeted PDS was put as high as Rs 6.68 (Dev and Evenson, 2003).

Hence the administrative identification exercise to classify all households into those above and below the poverty line has been implemented with several shortcomings. Its progress has been slow and inefficient, and the results are not always reliable. However, the classification based on this exercise is used by a majority of the schemes in operation today that are targeting poor households.

IMPACTS OF THE MAIN TARGETING PROGRAMS

This section provides a selective survey of five major targeting programs listed below.

1. Rural employment program – *Sampoorna Grameen Rozgar Yojana* (SGRY), or Comprehensive Rural Employment Scheme.
2. Self-employment scheme – *Swarn Jayanti Gram Swarozgar Yojana* (SGSY), or Golden Jubilee Rural Self Employment Scheme.
3. Rural Housing Scheme – *Indira Awas Yojana* (IAY).
4. National Old Age Pension Scheme (NOAPS).
5. Drought Prone Areas Program (DPAP).

The first scheme in the list is the main program for rural employment generation for the needy poor, and subsumes all food-for-work programs, while the second scheme is the national targeting program geared towards assisting the poor through asset creation to generate self-employment. The third and fourth schemes (IAY and NOAPS) are the most important schemes for pure income transfers, while the last scheme aims at creating infrastructure for the poor.

Rural Employment Programs – *Sampoorna Grameen Rozgar Yojana* (SGRY) and Others

The SGRY, targeting poverty reduction through employment generation, has a long history in India, spanning several incarnations. Its genesis lies in the National Rural Employment Program and the Rural Landless Employment Program, both of which were initiated in the early 1970s, but subsequently merged in 1989 into a new scheme called *Jawahar Rozgar Yojana* (JRY) or the *Jawahar* Employment Scheme. A number of different schemes have been used and Figure 2.3 charts their complex history and evolution.

Employment Guarantee Scheme (EGS)

Highly influential in thinking about employment creation programs in India was the initial experience in Maharashtra. An early food-for-work program implemented in the western Indian state of Maharashtra was widely regarded as very successful in its initial years, and indeed was the inspiration for later national efforts. The Employment Guarantee Scheme (EGS) started on a pilot basis in 1965 in one district (Sangli) and a modified EGS was implemented across the state in 1972, following one of the most severe droughts in the region in recent history. The scheme was soon suspended for two years, replaced by central government schemes, but in 1974 the state government decided to set up a permanent scheme using only state resources, leading to resumption of the EGS. It was provided a statutory basis with the enactment of the Maharashtra Employment Guarantee Act of 1977. The scheme is financed by urban taxes (on professionals and motor vehicles) with matching grants from the state government.

The EGS is unique for several reasons, including its age, being one of the oldest such schemes in the developing world, its large scale of operations at inception, and the fact that it guarantees employment (rather than merely assuring it). The EGS provides a guarantee of employment to all adults above 18 years of age who are willing to do unskilled manual labor on a piece-rate basis. Its primary objective is thus creation of employment opportunities with the secondary objective of creating rural assets to provide drought proofing, soil management and conservation. Starting

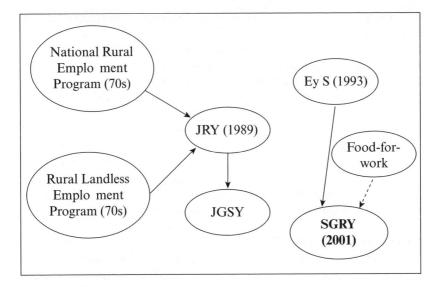

Figure 2.3   SGRY – scheme history

from 4.5 million person days of jobs created in its first year, the EGS was generating more than 100 million person days of employment by the early 1980s (190 million in 1986), before declining to 80–90 million person days after 1989 (Dev, 1995). Cumulatively, the scheme spent Rs 27 billion up to 1991 to create about 2.3 billion person days of employment in the state. Not surprisingly, the EGS is one of the most analyzed public-works programs in the literature, and received high marks in its initial years from most evaluations (Gaiha, 1996; Datt and Ravallion, 1994; and Dev, 1995).

There was a sharp decline in the coverage of the EGS after 1988 following a virtual doubling of the wage rates in May 1988. Prior to that, EGS wage rates were less than market wages but this was reversed with the wage hike. According to some studies, this resulted in rationing of employment opportunities, leading to exclusion of eligible participants (and thus eroding the nature of the 'guarantee'). In more recent years, observers have also noted a deterioration in other elements that translate the guarantee into actual delivery of the EGS benefits, including informal program guidelines, extensive monitoring, unscheduled field visits, vigilance tours by officials at various levels, and the advisory and supervisory roles of unofficial statutory committees. Although targeting errors of undercoverage (type one errors) are not considered a source of major concern, the declining coverage, quality and maintenance of rural assets created and problems of governance are noteworthy, given the exemplary history of the EGS.

For example, a recent review found wage employment generated through food-for-work continued to be important, contributing a significant 40 to 45 per cent of total family income of beneficiaries, but the work was not organized in the lean season, and bribes had to be paid to obtain the employment (PDI, 2000). Even more recently, a petition has been filed in the Bombay High Court accusing the state government of diverting money from the Employment Guarantee Fund of the EGS into its general-purpose budget (Bavadam, 2003). Ironically, the legal action has been brought by a former member of the Planning Commission who is also a member of the committee set up by the state government to review the Maharashtra Employment Guarantee Act 1977. The state government believes the trend decline in coverage of the EGS reflects a declining need for the scheme in view of improvements in rural economic conditions.

Jawahar Rozgar Yojana (JRY)
At a national level the subsequent scheme, the JRY, was meant to offer additional gainful employment to the unemployed and the under-employed people in rural areas through creation of rural economic infrastructure, although it fell short of the early achievements of the Maharashtra program. Employment generation was too inadequate to be meaningful, with an average of roughly 11 days of employment created per person according to an evaluation in 1994 (GOI, 2000). The resources available were spread too thinly to increase coverage without concern for duration of employment. The asset creation involved high material costs and was not particularly labor intensive, in flagrant violation of prescribed norms. Other routine violations included the use of contractors or middlemen who often hired outside laborers to lower the wage rates, and used trucks and tractors instead of labor-intensive techniques. Fudging of muster rolls and measurement books was thus rampant. Only 17 per cent of jobs generated under the JRY went to women, against a target ratio of 30 per cent.

According to estimates presented by Dev and Evenson (2003), the cost of transferring one rupee under the JRY was Rs 2.28. This can be compared to a cost of Rs 1.85 per rupee transferred under the Maharashtra Employment Guarantee Scheme, and the high ratio of Rs 6.68 per rupee transferred under the PDS. In view of its deficiencies, the JRY was restructured and transformed in 1999 into a new scheme – the Jawahar Gram Samridhi Yojana (JGSY) or the Jawahar Rural Advancement Scheme, which explicitly prioritized asset creation as the primary objective, followed by wage employment. No evaluation studies of JGSY are available since it lasted only a short time before being merged into a new scheme, the Sampoorna Grameen Rozgar Yojana (SGRY).

Employment Assurance Scheme (EAS)

The transformation of the JRY into the JGSY was preceded by a parallel scheme launched in 1993 – the Employment Assurance Scheme (EAS) – that had similar objectives as the JRY/JGSY, but with reversed priorities. The EAS, which was in implementation through most of the country by 1997–98, had the primary objective of creating additional wage employment for the rural poor through manual work in periods of acute shortage of employment opportunities, with asset creation as a secondary objective. The EAS relied on self-targeting by setting of wage rates below market wages. However, the EAS showed similar failings in implementation as its close variant, the JGSY. For example, the scheme generated on average only about 17 days of employment per person per year according to a study by the Controller and Auditor General of India (GOI, 2000). The objective of the EAS was, by comparison, to provide assured employment of 100 days per year at statutory minimum wages. The self-selection targeting was subverted by routine use of contractors in most states, fudging of the employment rolls, and violation of norms that called for a 60:40 split of wages and materials in asset creation. As a result, in three states – West Bengal, Gujarat and Haryana – the estimated unit cost of generating a day's employment was Rs 200 to Rs 300, far in excess of wage rates. For the country as a whole, the mid-term evaluation estimated that only Rs 15 of every Rs 100 expenditure reached the beneficiaries as wages, against a target of Rs 60. No inventory of assets was kept, making it difficult to ascertain whether assets created were community assets or for individual benefit. In addition, with deteriorating finances of state governments, allocated funds did not reach the ground in many cases, in part due to lack of matching funds from state governments.

Amongst similar problems in the implementation of the EAS, a review by the Planning Commission (PEO, 2000) found the effective rate of utilization of funds was only about 67 per cent of the notional minimum allocations to administrative blocks. This reflected in part lack of matching funds from state government preventing release of funds, and also ad hoc and untimely release of funds by the governments. For example, the first part of central government allocation (40 per cent of the total allocation) was to be provided at the beginning of the financial year, with the remainder to be released on receipt of utilization certificates. In practice, however, in more than half the 14 states studied, states received more than 50 per cent of their allocation in the last quarter of the year. There was also evidence of significant diversion of funds, reflected in a mismatch between allocation and expenditure of funds at different nodes of implementation of the scheme. This diversion was also noted by the report of the Controller and Auditor General of India (CAG, 1997). PEO (2000) also found only 32 per cent of villages were covered by the EAS in an average block, with little consistency in implementation within specific villages. Thus, only 5.4 per cent of villages covered in a block typically had the EAS operations in each year during the first four years of the EAS (1993–97). Thus, coverage of villages within specific blocks was ad hoc, allowing discretion to district administrations, and there was little credibility in terms of providing assurance of employment in the villages actually covered. In addition, the study estimated that on average the EAS implementation covered only 16 per cent of the target group in the chosen villages. Thus, the effective annual coverage of the target groups in ten of the 14 states was less than 10 per cent, being as low as 1 to 3 per cent in some states. Combined with the small number of days of employment generated per person on average, the impact of the EAS on household income was negligible. Although the EAS was quantitatively more significant as a source of income than other government wage employment programs running in parallel in the villages, it contributed only 11.5 per cent of household annual income to the extremely limited group of selected beneficiaries.

Sampoorna Grameen Rozgar Yojana (SGRY)

Thus, in practice, there was little difference between the JGSY and the EAS, in terms of both objectives and implementation failures, with the only substantive difference being administrative. The JGSY was implemented by village-level institutions (*Panchayti Raj* institutions), while the EAS relied on the state administrative apparatus.[10] In September 2001, on-going schemes under the EAS and the JGSY were merged into a new scheme – the SGRY. The objectives of SGRY are to provide additional wage employment in rural areas and also food security, alongside the creation of durable community, social and economic assets and infrastructure development. A part of wages to the workers is to be distributed in the form of 5 kilograms of food grains per day. The cash component is shared by the central and state governments in the ratio of 75:25, while the cost of food grains distributed to the states is borne entirely by the central government. The SGRY is implemented in two streams, with each stream receiving half of the total resources available. The first stream is implemented through district and intermediate elected bodies (such as *Zilla Parishads* and *Block Panchayats*), while in the other stream funds are allocated to the village *Panchayats* (see note 3).

The SGRY also encompasses all food-for-work programs in the country, since it includes a special component for augmenting food security through additional wage employment in calamity-affected rural areas. A certain percentage of foodgrains allotted under the SGRY is reserved for this purpose. Foodgrains under the Special Component can be utilized by any scheme of the central or state government that is implemented to generate additional employment in calamity-affected areas. Administrative arrangements for implementing the SGRY involve coordination among three central ministries, namely, Agriculture, Food and Rural Development. The Food Ministry releases grains at the direction of the Ministry of Agriculture, while the Rural Development Ministry is responsible for administration and supervision. The scheme is self-targeting and available to the rural poor, who are in need of wage employment and willing to take up unskilled, manual work at specified wage rates. Preference should be given to the poorest of the poor, women, and scheduled castes and tribes. The beneficiaries are selected by the *Gram Panchayat* during meetings of the village assembly (*Gram Sabha*).

The emphasis on payment in kind – via foodgrains – combined with the difficulty and cost of storing and transporting foodgrains reduces the scope for misappropriation of resources by officials. Nonetheless, responsibilities for storage, transport and distribution within districts are contracted out to fair price shops (which are part of the central government targeted public distribution system of subsidized foodgrains) and the associated contractors. This has created substantial scope for fraudulent practices due to the large gap between market prices and prices in fair price shops (though the gap has been declining of late). Nayak et al. (2002) estimate that the combination of malpractice among administrators at lower levels of government and contractors results in perhaps only 25 per cent of the wage funds to which beneficiaries are entitled actually reaching them.

SGRY, the latest incarnation of employment-based, food-for-work targeting in India, is too recent for any comprehensive evaluation studies to have been done. However, one recent study has reviewed the implementation of the SGRY in the state of Andhra Pradesh. Using primary data collected over 12 months between 2001 and 2002 from six villages, Deshingkar and Johnson (2003) find little has changed at the ground level in implementing the SGRY. Despite attempts at decentralization of decision-making in the SGRY, village-level governments (*Gram Sabhas and Panchayats*) are often controlled by the local landed elite. Beneficiaries were selected during meetings among the local officials (members of *Panchayat* and village heads) and contractors, and the decisions announced in the village meetings of the *Gram Sabha*. In three villages, the largest number of laborers were hired from the hamlet of the village head, while in another the largest share of hired labor belonged only to the caste of the village head.

There was also widespread use of contractors, contrary to the scheme guidelines, often in connivance with local officials. The contractors also obtained illegal profit by claiming the full rice quota for partially and poorly completed works, claiming rice for old assets already completed under some other scheme, 'double-dipping' by filing separate claims to different departments for the same work, and submitting inflated costs in works proposals. In addition, contractors often decided to pay labor only in cash either because rice was released late to the contractors, or because the contractor could sell the rice in the open market at a profit.[11]

The impact of the scheme varied across the six villages, being relatively high in one village (which also had the lowest corruption in implementation), but miniscule in most others. On an average, 24 per cent of households sampled in these villages had participated in the scheme (ranging from 65 per cent in one village to 3 per cent in the worst case). With the exception of the single village, the number of person days of employment created was also low, averaging less than 14 days per participating household. Two major reasons contributing to this, aside from corruption and leakage, were use of outside or migrant labor by contractors to minimize costs, and substantial use of labor-displacing machinery (often owned by contractors).

Impact of employment programs
This brief review of employment generation and food-for-work type of targeting in India paints a fairly bleak picture, and highlights several problems in implementation. Some of these problems are well known, such as the importance of appropriate wage setting in affecting screening efficiency. In the case of SGRY in Andhra Pradesh, Deshingkar and Johnson (2003) document that wages were too low in relatively prosperous villages, leading to the use of migrant labor and machinery, while in poor villages the wages were much higher than prevailing rates, leading to crowding out of the really poor. A well-designed scheme of self-selection (without quantitative rationing) should lead to virtually negligible levels of type one and type two errors, in that only the really poor would be willing to work at wages below prevailing rates, and all those willing to work at these rates would be accommodated. With only quantitative rationing (a ceiling on total funds available), some needy poor may not be able to access wage employment leading to undercoverage (a type one error in targeting). In relatively prosperous villages, with wages set too low, local labor may not have participated but presumably the migrant poor willing to work at these wages were a justifiable target, implying little leakage. In contrast, in poor villages where the targeting was really needed, the higher than prevailing market wage rates created room for leakage (type two error), with the poor crowded out by better off migrant workers.

However, problems other than wage setting are of deeper and greater concern, stemming from institutional and governance constraints, and magnifying both types of targeting errors. While the government has sought to decentralize scheme implementation to create greater ownership of resulting assets, the local level administration and the *Panchayti Raj* institutions are strongly susceptible to corruption. This has resulted in flagrant violations of government guidelines, including use of contractors and intermediaries, excessive reliance on labor-displacing machinery, payment in cash instead of kind, and doubtful quality of the assets created. Greater reliance on labor-displacing machinery and payment in cash rather than cash in kind magnifies type one errors leading to the exclusion from benefits of those who are really poor at the expense of funds diverted to owners of the machinery and middlemen. Other corrupt practices magnify type two errors by diverting funds and benefiting corrupt officials and middlemen who are not the intended beneficiaries of the program. Thus, even the most well-designed scheme, relying on self-selection, will fail in implementation if employment rolls can be falsified, assets shown as created when they actually are not, and payments made that are below those legally mandated. Although employment generation using food-for-work continues to be a critical element of poverty targeting in areas adversely affected, the leakage of funds, corruption and poor governance result in the impact of these interventions on poverty being substantially diluted.

Self-employment Schemes – *Swarn Jayanti Gram Swarozgar Yojana (SGSY) and Others*

SGSY or the Golden Jubilee Rural Self Employment Scheme is the main national scheme for rural self-employment and was launched by the government in April 1999 as a single, holistic program to cover all aspects of self-employment for the rural poor. The funding of the scheme was to be shared by the center and the states on a 75:25 basis and a central allocation of Rs 26.7 billion was provided for the period 1999–2002.

Integrated Rural Development Program (IRDP)

The SGSY too is not a new scheme but a reincarnation of an earlier scheme – the Integrated Rural Development Program (IRDP).[12] The IRDP was the first major intervention for creating an income generating asset base to promote self-employment, using a mix of subsidy and institutional credit from the formal financial system. It was launched in 1976 in 20 selected districts on a pilot basis and soon extended to cover all the blocks in the country by 1980. As many as 54 million families were assisted by IRDP between 1980–81 and 1998–99, by providing Rs 203 billion in credits with an average loan size in 1997 of Rs 5600. IRDP accounted for almost 35 per cent of all small borrowers' accounts in commercial banks in India.[13] The risk of the loans made by banks under IRDP was borne by the banks, and the recovery rates on these loans were poor, between 25 per cent and 33 per cent (Long and Srivastava, 2002). A concurrent evaluation of the

IRDP showed that of the 54 million beneficiaries, only one in seven (14.8 per cent) managed to cross the poverty line (CAG, 2003).

Studies reviewing the state-wise implementation of IRDP and its allied poverty-alleviation schemes for the Planning Commission showed substantial problems in implementation, which were also relatively consistent across the states. For example, MAKER (2002), reporting findings of a survey conducted in the states of Bihar and Jharkhand, found 24 per cent of the beneficiaries of poverty-alleviation programs had incomes above the poverty line while a large proportion of others were in the income group just below the poverty line. Implementation of poverty schemes in all zones was steeped in corruption. To access the programs, payment of bribes was an essential condition. Misutilization of funds was also prevalent since neither the authorities nor the beneficiaries took the schemes in the spirit intended. The authorities viewed them as a source of additional funds for their own priorities, while the beneficiaries took the assistance as a subsidy with no serious thought to the purpose of the assistance. In general, a considerable amount of funds were siphoned off by local authorities in connivance with local middlemen. Procedural delays and red-tape were also an endemic problem reported by beneficiaries. Similarly, a survey of 104 beneficiaries of four schemes in Maharashtra (including IRDP) found weak targeting with a third of the beneficiaries above the poverty line. A large proportion of the beneficiaries of other schemes in the survey also reported having to pay bribes to receive benefits.

Swarn Jayanti Gram Swarozgar Yojana (SGSY)

The newest version of self-employment schemes – the SGSY – is a holistic program covering different aspects of self-employment including organizing the poor into self-help groups, training, credit, technology, infrastructure and marketing. It aims to establish a large number of micro-enterprises in the rural areas, and provides great emphasis on mobilization of the poor through formation of self-help groups among potential recipients. In consolidating numerous schemes including the IRDP and its associated schemes, the SGSY also aims at integrating the activities of different agencies, including the district rural development agencies, banks, line departments, *Panchayti Raj* institutions and non-governmental organizations (NGOs). At the Block level, identification of key activities in selected villages, verification of assets and review of the recovery performance are to be undertaken by Block-level SGSY committees (working under district-level and state-level committees). The individual beneficiaries have to be selected in the village assembly with the involvement of banks and the district administration. There are also special safeguards under the SGSY for the vulnerable groups. For example, 50 per cent of the self-help groups to be formed are to be comprised exclusively of women and 40 per cent of the individual beneficiaries are to be women. In addition, scheduled castes and tribes and the physically disabled are to constitute 50 per cent and 3 per cent, respectively, of individual beneficiaries.

Financial assistance under the SGSY to individuals or groups is given in the form of a subsidy by the government and credit by banks, as was the case with the IRDP. Banks can classify their lending under the SGSY as (central bank mandated) priority-sector lending but are liable for all the risks of these loans.[14] The subsidy allowed under the program is uniform at the rate of 30 per cent of the project cost subject to a ceiling of Rs 7500 per individual, and 50 per cent of the project cost with a ceiling of Rs 125 000 for group projects. For irrigation projects there is no ceiling on the subsidy.

Instead of setting annual targets, the SGSY aimed at covering 30 per cent of below-poverty-line families, as classified by administrative identification, in five years of operations (1999–2004). As of 31 March, 2001, SGSY had 1.03 million beneficiaries with bank credit of Rs 14.5 billion along with government subsidies of Rs 6.9 billion. By the end of the third year (March 2002), only 2.56 million of the targeted poor families were covered, comprising less than 5 per cent of the five-year target. Thus there was no acceleration in coverage and pace of implementation; the number of poor families covered by the erstwhile IRDP in the last two years of its implementation was 17 per cent higher than covered in the first three years of SGSY implementation (CAG, 2003).

Impact of the SGSY
Several other problems exist with the implementation of the SGSY. The intended integration of activities of different agencies has not happened. In most states, there was no evidence of proper planning that was crucial to setting in motion the overall process identified for implementation. Selection of key activities was undertaken without involving concerned agencies, including banks, as specified in the guidelines. Project reports for the selected activities were either not prepared or were highly deficient. Even the identification of individual beneficiaries and the formation of groups lacked involvement of line departments and banks, as envisaged. There is also no evidence of an overall shift of focus, as planned, from individuals to groups, in part because implementing agencies have been unable to ensure proper evolution of self-help groups and there have been delays in release of funds to sustain their evolution.[15]

Subsidies combined with weak governance are an irresistible magnet for corruption, and the SGSY is no exception with pervasive malpractice by lower-level officials. State-wise surveys show a uniform pattern of deductions made by bank officials, as much as 10 per cent of the amount, on loans sanctioned under SGSY. With the cooperation of local officials, banks have also made illicit 'charges' on the beneficiaries. In other cases, over 20 per cent of the subsidy component was charged under different ways as 'speed money' or 'convenience charges'. Several instances have been found of local officials providing the assets to beneficiaries, in collusion with intermediaries, in contrast with the requirement that assets be purchased by beneficiaries from approved suppliers in exchange for cash payment by the beneficiaries.

Malpractice is pervasive not just at the micro-level of implementation of SGSY. According to an audit test check of Rs 9.9 billion spent on SGSY (of a total reported expenditure to date of Rs 30.6 billion) as much as 54 per cent of the funds (Rs 5.3 billion) were either diverted, misutilized or misreported (CAG, 2003). Of the Rs 5.3 billion, about Rs 1.2 billion were invested by the state governments in special term deposits, Personal Ledger Accounts and Civil Deposits. Rs. 1.1 billion were accounted for by inflated expenditures, and the remainder were attributable to irregularities in expenditure or misutilization of funds. This reflects both extremely low levels of governance in implementation and the desperate fiscal situation in most states, which are seeking funds in any manner possible to finance their deficits.

The design innovation in SGSY – relying on self-help groups rather than individuals – can help reduce leakage since the eligible groups are to comprise only members classified as poor under the administrative identification system. These groups are formed by a variety of sources, including village development officials, village government representatives and NGOs. This innovation can reduce leakage errors relative to those in the predecessor IRDP and associated schemes that were as high as 25 per cent to 33 per cent. However, the formation of such groups is time consuming and not always feasible. Groups, once formed, have to be in operation for at least six months before becoming eligible for SGSY loans. Often such groups cannot sustain themselves due to differences and even suspicion amongst members, making it difficult for a poor household to access the SGSY, and leading to higher targeting errors of undercoverage. It is expected that such type one errors will diminish over time if there is greater success in forming self-help groups. However, corruption and poor governance appear to have been immune to the design innovations of the SGSY. Their effect ultimately is to divert scheme resources to officials and middlemen, leading to higher leakage.

Finally, moving from implementation to the impact of the SGSY, there are important problems constraining creation of a sustainable productive asset base for the low-income self-employed. Despite attempts at a holistic approach, in practice there are no services available to support assets acquired by the beneficiaries, such as technical and advisory services and marketing. Due to the limited ability of government departments in identifying dynamic business opportunities, the implementation of SGSY has tended to focus excessively on one particular type of asset, such as dairy cows or sewing machines, and effective marketing of products is often difficult. In several situations, the lack of adequate insurance for acquired assets, such as livestock, can make it impossible for beneficiaries to repay loans in case of accidental death. The acquisition of assets that ultimately prove unfruitful, due to poor decisions by the beneficiary, inadequate support services, non-marketable output, or other constraints, can result in transforming a large number of intended beneficiaries from being simply poor, to being poor, as well as defaulters to the formal financial system.

Rural Housing Scheme – *Indira Awas Yojana* (IAY)

After being virtually neglected for the first three decades after Independence, rural housing was included as a major activity in the 1980s in the National Rural Employment Program and the Rural Landless Employment Guarantee Program, both early predecessors of the SGRY rural employment scheme. In 1985, for the first time specific proportions of rural employment funds were earmarked for construction of houses for Scheduled Castes and Scheduled Tribes and freed bonded labor. This was the origin of the IAY, which continued as a sub-scheme of the JRY – another predecessor of the SGRY.

According to the 1991 Census, 3.4 million households were without shelter of any kind while 10.3 million households were living in unserviceable houses. Adjusting for population growth, the central government projected a net housing shortage between 1997–2002 at 18.8 million units, of which 8.5 million new houses would need to be constructed and another 10.3 million upgraded. A National Housing and Habitat Policy was adopted in 1998, aimed at providing 'Housing for All' and proposing construction of almost 11 million units in the ninth five-year plan (1997–2002), against the projected shortage of 18.8 million units. The residual gap, along with the additional deficiency arising from population growth, was envisaged as a target to be met in the tenth plan. However, only five million units could be constructed between 1997–2002 under the IAY and other CSS schemes (CAG, 2003).

The objective of the IAY is to provide dwelling units free to the rural population below the poverty line. It specifically targets poor households belonging to scheduled castes and tribes, freed bonded laborers and other specified categories (the disabled and since 1996 families of members of the armed forces killed in action). Grants-in-aid are provided to beneficiaries with a ceiling of Rs 20000 in plain areas and Rs 22000 in hilly or difficult areas. The scheme also allows up to Rs 10000 for upgrading of temporary and unserviceable units. The house is registered in the name of the female household member, or jointly in the name of husband and wife of the beneficiary household. In addition, an integral requirement of the IAY scheme is provision of a smokeless cooking stove (*chulha*) and a sanitary latrine in the houses constructed.

The implementation of the IAY scheme follows the familiar pattern of delegation to local units, with the district rural development agencies and *Zilla Parishad* entrusted with implementation, coordination, monitoring and evaluation at the district level. Specifically, targets are decided at the state level based on estimates of number of people below the poverty line and the number of homeless, and district targets are developed based on the numbers of those eligible and estimates of rural income and productivity. Using these targets, the district rural development agencies and *Zilla Parishad* decide the number of houses to be constructed in each *Panchayat* and inform the *Gram Panchayat*. Local community-based organizations and NGOs with a proven track record, if available, are also associated with construction of IAY houses. The village assembly (*Gram Sabha*) in each village selects the beneficiaries restricted to the target allotted based on the list of eligible households, and forwards the list to the *Gram Panchayat*.

The IAY enjoys considerable support since it creates a visible and valuable asset for beneficiaries, leading to improved security and economic and social status. Unlike other schemes where beneficiaries have to work in return for assistance, the IAY provides grants with minimal requirements on the part of beneficiaries. Thus, in contrast to other targeting programs, the IAY has not undergone major transformations or reincarnations since its inception almost two decades ago.

Impact of IAY

Nonetheless, there are also severe problems in its implementation, caused in part by its design of large, unencumbered grants. The lump sum payment of Rs 20000 is large enough to again attract substantial corruption. Local politicians, including Members of Parliament, Members of Legislative Assemblies, and even village heads, view this as an important mechanism for patronage for supporters and there is clear evidence of a high proportion of benefits being manipulated towards this end. These machinations are a natural outcome of the context of the scheme, since the total allocation of grants-based IAY, although substantial, is miniscule relative to potential demand based on the number of poor households without housing in the country.[16]

The substantial size of individual grants also makes this a popular scheme with local officials, since it is large enough to withstand large 'unofficial' fees running into several thousands of rupees. As a consequence, safeguards built into the design of the scheme have stayed on paper. For example, payments for each stage of construction are to be made only when the preceding stage has been completed, and individuals are required to make their own arrangements for construction. In particular, officials are not allowed to engage contractors on behalf of the beneficiaries. According to a recent audit by the Auditor General, almost one-third (31 per cent) of IAY funds were misused (CAG, 2003). Of this, almost half was accounted for by the depositing of funds by state governments into current accounts, civil deposits, or treasuries outside the government account. The remainder was due to misappropriation, unapproved works, and unauthorized activities. Almost 20 per cent of the audited money was spent on construction of houses through contractors. Over-inflated expenditures combined with poor quality of dwellings was a natural outcome. In particular, only half the houses constructed were provided with smokeless stoves and 43 per cent of the houses were constructed without sanitary latrines.

Against this backdrop of corruption and poor governance in implementation of the IAY, it should be noted that the targeting performance of the IAY has not been too bad, with only about 2.2 per cent of the beneficiaries not being eligible.[17] The problem with the IAY is its small size relative to the eligible population (implying exclusion through rationing) and severe attrition in funds actually reaching the poor due to corruption (again raising type two targeting errors of leakage).

National Old Age Pension Scheme (NOAPS)

India has virtually no comprehensive system of old age protection. Less than 10 per cent of the labor force has pension coverage, primarily in the formal sector and there was no central government scheme relating to old-age security until recently (although many state governments had assistance schemes for the poor aged). The Government of India introduced the NOAPS in 1995 as part of the National Social Assistance Program.[18] The scheme is relatively small with an allocation of less than Rs 5 billion in 2000–01 relative to an estimated 70 million destitute-aged in the country. However, it is one of the few successful targeting programs in operation, with low leakage of benefits from intended beneficiaries.

The NOAPS targets old persons who are considered destitute in the sense of not having any regular means of subsistence on their own or through financial support from family members. Applicants have to be above 65 years, and beneficiaries are expected to provide certificates of age and proof of their destitute status. At the launch of the scheme, each state had an initial ceiling on number of beneficiaries, not exceeding half of the official below-the-poverty-line population in the state above age 65, as estimated through the administrative identification system. The targeting is done by selection of beneficiaries by *Gram Panchayats* based on targets communicated by state governments. The amount of the pension is modest – Rs 75 or US $1.60 per month per beneficiary – though the state governments can add to this amount from their own resources.

Implementation of the program is done by authorities at the district level with the assistance of *Panchayats*. The latter assist in selection of beneficiaries and are also responsible for reporting the death of a pensioner, and have the right to stop or recover payments sanctioned on the basis of false information. The central government transfers funds directly to the district administration through district rural development agencies in biannual installments, while beneficiaries are paid through accounts in banks or other financial institutions. Cash payments are also allowed, provided they are made in public before the village assembly.

Impact of NOAPS

Evaluations of NOAPS have shown the scheme is functioning well in terms of targeting and implementation without corruption and interference. The program has largely reached scheduled populations and women; the coverage of women was 40 per cent to 60 per cent across the states. In evaluations done of project beneficiaries, a third of beneficiaries were found to be neglected by their family or living alone, another third were found to have a dependent (mostly a spouse), and did not have a regular source of income in the remaining cases.

The delivery mechanisms for NOAPS benefits also appear to be functioning well. For example, benefits are transferred directly to beneficiaries through cheques, postal money orders or cash payments in public meetings. A review by IMI (2001) in Orissa found this process worked well with cash payments made by village workers in the presence of the village head (*Sarpanch*) at a fixed time each month.

The implementation problems of NOAPS are primarily bureaucratic. First, since many states had pension schemes before the introduction of NOAPS, the implementation of NOAPS is under different agencies across the states. Thus, although the Ministry of Rural Development is the executing agency at the center, the agencies at the state level may be departments of labor, social welfare, or health. These state departments have little or no interaction with the district rural development agencies, nor do they have any role in the flow of funds that are transferred directly from the center to these agencies. Consequently, state implementing agencies have little ownership in

NOAPS. There are too many entities involved in implementation without clear demarcation of responsibilities (ORG, 1998). Another outcome of this is irregular timing of payments to beneficiaries, which can be problematic if the recipients are severely liquidity constrained.

Further, given that birth certificates are still issued only to a small part of the population, documenting proof of age is an extremely cumbersome and arbitrary process. The registration procedure requires several proofs and certificates. This problem applies even more strongly to proving a destitute status, since criteria for identifying the destitute are not clear and different states follow their own norms. As a consequence, potential applicants have to undergo substantial transaction costs in dealing with the bureaucracy in the application process. The fact that the size of the pot available is so small relative to potential demand makes the problem of red-tape worse for applicants.

In sum, therefore, NOAPS is a welcome contrast from the typical targeting programs in India, actually transferring its modest benefits in entirety to intended beneficiaries, with little evidence of leakage to ineligible applicants. The absence of corruption can be related to the fact that the amounts involved are small and benefits may be transferred directly either into accounts of the beneficiaries or in cash. At the same time, given its modest benefits and delivery mechanism, resulting in minimal leakage, the scheme is unlikely to attract political backing, and grow in size.

Drought Prone Areas Program (DPAP)

The DPAP is another small but relatively more successful targeting activity in India, aimed at mitigating the adverse effects of drought on the production of crops and livestock. It also encourages restoration of an ecological balance and seeks to improve the economic and social conditions of the poor and disadvantaged sections of the rural community. Initiated like many other targeting programs in the early 1970s, the DPAP started as a Rural Works Program in 1970–71, aimed at creating assets to reduce severity of drought wherever it occurred, and to provide employment in drought prone areas. The Rural Works Program became the DPAP in 1973–74. Unlike other targeting, the program has retained its identity over time, though it was restructured in 1986–87 to focus more explicitly on a narrower objective: creating long-term assets aimed at drought prevention.

The program was supplemented by guidelines issued in 1994 that were intended for all watershed programs implemented by the government, but were taken up primarily by the Ministry of Rural Development in its schemes. These guidelines laid special emphasis on active mobilization and participation of stakeholders in the program, including planning, implementation and subsequent management of assets created. Thus, the DPAP appears to be one of the few programs where evaluations have actually led to 'enlightened' policy design (Nayak et al., 2002).

Under the DPAP, beneficiaries' villages are selected by district rural development agencies at the district level. User groups undertake area development by planning and implementing projects on a watershed basis through watershed associations and committees constituted from among themselves. Their efforts are facilitated at the district level by the development agencies, who provide funds and technical assistance. A project implementation agency, constituted by government, non-government or a private commercial entity and having requisite technical and social organizational skills, works with the watershed committee to prioritize, sequence and implement the rehabilitation over a five-year period. Funds are released directly to the district rural development agencies to sanction projects and release funds to watershed committees and project implementation agencies.

Impact of DPAP
Evaluations have shown the DPAP to be working well, though the performance is uneven. The transfer of funds directly to district rural development agencies and the involvement of the community through user groups and NGOs has tended to discourage misappropriation of funds. In cases where local officials and the local elite have strong influence, they can in principle and have in practice misutilized the funds. Local officials have contributed to diverting funds through providing misleading information about the status of work undertaken. In general, though, as noted by Rao (2000), context-specific factors have affected the performance of DPAP. In Gujarat, committed NGOs led to positive outcomes, while in Madhya Pradesh, success emanated due to a tradition of community participation in tribal regions. On the other hand, as noted by Mahapatra (2001), large sums of DPAP funds, up to 30 per cent to 40 per cent, were diverted in the state of Rajasthan.

Design-related implementation problems of the DPAP are, in part, due to efforts at making it more participatory, which has tended to contribute to its success while making implementation difficult in other situations. For example, there have been problems in identifying suitable project implementation agencies in several cases. Administrative field staff typically have no incentive in pursuing participatory approaches, leaving planning and execution of schemes to district officials. Strict orientation towards achieving physical targets has also led to too little time to undertake and promote social organization.

MACRO DEVELOPMENTS AND FINANCIAL SUSTAINABILITY

It is well recognized that sustained and equitable economic growth inevitably leads to poverty reduction. However, the impact of growth on poverty reduction can be lessened if the growth is accompanied by rising inequalities. In addition, substantial segments of the population may benefit less from growth, and may need targeted assistance. During the 1980s and 1990s, India saw the highest GDP growth rates in the five decades since Independence. At the same time, poverty rates have declined steadily from a peak of more than 60 per cent in the late 1960s to approximately half that in 1999. Substantial controversy has surrounded the latest estimates of poverty in India, but there is little doubt poverty declined in the 1990s, perhaps to roughly 30 per cent. Using this estimate, poverty incidence as measured by the headcount ratio declined by six to seven percentage points during the 1990s and by the same amount in the 1980s. The average GDP growth rate during the 1980s and 1990s was 5.7 per cent and 5.8 per cent respectively, placing India amongst some of the fastest-growing economies over these 20 years, though inequality as measured by the Gini coefficient worsened from 0.29 to 0.38 in the 1990s (UNDP/ESCAP 2003). This clearly exemplifies the correlation between economic growth and poverty reduction.

However, during the 1970s, with substantially lower growth rates, poverty declined equally sharply, from 56 per cent in 1970 to 43 per cent by 1983, with the largest decline occurring between 1978–83. This decline in poverty incidence coincides with the populist approach initiated by the Prime Minister at that time, Mrs Indira Gandhi, which included policies like nationalization of the banking sector and adoption of the slogan *'Garibi Hatao'* (or Eliminate Poverty). Many of the targeting programs in existence today were initiated in the first part of the 1970s. It is arguable that these schemes have continued to date, albeit with mergers, restructuring and reincarnations, due to their political utility to the government. Successive different governments at the center have not only continued with these interventions but have added to them, leading to proliferation and multiplicity. Although several other factors could contribute to the popularity of these schemes, this also suggests the schemes are having an impact on the ground. However, two important questions in this context are, are these expenditures sustainable and how effective are these programs?

In terms of financial sustainability, it is useful to distinguish the narrowly targeted programs and other CSS schemes of the government from the more broadly targeted expenditures due to subsidies. While the total size of the CSS is roughly Rs 350 billion, aggregate central budgetary subsidies are in the range of Rs 850 billion. This latter figure amounted to 4.6 per cent of

GDP and 53 per cent of net receipts of the government. When expenditure on subsidies by state governments is also included, the picture is far worse. Aggregate budgetary subsidies of central and state governments combined were almost 13.5 per cent of GDP in 1998–99. Some components of this aggregate, particularly the food subsidy, have been rising sharply in recent years. At the same time, budget deficits of the central government have ranged between 5 and 6 per cent of GDP through much of the 1990s, and in 2002 the total deficit of central and state governments combined exceeded 10 per cent of GDP. In this context, the large expenditures on subsidies are unlikely to be sustainable in the long run. Moreover, they will also tend to squeeze out expenditures in other areas, including narrowly defined targeting programs. Several recommendations have been made to streamline and reduce expenditures on subsidies, though the process will obviously face political constraints.

Among the targeting programs, the self-employment schemes (IRDP in the past and SGSY now) have had a credit component combined with a subsidy. The implementation of these schemes has involved bank loans, but repayment rates have been quite low. For example, almost 71 per cent of all bank accounts in the Indian banking system are Small Borrower Accounts, defined as accounts with credit outstanding of less than Rs 25 000. IRDP loans accounted for slightly more than one-third of all such accounts in the commercial banking sector. Low repayment rates on these accounts have contributed to a worsening position of banks in terms of non-performing assets. For the public banks, gross non-performing assets were 6 per cent of assets and 2.9 per cent net of provisions in 2000. For the Regional Rural Banks, catering specifically to rural areas, the figures were much worse with non-performing assets being 23.2 per cent of assets in 2000. The higher level of non-performing assets in the latter reflects the poor performance of priority credits (including the IRDP and SGSY), which have non-performing assets of 35 per cent, much higher than on non-priority loans. Only about half of the small accounts in total were classified as standard assets by banks, with the rest being sub-standard, doubtful or loss assets. Provisioning for non-performing assets may add between one and two percentage points to the cost of credit in India (Long and Srivastava, 2002).

CONCLUSIONS

Poverty targeting in India has achieved some modest success but in general the picture is highly disappointing with very considerable evidence, principally from official 'grey cover' reports, of high leakage and misappropriation.

Problems of implementation, whether at the center, the state or the district level are clearly evident. At the highest political level successive governments have failed to take responsibility for streamlining the system of CSS, presumably because it is not a genuine political priority and because they fear challenging the local vested interests that have built up behind the present inefficient system. The multiplicity of schemes, and their sheer numbers, contributes to the problem of poor governance. Each scheme, with its own paperwork and bureaucratic requirements, adds to the load on the point of convergence – the district-level administration – which is part of implementation irrespective of whether funds are transferred via state governments or directly from the center.

The delegation of implementation of CSS to officials at the local government level and the local village or community institutions in principle should lead to greater ownership of the programs, but in practice has often contributed to the problem of corruption and weak governance. Inadequate institutional capabilities of lower tiers of government and inequities in power within villages allow capture by local elites and the corruption of government officials. Decentralization, an appealing solution at the conceptual level to improving delivery on the ground, has faced severe problems at the level of actual implementation.

The central problem that emerges clearly from the evaluation studies on these programs is that of poor governance. Gross violations of prescribed norms and guidelines of implementation are common, resulting in use of intermediaries, falsification of records, and provision of false information. Targeting programs with a large component of individual subsidy or large income transfers attract the attention of corrupt officials and the local elite. Substantial proportions of funds in such schemes are extracted from beneficiaries through illegal means (bribes and other special levies), aside from manipulating the benefits towards those not eligible. The effect in both cases would be to increase leakage, diverting resources to those not intended for coverage under the schemes. However, problems of corruption and poor governance are not confined to the targeting programs alone, but also affect more broadly large segments of government expenditures.

There have also been technical difficulties in the operation of many schemes. The key means of identifying the poor has relied on the system of administrative identification, designed initially to provide food security through the public distribution program. Secondary targeting – using indicators such as social category, gender or geographical location – is used, but in conjunction with administrative identification. For the requirements of the targeted public distribution system, the government sought to implement administrative identification by dividing the population into those above and below the poverty line. However, this exercise has been implemented poorly, leading to ineligible families being included as poor and families actually below the poverty line being excluded. Given the immense poverty in the country, with almost 80 per cent of the population living at below US $2 per day and a comparable proportion malnourished, attempts to overcome information asymmetries by directly 'tagging' families as below the poverty line, have faced conceptual and operational problems, resulting in errors of both undercoverage and leakage.

Food-for-work schemes have used targeting based on self-selection, which in principle should lead to the absence of either type of targeting errors. However, there is ample evidence that such schemes have also been misused. The choice of assets in self-employment schemes has tended to be poor, leading to dissipation of the assets acquired. This often reflects the poor literacy and human capital level of the beneficiaries, but the problem is compounded by the absence of supporting services (technical, marketing and business support) to the recipients.

The life of community assets developed through schemes depends critically on the social mobilization and community ownership of the assets. Technical departments of the government are typically ill-equipped to provide support in this area, nor do they have incentives for doing so.

Some benefits for the poor have been achieved and some forms of scheme have had more success at minimizing targeting errors. More modest schemes with small regular payments to recipients have tended not to be worth the effort of funds diversion and hence show only very low leakage. There have been welcome initiatives in involving community and self-help groups and NGOs. Schemes where disbursal of benefits and scheme-related decisions are undertaken in public show fewer opportunities for corruption. Some NGOs may be better placed than government departments to provide the support needed by poor households in building up assets through employment creation schemes. There is some evidence that involvement of NGOs in targeting programs has been accompanied by relatively better implementation (although screening of NGOs is also critical). Also the operationalizing of self-help initiatives can be complex.

In short, as yet greater efforts at transparency and accountability have not materialized in parallel with the attempts at devolving powers to lower tiers of government. The combination of low literacy and human capital amongst the poorest of the poor, inequitable power structures within many rural areas, and lack of transparency, allow greater room for corruption to flourish amongst officials and the local elite. Greater involvement of beneficiary communities and community-based organizations such as NGOs should be attempted at each stage of implementation as part of program design. Shining a torch in areas darkened by lack of transparency will assist in curbing malpractice and corruption. The way forward is not easy, but for India a considerable amount is now known on the problems faced by poverty-targeting initiatives.

NOTES

1. In recent years surveys of varying detail are undertaken every five years.
2. For example, in 1996–97 state governments raised about 37 per cent of the combined revenues of the center and the states, but undertook over 58 per cent of total expenditures by the two tiers of government. For a more comprehensive discussion of the federal fiscal architecture, see Joshi (1999).
3. In addition to the Center and the States, a third tier of the government, namely local bodies, also exists but was not mentioned in the Constitution until 1993 when the 73rd and the 74th Constitutional Amendments assigned some functions to the local bodies. Under the 73rd Amendment to the Constitution, states were required to introduce a strengthened system of local government (*Panchayat Raj*). The government structure at the district level and below is now three tiered, though the names of each tier occasionally vary across states. The three tiers are (1) *Zilla Parishad* at the district level; (2) *Panchayat Samiti* at the block level; and (3) *Gram Panchayat* at the local level, typically comprising a group of villages. In addition, each village has a *Gram Sabha* or village assembly comprising all adults in the village, and to which certain development and other functions are allocated. Although the effective transfer of power to lower tiers of government has varied across states, most CSS including poverty-targeting programs are implemented through local government units.
4. The fiscal year in India is from 1 April to 31 March. These data refer to budget allocations. Actual utilization by the States is typically much lower due to various factors (Shariff et al., 2002).
5. Initially most of these schemes were fully financed by the central government but this has evolved over time into a shared burden with states contributing anywhere from 10 to 90 per cent of the scheme funding, with 25 per cent as the typical norm.
6. For example, during the ninth five-year plan the department of Agriculture and Cooperation ran 147 schemes with a five-year outlay of Rs 92.3 billion, implemented by 7500 people working in 182 offices across the country. Similarly, there were 17 independent schemes under the department of Women and Child Development, all aimed at development of women (GOI, 2000).
7. Under the Targeted PDS eligible families were issued with ration cards for use at fair price shops. They are entitled to a ration of foodgrains per month (set at 35 kg in 2002) at half the normal price in the PDS shops.
8. In a case study of three villages in Uttar Pradesh, one of the largest and poorest states in the country, Srivastava (2004) documents the process of identification of poor households. None of the villages had cards issued, though the survey was completed. In practice, the survey was substituted by a list of poor households in each village drawn up by the Village Development Officer in consultation with the village chief (instead of an open meeting of the village assembly) and forwarded to the district level. At the same time, it was expected some names from the list would be deleted at higher levels of administration due to a ceiling on the total number of poor. Meanwhile, many village residents were confused by a profusion of color-coded cards allowing different privileges, due to cards issued earlier as part of the PDS as well as other cards issued under a state-government scheme targeting poor households.
9. For example, according to the National Sample Survey, 70 per cent or more of the total population consumed less than 2100 calories per day in all available years since 1993–94. Data from the National Nutrition Monitoring Bureau shows that 48 per cent of all adults are malnourished, while according to the National Family Health Survey, almost 47 per cent of all children are malnourished (Karat, 2003).

10. Administratively those seeking to work in EAS had to first apply and register. A project report had to be prepared initially, submitted to the district administrator (the Collector), who then would seek funds from the central Ministry. In practice Collectors took key decisions on where and how the funds would be used (GOI, 2000).
11. In one of the six villages, the head was also the owner of the subsidized food outlet, while in another the local administration had close ties to the owner of a 'toddy' (country-liquor) shop. Instead of the mandated wage of Rs 56 per day, men in that village were given Rs 40 and two bottles of toddy and women received Rs 30 and one bottle (Deshingkar and Johnson, 2003).
12. A host of other schemes co-existing with the IRDP, such as the Training of Rural Youth for Self Employment, Development of Women and Children in Rural Areas, Supply of Improved Toolkits to Rural Artisans and the Million Wells Scheme, were merged into the SGSY.
13. Small borrower accounts are defined as accounts with less than Rs 25 000 outstanding, and accounted for 71 per cent of total bank deposits in 2001.
14. Commercial banks in India are required to target 40 per cent of their lending to priority sectors defined by the government.
15. Formally self-help groups may be formed by NGOs or by officials of local government (or even banks). However, once formed, members of a group have to meet regularly over a period of at least six months, make regular contributions of funds, and maintain proper books before becoming eligible to receive funding from banks under the SGSY scheme.
16. The popularity of IAY as a source of patronage is evidenced by requests by members of the national parliament for a larger quota of housing whose allocation is under their control (Nayak et al., 2002).
17. The CAG audit tested about a third of the expenditures under the IAY, which cumulatively built almost five million units during the reference period. An examination of a third of this amount, that is roughly 1.6 million units, found that roughly 2.2 per cent of the beneficiaries (34 542) were ineligible (CAG, 2003).
18. There are two other CSS schemes under the National Social Assistance Program, namely the National Family Benefit Scheme and the National Maternity Benefit Scheme. The government is also introducing pension reforms to increase fiscal sustainability of its pension liabilities and expand coverage to the informal sector.

REFERENCES

Bavadam, L. (2003), 'Undermining a scheme', *Frontline*, **20** (16), August.
CAG (1997), 'Report of the Controller and Auditor General for the Year ended March 1996 (Civil)', Office of the Controller and Auditor General, Government of India, 1997.
CAG (2000), 'Report of the Controller and Auditor General for the Year ended March 1999 (Civil)', Office of the Controller and Auditor General, Government of India, 2000.
CAG (2003), 'Report of the Controller and Auditor General for the Year ended March 2002 (Civil)', Office of the Controller and Auditor General, Government of India, 2003.
Datt, G. and M. Ravallion (1994), 'Transfer benefits from public works employment: evidence from rural India', *Economic Journal*, **104**, 1346–69, November.
Deaton, A. (2001), 'Adjusted Indian poverty estimates for 1999–2000', mimeo, Research Program in Development Studies, Princeton University, USA.

Deshingkar, P. and C. Johnson (2003), 'State transfers to the poor and back: the case of the food for work program in Andhra Pradesh', Working Paper No. 222, Overseas Development Institute, London.

Dev, M.S. (1995), 'India's (Maharashtra) Employment Guarantee Scheme: lessons from long experience', International Food Policy Research Institute, Washington DC, available at http://www.ifpri.org/pubs.

Dev, S.M. and R. Evenson (2003), 'Rural development in India', paper and powerpoint presentation at Conference on Indian Policy Reforms, June, Center for Research on Economic Development and Policy Reform, Stanford University.

Gaiha, R. (1996), 'How dependent are the rural poor on the Employment Guarantee Scheme in India?', *Journal of Development Studies*, **32** (5), 669–94.

GOI (2000), 'Mid-term appraisal of the 9th Five Year Plan', Planning Commission, Government of India, New Delhi (accessed at http://planningcommission. nic.in on 4 November 2003).

GOI (2003), 'Report of the High Level Committee on Long Term Grain Policy', Ministry of Food and Consumer Affairs, Government of India, available at http://fcamin.nic.in.

Hemming, R., N. Mates and B. Porter (1997), 'India', in T.T. Minassian (ed.), *Fiscal Federalism in Theory and Practice*, Washington DC: IMF.

IMI (2001), 'Impact assessment study of rural development programs in Jagatsinghpur district in Orissa', International Management Institute, mimeo.

Joshi, D.K. (1999), 'Government finances', paper presented at ADB-NCAER Conference 'Economic and Policy Reforms in India', mimeo, National Council of Applied Economic Research, New Delhi.

Karat, B. (2003) 'Some issues in the struggle for food security', People's Democracy, mimeo, available at http://pd.cpim.org/2003/0817/08172003_brinda_pds.htm.

Long, M. and P. Srivastava (2002), 'Improving the impact of the financial system on poverty alleviation', report for the Asian Development Bank, TA 3739 IND, Centennial Group Holdings, Washington DC.

Mahapatra, R. (2001), 'Drought of relief', *Down to Earth*, **10** (2), June.

MAKER (2002), 'An empirical study of poverty alleviation programmes in Bihar', Mathura Krishna Foundation for Economic and Social Opportunity and Human Resource Management (MAKER), available at http://planningcommission. nic.in/reports.

Nayak, R., N.C. Saxena and J. Farrington (2002), 'Reaching the poor: the influence of policy and administrative processes on the implementation of government poverty schemes in India', Working Paper 175, Overseas Development Institute, London, September.

ORG (1998), 'Evaluation of National Social Assistance Program in selected states', Operations Research Group, mimeo.

PDI (2000), 'Study on assessment of poverty alleviation schemes in Maharashtra', conducted by Policy and Development Initiatives (PDI) for Planning Commission, available at http://planningcommission.nic.in/reports.

PEO (2000), 'Study on employment assurance scheme', Program Evaluation Organization, Planning Commission, Government of India, available at http:// planningcommission.nic.in/reports.

Rao, G. and N. Singh (2000), 'The political economy of Center-State transfers in India', mimeo, University of California, Santa Cruz.

Rao, H. (2000), 'Watershed development in India: recent experience and emerging issues', *Economic and Political Weekly*, April.

Saxena, N.C. and J. Farrington (2003), 'Trends and prospects for poverty reduction in Rural India', Working Paper 198, Overseas Development Institute, London, May.

Shariff, A., P.K. Ghosh and S.K. Mondal (2002), 'Indian public expenditures on social sector and poverty alleviation programs during the 1990s', Working Paper 175, Overseas Development Institute, London, November.

Srivastava, D.K., C.B Rao, P. Chakraborty and T.S. Rangamannar (2003), 'Budgetary subsidies in India: subsidizing social and economic services', National Institute of Public Finance and Policy, New Delhi, March.

Srivastava, P. (2004), 'Rural finance and development in UP: a case study of three villages', mimeo, National Council of Applied Economic Research, New Delhi, India.

UNDP (2003), 'Human development report 2003', United Nations Development Program, UN, New York.

UNDP/ESCAP (2003), 'Promoting the MDGs in Asia and Pacific', United Nations Development Program, Economic and Social Commission for Asia and the Pacific, Bangkok.

World Bank (2003), 'Supporting sound policies with adequate and appropriate financing', paper prepared for the Development Committee of IMF and World Bank, mimeo World Bank, Washington DC.

3. Poverty targeting in Indonesia

Ari A. Perdana and John Maxwell

INTRODUCTION

Prior to the economic and financial crisis (henceforth the Crisis) that gripped Indonesia in the late 1990s the previous 30 years had seen a substantial reduction in poverty brought about largely through rapid economic growth rather than through special measures, that is programs and policies that were specifically targeted at the poorest sections of the community. The real gains in poverty reduction, and the accompanying significant improvement in a key range of socio-economic indicators – such as declining infant mortality and rising school enrollments, literacy rates, nutrition and living standards – were achieved against a backdrop of sustained economic growth and the general improvement and expansion of public infrastructure and community social services. Of particular importance were the provision of basic education and health facilities through an active construction program of schools and community health centers. Important also were the development and expansion of roads and communication networks, a rural electrification program, and the provision of supplies of clean water. These programs were all largely funded out of the public purse through the national development budget (see Booth, 2000 and Hill, 1996: 198–9, 1994: 105–7).

Despite the fact that Indonesia has always been a poor country where poverty has always been a fact of life, and although there had previously been a number of government general development programs that provided indirect assistance to those who were among the poorest sections of the community, especially in rural areas, it was not until 1994 that a government program was introduced that was specifically targeted to address the problems of poverty. In that year, as part of the Sixth Five Year Development Plan (*Rencana Pembangunan Lima Tahun* or REPELITA VI), the government announced an ambitious special assistance program, known as Inpres Desa Tertinggal (IDT), which was designed to assist all villages throughout the country that had been identified as poor. We include this initial program in our review of the targeting of anti-poverty programs below.

If the Indonesian government had been slow to initiate programs that were deliberately targeted at the poor, preferring general economic growth to provide the main mechanism to lift people out of poverty, this strategy suddenly had to be reassessed after the onset of the Crisis. It appeared that the combined flow-on effects of the meltdown in the financial sector had wiped out much of the gains of the past three decades. The sudden alarming increase in poverty made it imperative that some special assistance measures were put in place for those who were most exposed and at risk. As Indonesia had never developed an effective social security system that might offer protection for the poor and the most vulnerable during a period of sudden economic shock, there were grave fears about the social consequences of the crisis, especially as there was a surge in the prices of basic commodities, such as foodstuffs, during 1998 and real wages fell by about a third (Feridhanusetyawan, 2000). The response to the Crisis was the introduction of a package of measures under a general Social Safety Net program and these formed the core of the poverty targeting strategy. Prior to examining the effectiveness of these measures we first survey the data on poverty trends in Indonesia.

POVERTY IN INDONESIA: PRE AND POST THE CRISIS

During more than 30 years in power, the reduction of absolute poverty was one of the most significant achievements of the New Order government. In the mid-1970s, more than 50 million people, or around 40 per cent of the population, were living below the poverty line. In the late 1980s and early 1990s, poverty incidence has been reduced to below 30 million or less than 20 per cent of the population. In 1996, a year before the onset of the Crisis, the poverty level had been reduced to an estimated 22.5 million people or around 11 per cent of the population. The New Order's success in reducing poverty has been attributed to rapid economic growth, especially from the mid-1980s, after the government undertook a series of structural adjustment policies, including privatization and economic deregulation, combined with rural development and employment programs (Booth, 2000: 83–5).

In sharp contrast to these trends, the Crisis that began in late 1997 created widespread social distress in many parts of the country. A fall in GDP was accompanied by massive job losses as bankruptcies and cutbacks in production multiplied. This led to a sharp rise in open unemployment and underemployment. As a result, there was a significant increase in the number of people living below the poverty line and a marked deterioration in income distribution.

The household-level adjustments resulting from the Crisis took the form of changing patterns of household income and expenditure. The sharp reduction in real income forced people to accept work at lower rates of remuneration, consume their savings or sell their assets to cope with increasing levels of expenditure. The increase in prices was considerably larger than the increase in nominal urban wages. For low-income families, where much of their expenditure was absorbed by food, the sharp increase in food prices significantly reduced their purchasing power, lowered their food consumption, and reportedly, even led to cases of starvation in some areas.

Table 3.1 presents the results of the official poverty headcount calculation (proportion of the population below the poverty line).[1] It shows that the Crisis increased the number of people living below the poverty line from 34.5 million (17.7 per cent of total population) in 1996 to 49.5 million (or 24.2 per cent) in 1998.[2] After reaching a peak in 1998, poverty figures began to decline in the following years. A reduction in food prices from the second quarter of 1999 contributed significantly to this trend, with the poverty line falling by 2 and 6 percentage points in urban and rural areas respectively (Badan Pusat Statistik, 2001: 583). The Central Bureau of Statistics published two sets of official poverty figures for 1999. The first set of figures was based on the results of the full national Social Economic Survey (SUSENAS) conducted in February. A slight improvement in the economy, especially with a lower rate of inflation and the return to positive GDP growth, reduced poverty levels to 48.4 million (23.5 per cent). The second set of figures, based on a Mini-SUSENAS[3] conducted in August, revealed a more significant decline in poverty to 37.5 million (18.2 per cent).

Official poverty figures in the subsequent years were estimated based on the core database of the full SUSENAS, with both the number of the poor and the incidence of poverty continuing to show a declining trend after February 1999.[4] The incidence of poverty and the numbers of the poor continued to decline slightly in 2001. As the economy continued to recover, the average real incomes of the poor also began to rise. Hence, although the poverty line also rose, on average nominal income increases more than compensated for this.

There is need for caution in interpreting and drawing comparisons between the various sets of official poverty figures presented by the Central Bureau of Statistics, since some of the calculations were based on different surveys. For example, the estimates for December 1998 and August 1999 were drawn from Mini-SUSENAS data, which cover only about 10 000 households, compared with the 65 000 households covered by the SUSENAS consumption module. In an attempt to produce a comparable set of figures for the poverty rate since the emergence of the Crisis, the Social Monitoring

*Table 3.1   The official poverty line, poverty numbers and poverty incidence,
1996–2001*

Year	Poverty line (Rp per month)		Headcount poverty rate (%)			Poor population (million)		
	Urban	Rural	Urban	Rural	Total	Urban	Rural	Total
1996[a]	38246	27413	9.7	12.3	11.3	7.2	15.3	22.5
1996[b]	42032	31366	13.6	19.9	17.7	9.6	24.9	34.5
1998[c]	96959	72780	21.9	25.7	24.2	17.6	31.9	49.5
1999[d]	92409	74272	19.5	26.1	23.5	15.7	32.7	48.4
			(19.4)[h]	(26.0)	(23.4)	(15.6)	(32.3)	(48.0)
1999[e]	89845	69420	15.1	20.2	18.2	12.4	25.1	37.5
			(15.0)	(20.0)	(18.0)	(12.3)	(24.8)	(37.1)
2000[f]	91632	73648	14.6	22.1	18.9	12.1	25.2	37.3
2001[g]	100011	80832	9.8	24.9	18.4	8.5	28.6	37.1

Notes:
[a] Based on the 1996 SUSENAS database and standard.
[b] Based on the 1996 SUSENAS database, applying new (1998) standard.
[c] Based on the December 1998 Mini-SUSENAS.
[d] Based on the February 1999 SUSENAS.
[e] Based on the August 1999 Mini-SUSENAS.
[f] Estimated result based on the 2000 SUSENAS Core data, excluding Maluku and Aceh.
[g] Estimated result based on the 2001 SUSENAS Core data, excluding Maluku and Aceh.
[h] The numbers in parentheses are figures without East Timor.

Source: Badan Pusat Statistik, Statistics Indonesia (2000, 2001).

and Early Response Unit (SMERU) Research Institute has published a
consistent series of poverty measurements (Suryahadi et al., 2003a). The
study used the data from the SUSENAS and Mini-SUSENAS database,
the 100-Village Survey,[5] as well as several estimates by Gardiner (1999),[6]
and Frankenberg and Beegle (1999).[7] These independent poverty estimates
are presented in Figure 3.1. Despite the differences in results, both series
show similar poverty trends.

Regional Analysis

From the official poverty statistics in Table 3.1, we can see that both the
number of the poor and the headcount poverty rate have always been higher
in rural areas than in urban areas. But if we consider the relative changes
to poverty before and after the Crisis, it is apparent that urban poverty
rose faster than rural poverty. A comparison of the SUSENAS data in
February 1996 and 1999 shows that the numbers of poor households in

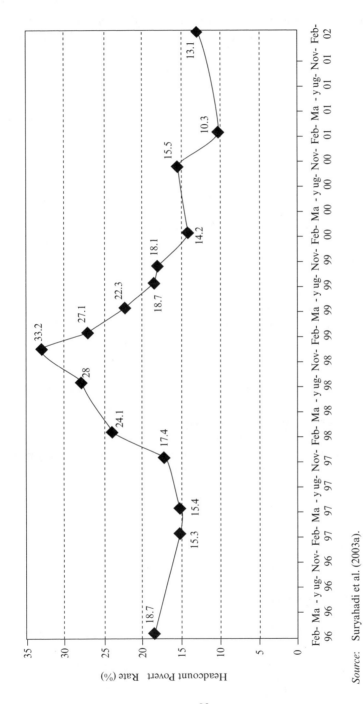

Source: Suryahadi et al. (2003a).

Figure 3.1 SMERU poverty headcount estimates

urban areas rose by 60 per cent, twice the rate of increase in rural areas. This reveals the nature of the Crisis as more of an urban phenomenon, and is consistent with the findings from the sectoral analysis of poverty. The sectoral analysis, presented in the following section, shows that the relative increase in poverty was higher in the modern sectors, which are mostly located in urban areas.

From a regional perspective, Table 3.2 illustrates that the increase in poverty during the Crisis was greatest in Java and Bali, and throughout western Indonesia in general. While the western part of Indonesia has a lower poverty rate compared with the eastern regions of the country, the increase in poverty was much greater in western Indonesia since most of the hard-hit modern sectors are located there. However, the figures in Table 3.2 only illustrate relative comparisons. In absolute terms, poverty rates remain larger in rural areas of Indonesia, and throughout eastern Indonesia.

Sectoral Analysis

The sectoral analysis of poverty is illustrated in Table 3.3 with the headcount poverty figures disaggregated by sectoral sources of household income between February 1996 and 1999, as calculated by Pradhan et al. (2000).[8] During the Crisis, an increase in the incidence of poverty was evident in all sectors. In absolute terms, the agriculture sector had the highest number of the poor both before and after the Crisis. It also consistently has the highest share of poor people within the total population. Pradhan et al. (2000: 20) argued that people working in agriculture have always been the poorest, relative to other sectors, and that poverty incidence in agriculture was still high after the Crisis, despite it not being as hard hit as the modern sectors. Since the agriculture sector is also the largest in terms of employment, although the Crisis seemed to have the greatest impact on the modern sectors of the economy, the numbers of those living in poverty in the agriculture sector remained the highest. However, after the Crisis, there was a decline in the agriculture sector's share of those living in poverty. On the other hand, the modern sectors' shares of poverty – especially manufacturing industry, trade, hotels and restaurants and financial services – all increased significantly.

Poverty Depth and Severity

As discussed in Chapter 1 the poverty gap and the squared poverty gap are used frequently to measure the depth and severity of poverty, respectively. Table 3.4 shows calculations of poverty gap and severity indices by the SMERU Research Institute.

Table 3.2   Headcount poverty rate and poverty numbers by islands and regions, 1996–99

Group of Islands	Headcount poverty rate (%)			Number of poor households (million)		
	1996[a]	1999	% change 1996–99	1996[a]	1999	% change 1996–99
Sumatra	15.46	19.81	28.14	6.3	8.6	36.51
Java and Bali	16.32	23.34	43.01	19.3	28.9	49.74
Kalimantan	15.01	19.87	32.38	1.6	2.2	37.50
Sulawesi	19.19	21.10	9.95	2.6	3.1	19.23
Other islands[b]	38.54	43.51(43.57)	12.90	4.7	5.6(5.2)	19.15
Western Indonesia	16.10	22.42	39.25	25.6	37.5	46.48
Eastern Indonesia[b]	24.42	28.21(27.87)	15.52	8.9	10.9(10.5)	22.36
Indonesia	**17.65**	**23.51(23.43)**	**33.20**	**34.5**	**48.4(48.0)**	**40.29**

Notes:
[a]   Based on the 1996 SUSENAS database, applying new (1998) standard.
[b]   The numbers in parentheses are figures without East Timor.

Source: BPS, Statistics Indonesia (2000, 2001).

Table 3.3 Headcount poverty by sector and contribution to total poverty

Sectors	Feb 1996		Feb 1999		Changes in the headcount rate, 1996–99 (%)
	Sectoral headcount poverty rate (%)	Share of poverty (%)	Sectoral headcount poverty rate (%)	Share of poverty (%)	
Agriculture	26.29	68.54	39.69	58.38	50.97
Other	13.29	0.10	32.00	0.27	140.78
Mining and quarrying	15.34	1.01	29.81	1.00	94.33
Construction	14.04	5.42	28.97	5.52	106.34
Transport and communication	8.85	3.32	24.02	5.58	171.41
Manufacturing industry	10.69	5.71	22.92	7.71	114.41
Trade, hotel, restaurant	7.96	8.10	17.63	11.13	121.48
Electricity, gas, water	6.10	0.16	14.18	0.17	132.46
Civil, social, and private services	5.73	5.72	13.13	7.36	129.14
Finance, insurance, leasing	1.24	0.06	5.23	0.23	321.77
Receiving transfer[a]	6.58	1.86	15.57	2.65	136.63
Total	**9.75**	**100.00**	**16.27**	**100.00**	**66.87**

Note: [a] Individuals that earn incomes from transfer.

Source: Pradhan et al. (2000).

Table 3.4   Poverty gap and severity indices, SMERU calculation, 1996–99

Year	Poverty gap			Squared poverty gap		
	Urban	Rural	Total	Urban	Rural	Total
1996	0.5	2.1	1.6	0.1	0.5	0.4
1997	0.3	2.7	2.3	0.1	0.8	0.6
1998	1.4	7.0	6.0	0.4	2.7	2.3
1999	1.5	3.6	2.8	0.4	1.0	0.8

Source: Suharyadi et al. (2000a).

The SMERU poverty estimates show that before the Crisis, the poverty gap had declined in urban areas but had worsened in rural areas. During the Crisis, all indices in both areas show a significant jump between 1997 and 1998, with those for urban areas increasing more rapidly than for rural areas. It is interesting to note that between 1998 and 1999 the rural poverty gap and severity index declined, while they remained relatively unchanged in urban areas, further evidence that the economic crisis was an urban phenomenon. However, in absolute terms, the poverty gap (and its relative change) in rural areas remained much greater than in urban areas.

Another way to illustrate the depth and severity of poverty is to calculate the incidence of chronic poverty. A household is considered to be in a state of chronic poverty – sometimes also referred to as 'structural poverty' – if the level of consumption is well below the poverty line. This segment of the poor does not possess adequate access to economic resources.[9] Sen (1999) defines such a condition as 'capability deprivation', which is more serious than just income or wealth deprivation.[10]

Suryahadi and Sumarto (2001) show that more than half of the increase in poverty between 1996 and 1999 was due to an increase in chronic poverty. The proportion of chronic poor within the total population increased from 3.2 per cent to 9.5 per cent during this period. Unlike transient poverty, improvements in general macroeconomic performance might not have a significant influence on the living conditions of the chronic poor. This means that the benefits of economic growth and the control of inflation may not affect the poorest segment of society. As a consequence, specific targeted interventions are required to tackle the problems of chronic poverty. Sumarto and Suryahadi (2001) also revealed that the Crisis not only increased poverty incidence, but it also significantly increased the number of Indonesian households with a high vulnerability to poverty, in the sense of a high probability of falling below the poverty line in the face of adverse shocks. They estimated that the proportion of households that were statistically not poor, but faced a relatively high probability of falling below the poverty line, increased from 6.8 per cent in 1996 to 18.4 per cent in 1999, an increase of more than 170 per cent over the pre-Crisis figure. This increase in vulnerability can be partially attributed to dis-saving on the part of the poor. As their savings diminished, this group became more exposed to future economic shocks. Adjustments to their pattern of expenditure have also increased the vulnerability of poor households, especially where they have been forced to reduce their spending on investment in education and health in favor of basic needs.

In summary, after significant improvements in poverty in previous decades in the late 1990s the number of households living below the poverty line increased substantially after the Crisis, as a result of lower real incomes and the absence of an effective social safety net. The magnitude of the impact of the crisis on poverty underlined the need for a comprehensive set of measures that would provide some level of special assistance for those families and individuals worst affected. Consequently, it suddenly became more crucial than ever for the government to identify as accurately as possible the most deserving sections of the community, and to make decisions about how to target assistance, so that this was delivered in an efficient and timely manner. The effective targeting of anti-poverty programs became an issue of national importance with the introduction of a package of social safety net measures in 1998.

DATA SOURCES FOR TARGETING

Accurate, reliable and up-to-date data about poverty are vital for both program planners and implementers as they seek to locate the precise whereabouts of the poor and ensure that program benefits are delivered to those who are most deserving of special assistance. Before we begin to consider the targeting of particular poverty alleviation programs in Indonesia in any detail, it is important to make some general observations about the particular problems associated with the data that have been used for the purposes of identifying poverty in Indonesia, both at a geographic level and at the household level.

In an archipelagic country as geographically diverse as Indonesia there have been considerable difficulties in accounting for poverty on a geographic basis. The official poverty statistics that are presently available provide poverty estimates to the provincial level and on an urban/rural divide, but do not break down poverty data beyond that point, for example to the district (*kabupaten*) and sub-district (*kecamatan*) levels.

In the immediate post-Crisis period, a precise account of the social impacts of the Crisis was not immediately available to the central government and its senior officials who tended to regard the whole of the country as being equally affected. In fact, by late 1998 information was appearing to show that the Crisis was quite heterogeneous in its impacts and that urban areas were hardest hit, as was Java-Bali, and much of eastern Indonesia.[11] However, there was a tendency for many of the emergency poverty alleviation measures that made up the government's Social Safety Net program to apply a safety blanket over the entire country, relying on local officials and program implementers to 'fine-tune' the targeting at lower levels of administrative authority.

Regarding information about poverty at the household level, the only available source of data that covers the entire country in a thoroughly comprehensive manner has been that produced by the National Family Planning Coordinating Board (BKKBN), which produces a classification of family welfare (*kesejahteraan*) compiled from a national registration based on the work of an army of village-based, family planning cadre. One of the major criticisms of the BKKBN registration is that, in marked contrast to the Central Board of Statistics (or BPS) socio-economic surveys and census that employ paid and trained data collectors and enumerators, the village cadre who carry out the BKKBN registration are unskilled and do the work in an honorary capacity. Although this is substantially true and must have some influence on the accuracy of the registration process, this must also be balanced against the advantages of local knowledge.[12] The data is collected on a regular basis and the results are updated annually.

The variables upon which this classification was originally based covered food consumption patterns, the type of health care family members were able to access, the possession of alternative sets of clothing, the material and size of the floor of the family home, and the ability of household members to practice their religion. Families that failed to meet certain minimum standards in any one of these five areas were registered in the lowest welfare category, referred to as 'pre-prosperous families' (*keluarga pra-sejahtera* or KPS).[13]

As a result of widespread criticisms from various quarters about the suitability of applying such a classification to determine socio-economic status for the purposes of targeting poverty programs, during 1999 BKKBN were persuaded to distinguish two additional categories of families based on particular 'economic' criteria. Consequently, from that year BKKBN have been producing a separate classification of those families in the two lowest welfare categories, 'pre-prosperous families' (*keluarga pra-sejahtera* or KPS) and 'level 1 prosperous families' (*keluarga sejahtera* 1 or KS-1) for economic reasons. These two additional classifications are referred to as KPS ALEK and KS-1 ALEK.[14] The indicators used by village-based, family planning cadres to determine which families fall into these categories are as follows: any family will be classified as KPS ALEK if it fails to meet any one of the following criteria:

- All family members are usually able to eat at least twice a day;
- All family members have different sets of clothing for home, for work or school, and for formal occasions;
- The largest section of the floor of the family home is not made of earth; and
- Sick children are able to receive modern medical attention and women of fertile age are able to access family planning services.

Any family will be classified as KS-1 ALEK if it fails to meet any one of the following criteria:

- At least once a week the family is able to eat meat, fish or eggs;
- Every family member has obtained at least one new set of clothes during the past year;
- There is at least 8 m^2 of floor space in the family home for every member of the household; and
- All children between seven and 15 years of age are presently attending school.

As we shall see in our account of specific programs, too close a dependence upon this classification has created some serious problems. However, in the difficult circumstance of mid-1998 when many of the safety net programs were being conceived in haste because of the prevailing sense of crisis – fueled by some alarming reports in both the domestic and international press that later proved to be unnecessarily alarmist and exaggerated – program planners really had no other option but to fall back on the BKKBN data as there was really no alternative listing at the village level of poverty or welfare status.

By contrast, the National Socio-Economic Survey (SUSENAS) data on consumption and expenditure, which has been widely used by both BPS and independent scholars to calculate poverty rates and poverty lines, is only available as part of a survey of a selected sample of the entire population. The SUSENAS is carried out on an annual basis (usually in February every year), and consists of a Core survey that is administered to over 200 000 households, and which is estimated to cover more than 800 000 individuals across the entire country. It collects data on a broad range of socio-economic indicators, including education, health and employment as well as consumption and expenditure. From this sample group, a subset of 65 000 households are surveyed on a certain topic or set of issues in much greater detail. This is referred to as the SUSENAS Module. Once every three years, as in 1999, the SUSENAS Module collects detailed information about consumption and expenditure, and this is widely regarded as the best data source for calculating poverty incidence as measured by consumption.

In addition, from time to time BPS uses the SUSENAS to collect data on other matters in what are referred to as Special Modules. In 1999 the SUSENAS included a Special Module on the government's Social Safety Net program. Consequently, the 1999 SUSENAS – both the Core survey and the Special Module – has been an invaluable tool of analysis for those observers who have monitored and analyzed the effectiveness of the targeting and program performance. We consider the results of these studies below. However, it is important to bear in mind some important limitations of this data source.

The 1999 Special Module consisted of a set of special survey items designed to test each respondent's awareness of and participation in the Social Safety Net programs (Badan Pusat Statistik, 1999). Yet some of the questions were framed in a deliberately general manner, avoiding, for example, reference to the official names of specific programs that were not likely to be widely known by village respondents. Yet there was still the possibility of confusion about which actual programs or poverty alleviation measures were being surveyed.

Another issue of particular importance is the precise period of time being covered by the 1999 SUSENAS Special Module. Respondents were surveyed in February about their knowledge of and participation in the Social Safety Net programs during the preceding six months (that is from August–September 1998). However, many programs did not properly get underway until well after July 1998, and the actual implementation of some measures, and the delivery of assistance to beneficiaries, did not really begin until early 1999. This means that since only the first period of the implementation of the safety net programs is covered by the survey, any conclusions that extrapolate to the period after that date should be treated with caution. No further questions about participation in these programs were included within the annual SUSENAS until the 2002 round when a further limited series of items were included as part of the SUSENAS Core. This has enabled some comparison of performance across a wider time frame and has been used in at least one of the most recent analytical studies (Sparrow, 2003a).

Another data source, the 100 Village Survey conducted by the Central Board of Statistics and UNICEF, also contained some questions about Social Safety Net program participation in its October 1998 round and

several of the earliest studies assessing these programs were based on an
analysis of the results (Cameron, 2001 and Suryahadi et al., 1999). However,
this survey of 12 000 households in 100 relatively poor rural villages located
in 10 districts and 8 provinces was far more limited in its scope. Moreover,
the original selection of locations had not been designed to be statistically
representative of the entire country. As a result, the findings from these
studies, although they gave some indication of important trends, are not as
reliable as the later studies that were based on the full 1999 SUSENAS.

TARGETED POVERTY PROGRAMS

As far as actual poverty alleviation programs are concerned, it has not
been possible to include in this chapter all those programs that have been
implemented in Indonesia at various times – before, during and after the
Crisis – especially since some of these programs have not been independently
and rigorously evaluated. A complete list of such programs would also
include some of the major donor-funded initiatives, in particular several
infrastructure and community development loan projects such as the World
Bank's Village Infrastructure Project (VIP/P3DT), Kecamatan Development
Program (KDP/PPK), and Urban Poverty Project (P2KP).[15] Some of these
programs had broader community development aims and were not intended
simply as poverty alleviation measures, although this was still an important
consideration. There were also several 1998 donor-funded drought relief
programs that directed special assistance to poor rural villages. We
concentrate, however, here on those key programs that have already been
subjected to some serious analysis, and in particular where there have been
published studies of the effectiveness of program targeting.

   Although the combination of the Crisis, and the accompanying political
and social turmoil of the early months of 1998 contributed to a delay
of nearly a year before any significant action was taken, in mid-1998 the
government announced a package of social safety net measures designed
to cover the following areas of need:

- Employment – emergency job creation schemes to provide work
  opportunities for the poor
- Food security – a program to provide certainty over both the availability
  and affordability of the rice staple throughout the entire country
- Education – special assistance both to poor families and poor
  schools
- Health – a package of measures designed to ensure that public health
  care services were accessible and affordable for the poor.

While the initial plans were announced in June and given further substance with the announcement of the details of the IMF reform package in July, various authors have pointed out that neither the Indonesian government nor its senior officials within the responsible ministries were well prepared for the implementation of this social rescue package. In fact, the bureaucracy itself lacked the necessary experience in such matters, and regrettably, it was inevitably caught up in the political turmoil of mid-1998 to the point where demoralization frequently contributed to inaction (Feridhanusetyawan, 2000: 155–8).

Further announcements from the National Planning Board (*Badan Perencana Pembangunan Nasional* or BAPPENAS) about the social safety net, outlining a planned expenditure of Rp 17 trillion in September 1998 created the impression that this body was closely coordinating the entire program. Although BAPPENAS spokespersons continued to give the impression in public pronouncements that this was the case, in reality the safety nets announced were little more than a collection of disparate programs that were planned and implemented by separate government agencies with little or no effective coordination between them. The entire package of measures was supported both as a whole and in its component parts by donor assistance, including a controversial World Bank loan known as the Social Safety Net Adjustment Loan. During late 1998 and throughout 1999 there were frequent allegations in the press and protest demonstrations from civil society groups claiming that the Social Safety Net program was being poorly implemented and the funds misdirected. The reputation of the entire Social Safety Net program was adversely affected by these campaigns, even though the protests were usually directed at one or two particular programs that had gained particular notoriety in the press and were the subject of allegations of corruption on the part of local officials.[16] We will consider the targeting of the most important of these programs in the following section. A summary of the programs is presented in Table 3.5.

Village Programs

The *Inpres Desa Tertinggal* (IDT), literally translated as the Neglected Villages Program, was an attempt by the New Order government to reach out to those parts of the country that had not yet shared in the benefits of its development policies and the steady economic growth of the previous two decades. By targeting direct assistance to the poorest sections of society in these locations, the government aimed to speed up the reduction of Indonesia's already declining poverty rate. The program formally began in 1994 with the strong backing of President Suharto through the announcement of a Presidential Decree (*Instruksi Presiden* or INPRES).[17]

Table 3.5 *Summary of the main poverty-targeting programs*

Area	Program description	Targeting	Database	Period	Costs (& budget share) 1998/99[a]
Village Improvement	Inpres Desa Tertinggal (IDT): provision of small-scale credit to poor households living in the poorest or most neglected villages	Geographic	Village Potential Survey (Podes)	1994–96	
Food Security	OPK/Raskin Program: sale of subsidized rice to targeted households. Eligible households are able to purchase 10–20kg of rice at lower than market price	Geographic Household	BKKBN list, with flexibility	1998–2003	Rp 5 450 000 (3.7% of total government expenditure)
Community Empowerment	PDM-DKE: a 'community fund' program providing block grants for either public works or revolving credit funds	Geographic Household	Pre-Crisis data (then updated) combined with local decision making	1998–2000	Rp 1 701 470 (1.16%)

Employment Creation	'Padat karya': a loose, uncoordinated collection of several labor-intensive programs under various government agencies	Household Self-selections	Various ministries, based on urban unemployment	1998–2000	Rp 2 066 000 (1.62%)
Education	• Scholarships for elementary, lower and upper secondary level students worth Rp 10000, Rp 20000 and Rp 30000/month • Block grants to selected schools	Geographic Household	SUSENAS data on enrollment, poverty data updated to 1998, combined with local criteria	1998/99– 2002/03 academic year	Rp 1 138 000 (1.06%)
Health	JPS-BK, a program providing subsidies for: • Medical and family planning services • Nutrition (supplementary food) • Operational support for health centers and midwives	Geographic Household	BKKBN list with flexibility	1998–2002/03	Rp 1 043 000 (0.97%)

Note: [a] The budget data for 1998/99 have been compiled from various sources; for further details, see Daley and Fane (2002: 311).

95

IDT applied geographic targeting to provide small-scale credit to poor households living in the poorest or most neglected villages throughout the entire country. The program channeled funds worth US$200 million per year over a three-year period (1994, 1995 and 1996), which were targeted to more than 20000 poor villages across Indonesia (Pangestu and Azis, 1994; World Bank, 1995). Each participating village received a block grant of Rp 20 million (US $8700)[18] that was to be used as a base fund for small-scale revolving credit (*dana bergulir*) to be made available to selected groups of people within the village. The credit was to be directed at a range of self-employment activities (Alatas, 1999: 1).

The identification of the poor who were the intended targets of the program was carried out through a two-stage process. Firstly, the IDT villages were selected, and then secondly, community organizations within the villages decided which particular households should receive the funds. The initial village selection process was carried out in June 1993, drawing on data obtained from the 1990 Podes survey conducted by BPS.[19] The irregular Podes surveys ('Village Potential', *Potensi Desa* or Podes) are a complete enumeration of every village in the country, and collect basic information and data about village characteristics. This includes crude population statistics, data about local economic characteristics, and the presence or absence of basic infrastructure and government-provided facilities such as health services, schools, marketplaces, potable water, electricity and roads. For the IDT village selection process, BPS extracted some 25 relevant variables for urban areas and 27 variables for rural areas to make a classification of neglected and non-neglected villages.[20] For each of these variables, villages were assigned scores from 0 to 5 to indicate their status.

The determination of whether a particular village was classified as 'neglected' was based upon two different types of assessments, an examination of the range and standard deviation of village scores within the provinces, as well as the results of field-based qualitative assessments by local officials. To be listed as an IDT recipient, a village had to satisfy two of the following three conditions:

• a score less than or equal to the provincial average score minus one standard deviation,
• a score less than or equal to the provincial maximum score minus 0.6 times the provincial range,
• an assessment by local officials that the village was poor, following a field inspection.[21]

Based on the June 1993 methods, 20 622 villages were classified as 'neglected' (31 per cent of all villages in Indonesia). Of these neglected villages, 19 615 were in rural areas, and 1007 in urban areas (see Tables 3.6 and 3.7). It needs to be pointed out that the allocation of IDT funds was not entirely free of political considerations, for in two of Indonesia's most troubled provinces, Irian Jaya (now Papua) and East Timor (now an independent country), all villages were included as recipients of IDT funds at the 1994 selection.

Table 3.6   Number of neglected villages in rural areas 1993–95

| | Rural | | | | | |
| | 1993 | | 1994 | | 1995 | |
	Village	%	Village	%	Village	%
Western Indonesia	12 087	61.6	12 709	60.7	11 355	54.8
Java	5 427	27.7	5 648	27.0	5 610	27.1
Bali	81	0.4	92	0.4	91	0.4
Sumatra	6 579	33.5	6 969	33.3	5 654	27.3
Eastern Indonesia	7 528	38.4	8 242	39.3	9 366	45.2
Total	**19 615**	**100.0**	**20 951**	**100.0**	**20 721**	**100.0**

Note: Data in 1993, 1994 and 1995 are not comparable because of a modification in the method of determining poor villages.

Source: Sumarto et al. (1997: Tables 2.6, 2.7, 2.8).

Table 3.7   Number of neglected villages in urban areas 1993–95

| | Urban | | | | | |
| | 1993 | | 1994 | | 1995 | |
	Village	%	Village	%	Village	%
Western Indonesia	853	84.7	928	81.2	905	68.6
Java	663	65.8	681	59.6	666	50.5
Bali	17	1.7	19	1.7	18	1.4
Sumatra	173	17.2	228	19.9	221	16.7
Eastern Indonesia	154	15.3	215	18.8	415	31.4
Total	**1007**	**100.0**	**1143**	**100.0**	**1320**	**100.0**

Note: Data in 1993, 1994 and 1995 are not comparable because of a modification in the method of determining poor villages.

Source: Sumarto et al. (1997: Tables 2.6, 2.7, 2.8).

The second stage in the process of delivering the IDT assistance to the poor occurred at the village level. The program was designed to give village communities a certain degree of freedom to set their own rules and procedures concerning the allocation of the funds within the village, although this meant that the process was not always accountable and that credit could be misdirected, especially since supervision and monitoring were notoriously lax and ineffective.

In the recipient villages, community groups (*Kelompok Masyarakat* or Pokmas) of poor households were established. According to anecdotal evidence, village leaders played a decisive role in the formation of these Pokmas, which were usually based on the geographic distribution of poor households within a village. Each Pokmas had to submit a proposal explaining their plans for using the funds, and how the funds were to be distributed among members. These plans were subjected to scrutiny by the village council and its officials. According to IDT program guidelines, the available funds were intended for small-scale investment activities that were to be quick-yielding (so that credit could be rolled over to other poor households), reliant on available local resources, easy to market and contributed 'value-added' through generating additional household income. However, in reality there was a considerable tolerance and a wide degree of freedom for the Pokmas to include almost anything in the proposal. In cases of immediate need, proposals could even be used to meet the basic needs of poor households, and only physical village infrastructure projects were explicitly excluded from the IDT program. We are unaware of any comprehensive studies of the allocation of IDT funds at the household level within villages. Hence, our analysis focuses on the effectiveness of the targeting at the broader level.

Effectiveness of targeting through village programs

If we compare the proportion of neglected villages with the proportion of poor households throughout the country using the BPS headcount poverty rate, it is apparent that the percentage of villages classified under the IDT program as 'neglected' (31 per cent) was significantly higher than the percentage of poor households in 1993 (13.7 per cent according to the BPS data). Sumarto et al. (1997: 12–13) have argued that the striking difference between these two figures was due to the quite different concepts used to determine poor households and 'neglected' villages.[22] Household poverty is established using an 'absolute' measurement; a household is considered poor if its average consumption and expenditure falls below a given threshold (the official poverty line). In contrast, the 'neglected' village status was determined using a relative measure; a village was deemed to be 'neglected' if its Podes-derived score is one standard deviation from the provincial mean. However by the theory of probability, about 30 per cent of any distribution will be one standard deviation from the mean. Hence, using this procedure, in every province, there must always be some villages that will be defined as neglected, regardless of their actual condition. Moreover, two villages of broadly similar socio-economic condition, but located in different provinces, could be treated differently because of their relative position within their respective provinces (Alatas, 1999).

Another problem that resulted from the method used to determine 'neglected' village status was a marked geographic disproportion. Half of all poor households in Indonesia (around 50 per cent) are in Java while more than 70 per cent of all the IDT villages were located outside Java. This occurred because villages outside Java are mostly smaller in size and population than villages on Java (Sumarto et al., 1997; World Bank, 1996: 3). As a result, in terms of the number of IDT villages, there was a significant disproportion in the number of 'neglected' villages on average per province off Java than on Java.

Drawing on the results of a 1996 BPS pilot study of IDT in 384 villages in six provinces, Sumarto et al. (1997) demonstrate that the effectiveness of the IDT program in targeting poor households was indeed quite low, at least in the first year of the program. Citing the results of the targeting in two provinces, Central Java and West Nusa Tenggara, as examples, their study shows that there were still a large proportion of the poor excluded from the program (see Table 3.8). In Central Java, about 30 per cent of villages were classified as 'neglected', and 54 per cent of poor households lived in these villages. However, the remaining 46 per cent of poor households did not live in the IDT recipient villages and therefore did not benefit from the program. In West Nusa Tenggara, 58 per cent of all households in IDT villages were poor – only slightly more than the percentage in Central Java, but the percentage of IDT village was almost double that in Central Java. Nevertheless, about 46 per cent of poor households in West Nusa Tenggara lived in non-IDT villages.

Since this study only considers the experience of two selected provinces, caution should be exercised in drawing conclusions about the entire IDT program. However, these two cases certainly illustrate the mis-targeting problem that arose as a result of the selection process. The two provinces selected as examples are also important for poverty analysis. Central Java is one of the most heavily populated provinces with a high incidence of poverty in rural areas, while West Nusa Tenggara is one of the poorest provinces in the country. Unfortunately, we do not have similar data to assess the 1994 and 1995 programs.

Table 3.8   Comparison between neglected villages and location of poor population in IDT and non-IDT villages, in Central Java and West Nusa Tenggara, 1993

Type of village	Central Java				West Nusa Tenggara			
	Number of villages	%	Number of poor people (million)	%	Number of villages	%	Number of poor households	%
IDT villages	2524	30	2.47	54	330	56	65274	58
Non-IDT villages	6006	70	2.13	46	262	44	46850	42
Total	**8530**	**100**	**4.6**	**100**	**592**	**100**	**112124**	**100**

Source: Sumarto et al. (1997: Tables 2.9 and 2.10).

During the second and third years of the program, the selection procedures were revised to eliminate flaws that had been identified in the selection criteria that made it difficult to give sufficient consideration to the level of household consumption (World Bank, 1996). In the initial selection process, too much weight had been given to infrastructure deficiencies that do not always reflect low levels of household consumption. Consequently, in late 1994, the field observation criterion was dropped, and a smaller list of variables more closely related to economic welfare was used to obtain village scores. This new method may have been better at targeting poverty, since it was a more accurate reflection of the social and economic condition of the inhabitants rather than physical location. In addition, villages with fewer than 50 families were eliminated from the program for the 1995 round. As a result, almost a third of the villages that had been selected in 1994 changed for the 1995 program. However, due to the change in the selection criteria, the 1995 and 1996 data could not be directly compared with the 1994 data.

Despite the problems identified in targeting the poor, the IDT program still had positive impacts for the recipients. Alatas (1999: 25–6) revealed that the IDT program increased the per capita total expenditure of village recipients, although not per capita expenditure on health care. The program also had a positive impact on employment, especially on female workers in rural areas, indicating a loosening of the traditional labor market constraints for females in some rural areas. There was also a small positive impact on the school attendance rate. In addition, Akita and Setto (2000) have argued that the IDT program has been a relatively successful fiscal decentralization, which channeled funds from the center to regions, and has had some significant impact in reducing regional disparities, especially between the western and eastern regions of Indonesia.

Employment Programs

Emergency job creation measures to provide assistance to those who had lost their positions in the formal sector as a result of the Crisis became one of the key planks in the government's official 1998/99 Social Safety Net program. However, there was really no single program of this kind, but an odd assortment of programs that were lumped together under this category in the official pronouncements of the government's policies. This collection of quite disparate programs – some of them were programs that had their origins before the Crisis erupted, while many more were rapidly brought into existence in the troubled months of 1998 – nevertheless shared certain common attributes. In theory, all drew upon labor-intensive methods, widely referred to in Indonesia by the term *padat karya*,[23] usually to undertake some small-scale village-based infrastructure or public works projects, thus providing the maximum opportunities to absorb local unemployed or underemployed labor.

Some of these labor-intensive programs using the *padat karya* label were hastily developed by sectoral or line ministries to absorb recently retrenched workers, especially in rural areas. According to one estimate, the total number of programs that fell under this category may have been as many as 16 in the 1998/99 fiscal year, but by 1999/2000 the number of *padat karya* style programs had been reduced to two (Sumarto et al., 2001: 8). However, in the first year of the Social Safety Net program, there were *padat karya* programs announced by ministries such as Forestry, Religious Affairs and Public Works, sections of the national bureaucracy with little or no previous experience or record of accomplishment in the delivery of social welfare assistance. It has also been suggested that certain ministries took the opportunity presented by the government's announcement of its intention to introduce a Social Safety Net program to capture a share of the budget that had been set aside for this form of social expenditure (Daley and Fane, 2002: 314).

It should therefore come as no surprise that many of these programs were widely criticized for their poor performance. Many of them did not last more than a few months before disappearing. There were numerous reports in the Indonesian press during the final months of 1998 and throughout 1999, instancing examples of poor and hasty planning, inadequate or non-existent monitoring and supervision, and unsatisfactory implementation. Many of the projects were reportedly selected without adequate consultation with the local community, especially the poor and those who were most in need of even short-term employment opportunities. As a result, much of the work on some of these *padat karya* programs was menial and mindless. There were also frequent complaints that a large proportion of the funds were being diverted into materials and equipment rather than being directed at labor-intensive tasks. This is in addition to widespread allegations of malfeasance on the part of local officials.

We should also bear in mind that during the second half of 1998 and into 1999, some other programs were operating that were not actually intended to be listed as part of the government's official Social Safety Net program, but were nevertheless also applying *padat karya* principles. Some of these were development programs of a longer-term nature that had already been put in place before the Crisis began. This includes the second phase of the Village Infrastructure Project (VIP/P3DT), a program funded by a World Bank loan to deliver assistance to 2600 poor rural villages throughout Java and Sumatra (World Bank, 1996). To a certain extent, this program was building on the IDT model, but was much more closely supervised and monitored. During the second half of 1998, and continuing in some locations into the early months of 1999, an emergency drought relief 'crash' program known as the *Padat Karya Desa* Program (PKDP) was operating in nearly 2000 villages in four eastern Indonesian provinces. This program was funded by a World Bank loan package, and directed at those rural villages that had been seriously affected by the 1997–98 El Niño-related drought (Swisher, 1999).

Although not a formal part of the Social Safety Net program, both these programs delivered block grants to fund small-scale infrastructure projects using labor-intensive methods. Drawing on both geographic and administrative targeting criteria, the villages selected to receive these programs were intended to be among the poorest, in the case of VIP, or suffering serious food shortages in the case of PKDP. It should be kept in mind that participation in both programs might well have been captured by the questions about participation in *padat karya* activities contained in the 1999 SUSENAS Special Module on the Social Safety Net program.

The targeting criteria that were used in many of the Social Safety Net labor-intensive programs were often poorly formulated. This applies especially to those schemes that were conceived in haste by the sectoral ministries in mid-1998. However, one common feature of all the *padat karya* type programs was a strong element of self-targeting or self-selection. Wage rates were supposed to be kept deliberately low, well below prevailing wages for unskilled agricultural labor in rural areas. This way, only those who were in real need would consider registering for the work gangs that were being formed. This was a conscious attempt to attract to the programs only those members of the village community who really were unemployed and desperate for some temporary work, rather than those who had sufficient resources or who were still gainfully employed. In practice, as with much else about these *padat karya* schemes, these rules were reportedly often flouted, while supervision and sanctions were usually lax or non-existent.

Impact of employment programs

How effective were the targeting outcomes in these labor-intensive employment safety net programs? Several preliminary studies drew on the results of the 100 Village Survey,[24] but the most complete analysis has been by Sumarto et al. (2001), drawing on data provided by the SUSENAS Special Module. This reveals that only 8.3 per cent of poor households (as defined by those households in the lowest quintile of per capita expenditure) were covered by these programs in the six months before February 1999. Meanwhile, 70 per cent of those who took part in *padat karya* activities were from non-poor households, even though participation dropped off among the better-off sections of the community.

The authors use a simple targeting ratio to judge the effectiveness of the schemes. This is defined as 'the ratio of participation of the non-poor in a program compared to the fraction of non-poor in the sample.' It is derived by dividing the proportion of non-poor beneficiaries for each program by 0.8, which is the proportion of non-poor in the sample (as the poor are the bottom quintile); see Sumarto et al. (2001: 14–18). If all recipients are non-poor, the targeting ratio will be 1.25, whilst perfect targeting, where all beneficiaries are poor, will mean a targeting ratio of zero. Random targeting, where the non-poor and poor are equally likely to be beneficiaries, will produce a targeting ratio equal to unity. For the employment creation schemes the result was a targeting ratio of 0.88, leading to the conclusion that targeting, far from being effective, was near to random. Table 3.9 gives their estimates of targeting ratios for a number of anti-poverty programs. Overall, ratios are high and relatively close to unity for all schemes, with the lowest ratio of 0.83 found for the Health Card program (see below). Although these results refer to a relatively brief and early period for these schemes, the weak coverage of the poor relative to the better-off suggests that these Social Safety Net programs were relatively ineffective.

Some other valuable insights gleaned from the SUSENAS data included the low participation rates for women (19 per cent) compared with men (81 per cent), almost certainly a reflection of the overwhelmingly heavy physical labor that was offered by these programs. The wage rates on offer appear to have not been very far below average wages for agricultural laborers, perhaps helping to explain why so many non-poor were attracted to the programs (giving a high leakage or type two error).

Table 3.9   Coverage and targeting of anti-poverty programs, August 1998–February 1999

Programs	Total number of potential recipients[a]	Program coverage (%)				Program targeting	
		Poorest 20%	Richest 20%	Non-poor (upper 80%)	Coverage of all potential recipients	Proportion of total recipients from non-poor	Targeting ratio[b]
	(1)	(2)	(3)	(4)	(5)	(6)	(7)
Subsidized rice	50 385 444	52.64	24.33	36.90	40.09	0.74	0.92
Employment creation	50 385 444	8.31	2.53	4.94	5.61	0.70	0.88
Primary scholarships	29 745 369	5.80	2.04	3.60	4.03	0.71	0.89
Lower secondary scholarships	10 394 621	12.15	4.85	7.53	8.42	0.71	0.89
Upper secondary scholarships	6 430 146	5.40	1.96	3.32	3.71	0.71	0.90
Health Card	27 567 138	10.60	3.09	5.28	6.33	0.67	0.83
Nutrition	19 970 948	16.54	14.24	15.79	15.94	0.79	0.99

Note:
a   The total number of potential recipients for each program:

- Subsidized rice and job creation programs: all 50.4 million Indonesian households.
- Scholarships: the total number of individual students enrolled at each school level: primary, lower secondary and upper secondary.
- Health care: all those individuals estimated to have visited a health care provider in the three months prior to the SUSENAS survey.
- Nutrition: the total number of individuals in the 'pregnant women and children under three years old' category.

b   Targeting ratio is column (6) divided by the fraction of the non-poor in the population. By definition, non-poor households are 80 per cent of the population, hence the targeting ratio is column(6) is divided by 0.8.

Source: Sumarto et al. (2001: Table Appendix 2), based on the 1999 SUSENAS.

PDM-PKE program

Mention should also be made of one particularly important social safety net program that, at least in part, can be included in the labor-intensive employment creation category although for reasons of its timing cannot be considered from a quantitative analytical perspective. This was the awkwardly named Empowering the Regions to Overcome the Impact of the Economic Crisis Program (*Pemberdayaan Daerah dalam Mengatasi Dampak Krisis Ekonomi* or PDM-DKE).[25] With a total budget of Rp 1.7 trillion, the program consisted of block grants delivered through a decentralized disbursement process, under the supervision of district-level committees and village implementation teams. The block grants were intended for local infrastructure improvements that would generate temporary employment opportunities using labor-intensive methods, and for the creation of revolving funds to provide credit to the poor and unemployed to support income-generating small-scale business activities. The size of the funds made available to villages varied from Rp 10 million to as much as Rp 1 billion, depending on size and the estimated numbers of the poor and unemployed.

This program was conceived by BAPPENAS to be one of the centerpieces of the government's social rescue package. It seems to have been designed by that agency's planners to create the impression that this arm of the central government bureaucracy was really in charge of the coordination of the entire Social Safety Net program. However, the PDM-DKE program soon attracted considerable negative attention as one of the worst of the safety nets and was quickly mired in controversy with allegations of corruption and 'money politics'. Much of the final stages of the implementation of the program, in particular the disbursement of significant amounts of cash at the district level to thousands of specially created community groups in rural and urban villages throughout the entire country, occurred in the lead up to the 1999 national elections. Consequently, in the heated political atmosphere of the country's first democratic election campaign since the mid-1950s, charges of blatant pork barreling were leveled at the government and those officials who were directly in charge of the program.

The plans for the PDM-DKE program had been announced in November 1998, and the program's planners had stressed that this package was intended to be delivered as rapidly as possible, ostensibly to provide support to the poor and disadvantaged throughout the country who were still suffering from the economic impact of the crisis. However, the actual disbursement of funds did not begin to take place until March of the following year. As a result, although the various essential administrative preparations had started shortly after the program was announced, the actual physical work on any of the labor-intensive public infrastructure projects funded by this program had not yet started when the February SUSENAS was conducted by BPS. Unfortunately, this means that participation in *padat karya* activities under PDM-DKE was not captured by the question asked of respondents in the SUSENAS Special Module on the Social Safety Net program.

This point has never been made explicit in any of those published quantitative analyses of the targeting of social safety net activities based on the data derived from the Special Module, even though frequent reference is made to the PDM-DKE program in these studies. The only specific analysis of this program was a rapid appraisal conducted by a team from SMERU in late 1998, the period when the administrative preparations and structures were being put in place at the local level.[26] This qualitative field survey study examined the operations of the PDM-DKE in 13 villages located within six districts across four different provinces.

In addition to reporting on the many problems that were already evident because of the excessive haste with which such a complex and difficult program was being put into effect, the SMERU study revealed some of the serious targeting anomalies that were already becoming apparent. Although the intended beneficiaries of the PDM-DKE program were the rural and urban poor and unemployed, it was apparent that in the villages in the rapid appraisal, credit was being directed instead to those who were better off and who were considered more likely to repay their loans. As for the employment-generating infrastructure component, there was little evidence that the poor were being consulted over the selection of projects, and as a result, many infrastructure projects were being selected that did not provide benefits to the poorest section of the community. There were strong indications that excessive amounts were being diverted into materials and equipment instead of being made available for labor. These preliminary findings appear to have been confirmed by the many problems observed as the program funds were released in the months that followed. Serious shortcomings in the PDM-DKE program were a strong element in the World Bank's decision to cancel the second tranche of the Social Safety Net Adjustment Loan.

Food Security

Food security was one of the most important issues to be addressed during the 1998 Social Safety Net program that had followed in the wake of the Crisis. There was serious concern that poor families, those most affected by falling real incomes and rising food prices, would be unable to afford to purchase rice, the staple foodstuff for Indonesians in most parts of the country. As a result, a special food assistance program was designed that was intended to deliver a quantity of medium quality rice every month to poor and needy families at a heavily subsidized price. The situation was compounded by the 1997–98 El Niño-related drought which had adversely affected agricultural output and food production, especially in the eastern regions of the archipelago.

The program was known until 2002 by its Indonesian abbreviation OPK (*Operasi Pasar Khusus* or Special Market Operations).[27] It was originally planned and put into effect by officials from the Ministry of Food and Horticulture working in close collaboration with the National Logistics Agency (Bulog). Rice began to be delivered in selected parts of the country in July 1998, gradually spreading throughout every province, district and sub-district in the archipelago over the following months as the program was brought up to full scale. By mid-1999, Bulog had assumed full responsibility for the OPK program's implementation.

When the program first began, OPK aimed to deliver 10 kg of rice per month to poor families at Rp 1000 per kg. The targeting of those families who were to receive the assistance was based on the National Family Planning Coordinating Board (BKKBN) classification of family socio-economic status. The intended beneficiaries were those families listed in the lowest welfare category of the BKKBN classification, those who were referred to as 'pre-prosperous families' (*keluarga pra-sejahtera* or KPS). As the government became increasingly concerned about the extent of the social and economic impact of the Crisis, particularly with rising rice prices, the program's national allocation of rice was steadily increased so that 'level 1 prosperous families' (*keluarga sejahtera* 1 or KS-1) could also be included as program beneficiaries. From December 1998, the monthly amount that each participating family was to receive was also increased to 20 kg at the same subsidized price of Rp 1000 per kg.[28] If this intended allocation had indeed been achieved, it would have constituted an indirect net monthly income transfer of approximately Rp 20 000 to Rp 30 000 per family.

Impact of the OPK program

However, a number of studies subsequently revealed that the OPK program failed to achieve its objective of providing food security for the poorest sections of society. The first independent assessment of OPK, a rapid appraisal conducted in five provinces in late 1998, revealed a lack of effective public information about the program at the local community level and identified serious shortcomings in the program's administrative procedures. Most importantly, it was apparent that the approach that had been taken to target the beneficiaries was ineffective since many poor families were identified in the areas surveyed that were not receiving the subsidized rice.[29]

Following widespread criticism of many of the safety net programs during 1999, the government responded with attempts to improve the targeting procedures and to tighten the eligibility criteria for programs such as OPK. As outlined earlier, the BKKBN classification was revised to produce two additional categories of families based on 'economic' criteria – KPS ALEK and KS-1 ALEK.

The reliability of the OPK program's targeting of the poor was subjected to scrutiny in a number of analytical studies that appeared over the following two years. Of particular importance were the papers published by SMERU researchers that established that the coverage and targeting of the OPK program was seriously deficient (Suryahadi et al., 1999; Sumarto et al., 2000; Sumarto et al., 2001). These studies used panel data from several rounds of the 100 Village Survey as well as data from the February 2000 SUSENAS Special Module. According to one assessment, an estimated 20.2 million households across Indonesia had received OPK rice during one six-month period, almost double the number of beneficiaries recorded in various official reports (Sumarto et al., 2000: 20). For comparison, see the figures in Irawan (2001: 19–20).

Furthermore, the OPK program's coverage of poor families – those in the lowest quintile, defined by levels of household expenditure – was disappointingly low, as only 52.6 per cent of poor families had received OPK rice (see Table 3.9). Hence type one errors of undercoverage were high. An unacceptably high level of program leakage or type two error was also evident, since a significant proportion of the subsidized rice was received by non-poor families, those in the top four quintiles of household expenditure levels, and who accounted for about three-quarters of all recipients. Far from fulfilling the aims of the program planners, the benefits of the program were spread almost equally between poor and non-poor families, producing a targeting ratio of 0.92 which is indicative of random rather than effective targeting.

In sharp contrast, an adjunct food security program distributing cheap rice to poor families being conducted by the World Food Program in a limited number of urban localities in Java during 1999–2000, seemed to have largely overcome the targeting problem. This program contracted local non-governmental organizations to compile the list of recipients and execute the regular distribution, under close supervision and monitoring from World Food Program staff. A field study of this program suggests that it was successful in delivering the subsidized rice to the poorest and most needy sections of the community in these areas. The comparison with the official program is instructive.[30]

Although the studies of the OPK program drew on data derived from a limited and early period of the program's operations, subsequent field-based observations confirmed these findings. Several studies conducted in many different locations all reported that rice continued to be dispersed to a far larger number of recipients – and hence in much smaller monthly allocations – than the program guidelines had stipulated (LP3ES and MENPHOR, 2000; Tim Dampak Krisis, 2000; Olken et al., 2001). As a result, when the official guidelines were released for the 2000 and 2001 OPK program, program planners appeared to have accepted the overwhelming evidence of what was occurring in the villages throughout Indonesia as the total allocations for each recipient had been changed from 20 kg for each family to a maximum of 20 kg and a minimum of 10 kg.

Raskin – the 2002 food program

In preparation for the 2002 phase of the program, an attempt was made by Bulog to revisit the targeting issue and find a solution to the problems that had prevented many of the nation's poorest families receiving the benefits of the subsidized rice program. Some of the changes that were agreed upon were simply 'window-dressing': the name of the program was changed to emphasize the fact that the cheap rice was really intended only for the poorest families (Raskin, abbreviated from *Beras untuk Keluarga Miskin* or Rice for Poor Families). This message was reinforced by a limited national television advertising campaign.

Other more radical approaches to targeting were considered but failed to win sufficient political support.[31] In essence, the basic principles set out in the 2002 official program guidelines were little different from the earlier versions of the subsidized rice program (Badan Urusan Logistik, 2001). The Raskin program returned to the formula of 20 kg of rice for poor families every month at Rp 1000 per kg, but it is worth noting that central government planners had passed the ultimate responsibility for the selection of the recipient families down to decision-makers at the village level. The Bulog program guidelines simply stipulated that the determination of actual beneficiaries should be made with reference to the BKKBN data on those families classified as KPS ALEK and KS-1 ALEK, but that this matter was to be the subject of a process of discussion and consultation involving village officials, community leaders and representatives of the wider village community.

Nevertheless, although village decision-makers were given authority over the actual composition of the lists, the program guidelines stipulated that they were also expected to work within the limitations of the ceiling or quota of rice that each village would receive. Every village was to receive a specific monthly allocation of rice that was intended to supply a finite number of families with a 20 kg allotment, and so the total number of families to be listed by each village as recipients of the Raskin program should not exceed that number.

Under the 2002 Raskin program, a national level quota was determined after consultation between Bulog and other government agencies, in particular the Ministry of Finance and the National Planning Board (BAPPENAS), drawing on data from both the Central Bureau of Statistics (BPS) and BKKBN. It was estimated that this quota was sufficient to provide a 20 kg monthly allocation of rice to just over 9 million families – roughly 19 per cent of the total number of families in the country. The central government decided upon the quotas for each of the provinces, calculated proportionally according to the BKKBN data on KPS ALEK and KS-1 ALEK, and every provincial government was asked to determine the quotas for each *kabupaten* and *kota* within its area of jurisdiction, again drawing on BKKBN data. Finally, at the *kabupaten* and *kota* level, the local administration was given the task of deciding on the exact quotas for each of the distribution points within their region.[32]

Official records indicate that Bulog and its branches in the regions had succeeded in improving the distribution system, so that an impressive tonnage of rice was delivered on a monthly basis to over 44 000 distribution points throughout the archipelago during 2002. However, achieving satisfactory targeting of the program so that the rice really reaches the poorest and most needy sections of the community is a far more intractable problem.

A complete analysis of the targeting effectiveness of the Raskin version of the subsidized rice program has not been possible, since there have been no available data comparable to the February 2000 SUSENAS Special Module. Nevertheless, some indication can be derived from the only study to date, a rapid appraisal conducted in 2002 based upon field studies in ten villages located in three districts in two sample provinces (Hastuti and Maxwell, 2003). The study was a wide-ranging and detailed examination of all aspects of the program, and particular emphasis was given to the issue of who was receiving the rice in the villages that were surveyed, and the precise quantity of the monthly allocations obtained by beneficiaries.

It is apparent that there was once more a considerable amount of program leakage: although many poor families were able to secure some of the benefits of the program, far too many of the non-poor members of village communities also managed to obtain a share of the subsidized rice delivered to the village distribution points. Consequently, many more families were still participating in the Raskin program than was ever intended by the central government planners at Bulog. The evidence from the villages in the survey area suggests that the actual number of recipients amounted to about double the target number that was decided upon when national, provincial and district quotas were established in late 2001 using the BKKBN data.

This estimate was confirmed by those local government officials who were responsible for conducting the monthly rice distribution at province and district level, especially as some of these officials had been collecting their own statistics about the actual number of families receiving Raskin rice in an attempt to verify what had actually been occurring.

At the local level, the precise details of how the distribution to beneficiaries was conducted varied from village to village and depended on a range of local factors, but two main trends stand out. Firstly, in one group of villages any attempt at targeting particular families had been abandoned and the Raskin rice was being offered to all families more or less equally on a 'first come, first served' basis, so that any family who wished to do so was able to purchase rice irrespective of any assessment of their real need. Secondly, in another group of villages, although the rice was being allocated to a significantly larger group than those identified by the BKKBN lists, an attempt had been made to identify all families considered to be the most deserving cases, and once this list had been compiled, to limit the distribution to those beneficiaries (Hastuti and Maxwell, 2003: 26–33).

Where villages were no longer making any effort to target the distribution of Raskin rice, local officials argued that this was a result of community pressure and the threat of communal conflict. In those villages where an attempt had been made by village officials and community leaders to produce their own local solutions to the difficult targeting problem, there had been widespread opposition to the strict application of BKKBN data on poor families. Many of the objections that were raised appeared to be sound and justifiable criticism. In any case, the size of the village allocations – which were a direct result of the quota decided upon by the central government – were insufficient to include all those families in the KPS ALEK and KS-1 ALEK categories. Consequently even in the villages where local targeting had not been abandoned, villages had decided upon a final number of beneficiaries that was much greater than the target number set by the government, and so beneficiaries were usually receiving considerably less than the target of 20 kg.

Despite the powerful arguments in favor of villages making their own decisions about which families are most in need of this assistance, it remains a matter of concern that a large amount of the subsidized rice was being accessed by families for whom it was clearly not intended. This was most evident in those villages were the rice was made available to anyone on a 'first come, first served' basis. But it was apparently also occurring in those villages where the poorest families had often had difficulty collecting the required amount of cash in the limited time allowed them by local officials before the rice was delivered and the distribution was completed.

In some villages, the subsidized rice had been distributed to such large numbers of recipients that the actual amount of rice received had been reduced to only a few kilograms. In these cases, the local targeting had been so distorted that the program's central aim of providing a certain degree of food security and a useful indirect income transfer to the poorest sections of the community was clearly a lost cause.

During 2002, the operation and implementation of the Raskin program at the village level was still largely under the direct jurisdiction of a small group of village officials, with the village head in a dominant position of authority. Although the reform of village-level political institutions throughout the country is now underway, the new institutions have not yet had any experience with the implementation of social welfare programs. Nor are these yet able to provide a check on the power and authority of program implementers at the village level, although this may happen in the future. At present, the direction of a program such as Raskin is still largely in the hands of the village heads and their staff. The personal qualities and capacities of these village officials seem to have a direct bearing on whether local communities are successful at solving the targeting issue and arriving at an acceptable solution that ensures that the benefits of the program are really directed at the poorest sections of the community. In those villages where local officials are people of integrity and honesty, where they have a solid grasp of the central purpose of the program, and where their own reputation and standing within their community is secure, the chances of successful targeting occurring followed by effective implementation seem to be immeasurably strengthened.

The targeting issue is fundamental to the success of a program such as Raskin. Yet it seems that there are no simple solutions. To some extent, effective publicity campaigns and careful monitoring may also have some impact on village-based decisions about the targeting of such a program.

Education

The Scholarships and Grants Program (SGP) component of the safety net measures aimed to reduce the feared adverse impact of the Crisis on the quality and effectiveness of the education system. The SGP began in the 1998/99 academic year, and provided special assistance both to students from poor families and to selected schools. Since the early 1990s, education statistics have shown a trend of increasing enrollment ratios at the primary, lower and upper secondary levels (see Table 3.10). The national 9-year compulsory education program (*program wajib belajar nasional 9 tahun*) established by the government in the mid-1990s resulted in a net primary school enrollment ratio hovering around 94 per cent, and a rapid increase in the enrollment ratio at the lower secondary level, from 69 to 79 per cent in less then a decade.

Table 3.10   School enrollment ratios, 1993–99

	SUSENAS year						
	1993	1994	1995	1996	1997	1998	1999
School level	Academic year						
	1992/93	1993/94	1994/95	1995/96	1996/97	1997/98	1998/99
Primary	92.8	94.1	93.9	94.4	95.4	95.1	95.2
Lower secondary	68.9	72.4	73.2	75.8	77.5	77.2	79.1
Upper secondary	42.6	45.3	44.6	47.6	48.6	49.3	51.2

Source: Cameron (2002: Table 1).

At the beginning of the Crisis, there was a serious concern on the part of the government that the Crisis would trigger a significant increase in school dropout rates, with fears that parents would be forced to withdraw their children from school as a way of coping with falling incomes and rising costs. However, as we can see in Table 3.10, between the 1996/97 and 1997/98 academic years, there was only a small dip in enrollment rates at the primary level and only a slightly larger decline at the lower secondary level. Meanwhile, upper secondary enrollment rates actually increased over the same period.

Table 3.11 compares the 1997, 1998 and 1998 SUSENAS data on enrollment rates, broken down by five expenditure quintiles to approximate socio-economic groups. It shows that the Crisis did not have a very dramatic effect on enrollment rates up to the 1997/98 school year, even on the poorest quintiles of the population in all school levels.[33] While these figures provide evidence that the Crisis did not lead to a serious decline in enrollment ratios, it has nevertheless stalled the growth of enrollment ratios at the primary and lower secondary levels, one of the government's central aims for the education system before the Crisis struck. This is one measure of the educational cost of the Crisis (Jones and Hagul, 2001: 218).

There is, however, evidence that the Crisis had some negative impacts on the quality of education. A field survey by the SMERU Research Institute found that after the Crisis, there was a slight decline in students' average scores at the National Final Examinations (*Nilai Ebtanas Murni*). There was also a reduction in teachers' real incomes, fewer extra-curricular activities and signs of declining health and nutrition levels among some students, affecting their capacity to absorb school lessons (Jones, 2003: 79). The

Poverty targeting in Asia

Table 3.11   *Age-specific enrollment rates by expenditure quintiles,*
1996/97–1998/99

| | Academic year | | |
Age and quintile	1996/7	1997/8	1998/9
5–6 years	*22.5*	*22.2*	*21.2*
Poorest	16.7	16.0	16.4
Second	20.4	20.9	19.2
Third	23.1	22.4	20.9
Fourth	25.8	25.6	24.6
Richest	31.0	31.1	28.6
7–12 years	*95.3*	*95.0*	*95.3*
Poorest	91.9	91.5	92.1
Second	95.2	94.8	94.8
Third	96.1	96.0	96.1
Fourth	97.2	96.7	97.4
Richest	97.8	97.9	98.0
13–15 years	*77.5*	*77.1*	*79.0*
Poorest	65.6	66.3	6837.0
Second	74.7	74.0	76.7
Third	79.7	79.2	80.5
Fourth	83.4	82.6	85.0
Richest	87.5	87.1	87.6
16–18 years	*48.6*	*49.2*	*51.1*
Poorest	32.2	31.5	34.9
Second	42.6	42.1	45.2
Third	49.4	49.9	52.9
Fourth	56.3	57.9	58.9
Richest	62.4	68.7	64.2

Source: Jones and Hagul (2001: Table 2).

Crisis also placed a considerable burden on parents, reducing the amount of time and money that they could afford to allocate to their children's education, thereby risking further negative impacts on children's schooling. Some families found it difficult to afford the regular, compulsory school payments, widely known throughout Indonesia as the BP3 contribution (*Badan Pembantu Penyelenggara Pendidikan* or Board of Education Assistance). Other families were unable to afford travel expenses, or the purchase of school uniforms or textbooks, forcing students to rely on inferior quality school package textbooks. Some students were unable to collect their graduation certificates, as they could not afford to pay the fees for the final examinations.

Alarmed by the situation, the government was prompted to establish the Scholarships and Grants Program (SGP) beginning in the 1998/99 academic year, with several donor agencies providing budgetary support for the package through special loans. The program has two components: scholarships for students from poor families and block grants for selected schools (see Table 3.12).

Table 3.12   Value and coverage of the SGP program

	Primary	Lower secondary	Upper secondary
Student scholarships			
Estimated number of children projected to receive scholarships over five years	3 000 000	2 750 000	830 000
Number of annual scholarships provided over five years	7 400 000	6 600 000	2 000 000
Approx. proportion of enrolled children receiving scholarship	6%	17%	10%
Scholarship amount per child per year[a]	Rp 120 000 (US $16)	Rp 240 000 (US $32)	Rp 300 000 (US $40)
School grants			
Schools receiving grants per year	104 340	18 240	9400
Percentage of schools receiving grants per year	60%	60%	60%
Amount of grants per school per year[a]	Rp 2 000 000 (US $267)	Rp 4 000 000 (US $533)	Rp 10 000 000 (US $1333)

Note: [a] Dollar equivalent computed at Rp 7500 per US $.

Source: CIMU (2000a: 7).

The scholarships program

The scholarships program was designed to encourage children to remain at school. It was designed as a direct cash transfer to students to increase the possibility of their continuing their studies on to the next school level. No restrictions were placed on how the money was to be spent, and students or their families were able to use it for any other expenses in addition to school fees. The scholarships provide monthly cash payments of Rp 10 000, Rp 20 000 and Rp 25 000 for primary, lower secondary and upper secondary school students respectively. This was equivalent to only US $1.33, US $2.67 and US $3.33, respectively, using the exchange rate of Rp 7500 per US $1 that applied at the establishment of the program in 1998. Nonetheless according to one estimate, these amounts generally covered the cost of school fees and charges.[34]

The government planned that the scholarships would reach a target of around 6 per cent of all elementary school students, 17 per cent of all lower secondary school students, and 10 per cent of all upper secondary school students nationwide, including students attending private and religious schools. Scholarships were only to be made available to those students who were:

- Enrolled as students in the final three grades in primary school and all three grades in both lower and upper secondary school,
- Recent dropouts or those students in danger of leaving school because of economic factors, and
- Not in receipt of any other scholarships.

Also as an additional criterion at least 50 per cent of the scholarships were to be allocated to female students.

Authority to decide upon the allocation of the scholarship funds was decentralized to district and school committees, but the funds themselves were distributed directly to the student beneficiaries through local post offices. This mechanism of channeling funds directly from the central government to the recipients was one of the program's most innovative measures, overcoming unnecessary delays in receiving payments and reducing leakage.[35]

The allocation of scholarships to districts and to schools was based on the estimated impact of the Crisis on poverty in each district. Poorer districts and schools received a relatively larger allocation of scholarships. However, the original allocations to districts in 1998 were based on school population and 1996 district poverty indices. These criteria proved to be only partially effective, and did not reflect the actual impact of the Crisis, which, as we have seen, affected some parts of the country far more seriously than others, such as the urban areas of Java (CIMU, 2000a: 15).

The number of scholarships to particular schools and the distribution of these to students relied heavily on local knowledge and community participation. This decision was based on the premise that local authorities are more capable of identifying the poor. Much of the criticism of the program focused on the fact that, initially, it failed to identify the poorest districts and those areas hit hardest by the Crisis (Sparrow, 2003b). School committees, consisting of teachers, parents and respected figures in the community, were established in the schools to which the scholarships were allocated. These committees were required to select the children to receive the scholarships, based on a consideration of family socio-economic background, emphasizing criteria such as families living in poverty, single parents and large households, or the family's welfare status according to the BKKBN classification. Generally, each school nominated as many students as possible. However, as there were far more potential applicants than available scholarships, the school committees were given some freedom to modify the guidelines they used to determine scholarship recipients (Jones, 2003: 81–2). In many cases, school committees also considered several additional factors such as the travel distance to and from school, the history of children dropping out, academic performance, and the submission of a poverty statement from the head of the village. Some schools even rotated the scholarships between student recipients on a monthly basis so that a larger number of students were able to receive some assistance, even though this was not strictly in conformity with the program guidelines.

Impact of the SGP
In the initial period of the SGP implementation, the coverage of the program was lower than had been targeted. Drawing on data from the 1999 SUSENAS Special Module, Sumarto et al. (2001) found that the program only covered 4 per cent of students at the primary school level, 8 per cent at lower secondary, and 4 per cent at upper secondary level, compared with the targeted 6, 17 and 10 per cents.[36] Moreover, despite an evident bias towards the poorest segments, there was also clear evidence of leakage, since a relatively large proportion of the recipients also came from better-off households. While the program reached 6 per cent of primary school students at the lowest quintile of per capita consumption, 4 per cent of students at the higher quintiles (and 2 per cent in the top quintile) were also allocated scholarships. At the lower secondary school level, 12 per cent of students at the poorest quintile received scholarships, but 7.5 per cent of students at the higher quintiles (and 5 per cent at the top quintile) also benefited. Meanwhile at the upper secondary level, 5 per cent of students at the poorest quintile received the scholarship, as well as around 4 per cent of students at the higher quintiles, (including 2 per cent of students at the

top quintile). Given these findings, the authors argued that the targeting of SGP was near to random (see Table 3.9).

According to CIMU (2000a: 16), apart from the data problem, one possible explanation for the evident mis-targeting among upper secondary students was the fact that at this level students who received scholarships might have been among the poorest at their school, but they are not always from the poorest segments of society. Although a high percentage of primary students come from poor families, this proportion drops dramatically at the lower and upper secondary levels. Thus, while 72 per cent of scholarship recipients at the primary school level come from the two lowest expenditure quintiles, the figure falls to 58 and 42 per cent at subsequent levels. Another problem mentioned in the CIMU report was that by directing scholarships to those who were already in school, a substantial number of the poorest young people of school age who had already dropped out, who were not attending school or attending 'open junior high school' (*SMP Terbuka*), were not eligible for the scholarships. Hence, such poor students were never likely to receive support from the program.

We should also again note that the SMERU study was based on the SUSENAS data that were collected in February 1999, covering only the previous six-month period. Hence, it only provides limited information on the implementation of the program, and only focuses on the issue of the targeting coverage of the SGP. It does not consider some of the other factors that may be important in making an overall evaluation of the program.

Other studies of the scholarship program have suggested findings that are more positive. While the SGP had initially contributed to preventing enrollment rates from declining sharply between the 1997/98 to 1998/99 academic years, it may have played a major role in increasing enrollment rates in subsequent years. In the 1999/2000 and 2000/01 academic years, the enrollment rate for all age groups increased, with the largest increase enjoyed by students from the poorest expenditure quintile (CIMU, 2001b: 3).

Another study by Cameron (2002), applying regression analysis of the probability of students becoming school dropouts using the 100 Village Survey data, argued that the scholarships significantly reduced the probability of dropout at the lower secondary level, but did not affect dropout rates in primary and upper secondary schools, at least during the first few months of the program's operations. However, some care should be taken when interpreting her findings or comparing these with other studies. Firstly, the study used the 100 Village Survey data, which is more limited and focused on poor villages in comparison with the SUSENAS Special Module.[37] Secondly, as Daley and Fane (2002) have argued, Cameron's results seemed to underestimate the effects of the scholarships in reducing dropouts since her results relate only to dropouts in the course of a school year. Using her data set, it is impossible to estimate the presumably larger impact of the offer of a scholarship on the probability of re-enrollment at the start of a school year.

Some modifications to the allocation rules, including a better representation of poor private and religious schools, improved the coverage and targeting of the SGP in later years of the program. This was assisted by better performance of the allocation committees, increased community participation and local awareness. In a nationwide survey, CIMU found that 7 per cent of all primary school students, 20 per cent of all lower secondary school students and 11 per cent of all upper secondary school students received SGP scholarships in the 1999/2000 academic year (CIMU, 2001a: 8). In terms of targeting, using data obtained from the 2002 SUSENAS, Sparrow (2003a: 20) has calculated that in the academic year 2001/02, 70 per cent of the scholarships went to the poorest two expenditure quintiles, an increase from 60 per cent in the first year of the program as revealed by the 1999 SUSENAS data. Meanwhile, the percentage of scholarships going to the richest quintile decreased from 6 to 3 per cent.

Block grants

The aim of the block grant component of SGP was to help schools maintain the quality of their program in the face of the sudden sharp rise in the cost of school equipment and other essential items. Only registered public or private schools were eligible to receive block grants, and all elite schools were excluded. Block grants were only to be allocated to schools with minimum levels of student enrollments. For schools in Java, this was set at 90 for primary schools, 60 for lower secondary and upper secondary schools, while in the outer islands minimum levels were slightly lower.

Surveys by CIMU have established that many schools would have found it very difficult to survive and provide adequate educational services without the grant. Most schools used some of the block grant they received to purchase teaching aids and stationery (over 85 per cent) and to fund essential maintenance of school buildings (over 85 per cent). Many schools (64 per cent) also used some of the grant to assist those students who had not been offered scholarships, usually with a scholarship-style fee relief (CIMU, 2000b: 13). By meeting the costs of some essential materials and some of the shortfall in income from outstanding student fees, the block grant has no doubt enabled some schools to keep fees lower than they would otherwise have been. This may in turn have enabled more children to stay in school (Jones and Hagul, 2001: 225–6).

In 2001, a second large-scale education assistance package was announced to supplement the existing Scholarships and Grants Program. The new program also had two components, Special Assistance for Students

(*Bantuan Khusus Murid*) and Special Assistance for Schools (*Bantuan Khusus Sekolah*), and was funded by the reduction in fuel subsidies that had recently been introduced. The program was designed to complement SGP and to operate in its place when that program ended in August 2003. There have been no studies to date to evaluate the coverage and targeting performance of these new programs.

Health

The health component of the safety net program, the Health Sector Social Safety Net program (*Jaring Pengaman Sosial Bidang Kesehatan* or JPS-BK), was an extremely broad set of measures consisting of a number of separate sub-components that aimed to provide subsidies for medical services, operational support for health centers, medicine and imported medical equipment, family planning services, supplementary food and midwife services. Unlike the other safety net programs, only a limited part of the JPS-BK program was actually targeted directly at the poor. As we shall see, this restricted the effectiveness of the program as an anti-poverty measure and also made the monitoring and reporting process difficult.

At the onset of the Crisis there were serious concerns that falling real incomes and sharp increases in the cost of both medicine and medical services would place modern medical services out of reach for poor households, contributing to a general decline in public health and reversing all the improvements in this sector over recent decades. Data from the 1999 SUSENAS certainly indicated a sharp decline in the use of modern health care facilities between 1997 and 1998, especially in the public sector (see Figure 3.2).

In an attempt to overcome these problems, the government established the JPS-BK program, inaugurated by the Minister of Health in August 1998. Funding for the program, Rp 1.4 trillion for the fiscal year 1998/99, came from the Asian Development Bank and the State Budget.[38] The separate components of the JPS-BK included the following:

- improvement of nutritional standards through the provision of supplementary foods for babies, young children, and malnourished and pregnant women.
- support for midwifery services,
- support for community health centre (Puskesmas) services,[39] and
- a Community Health Care Guarantee program (*Jaminan Pelayanan Kesehatan Masyarakat*, JPKM), with funding administered through district-level committees.

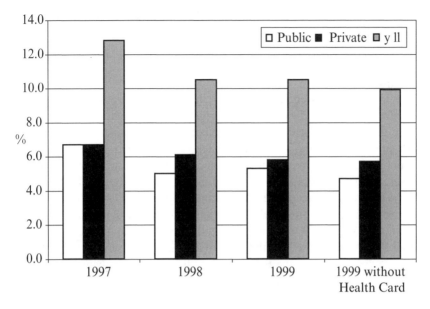

Source: Pradhan et al. (2002: Figure 1).

Figure 3.2 *Proportion of people that consulted a health care provider at least once, on an outpatient basis*

The funds for most of the JPS-BK program were paid directly into the accounts of the Head of Puskesmas and the village midwife at the local post office. In addition to the above, there was also a hospital referral program, with funding distributed directly to all public hospitals at the district (*kabupaten*) and provincial level.

Although the essential aim of JPS-BK was to reduce the adverse impact of the Crisis on public health for the poorest sections of the community, there were two major problems with the design of the program which created difficulties for both implementation and analysis. Firstly, for a crisis-induced emergency safety net program, JPS-BK was far too complex and cumbersome, with numerous separate sub-programs and no simple message that could be communicated directly at the community level. Secondly – and most importantly – the poor were not the immediate recipients of most of the program benefits. The only parts of the program targeted directly at the poor were the scheme to distribute Health Cards to poor households, and the nutrition component. The other parts of JPS-BK delivered funding directly to health care service providers (Heads of Puskesmas and village midwives), and the benefits of these components of the program could be indirectly shared by anyone who used these facilities, poor and non-poor alike. Hence, in terms of targeting performance, we are only able to consider the effectiveness of the Health Card and the nutrition components.

Health Cards

The Health Cards entitled recipient households (including all family members) to free medical treatment at public health facilities. This included visits to community health centers, contraceptives for women of childbearing age, pre-natal care and assistance at birth, and patient and outpatient visits at public hospitals. The implementation of the Health Card scheme involved several stages (see Pradhan et al., 2002: 4–5; CIMU, 2002a: 17–18). Every district (*kabupaten*) received an allocation of cards based on the BKKBN list of pre-prosperous households. The Health Cards were delivered to districts starting in August 1998, along with guidelines explaining the criteria to be used for allocating the Health Cards to individual households. The official criteria were based on the BKKBN classification of family welfare, but in practice many local officials combined this information with various local criteria in deciding how Health Cards should be allocated in their area (CIMU, 2002b: 9–10).

The first independent studies of the Health Card suggested that only a small fraction of the poorest households were covered by the scheme, at least in the first six months of the program. The SMERU analysis of the 1999 SUSENAS Special Module data showed that the Health Card covered only 10.6 per cent of households in the poorest 20 per cent of the population (Sumarto et al., 2001). In addition, mis-targeting resulted in some leakage to the non-poor as the data revealed that the Health Card was also distributed to around 3 per cent of the richest 20 per cent of the population. In total, some 5 per cent of all households in the richest 80 per cent received the Health Cards (see Table 3.9).

Researchers who have looked carefully at the Health Card issue have identified a number of factors contributing to the relatively weak coverage of the poor and the mis-targeting that occurred (Soelaksono et al., 2003: 40–41). Firstly, there were clearly deficiencies in the procedures used to identify the intended recipients. In most provinces, the village midwives or the staff from the local community health center, together with family planning cadres and the heads of villages, identified the households who were to receive a card. However, according to field surveys, the village midwives did not always understand the criteria in the program guidelines or appreciate the intended emphasis on poverty. Secondly, there was a lack of correlation between the BKKBN household classification and poverty incidence according to consumption and expenditure data. Thirdly, there were reports from a number of areas of recipients who sold their Health Cards to others who were not eligible to receive cards but who were in urgent need of health care (CIMU, 2002a: 17).

In addition, there were problems with the actual distribution of the cards in some localities, as the cards were supposed to be delivered directly to the recipients. Reportedly, the distribution did not always work smoothly, especially since there were no specific funds to support this process. In many instances, the head of the Puskesmas allocated the Health Cards only when poor patients arrived at the Puskesmas seeking treatment. According to one report, in Irian Jaya province (now Papua) some village heads were found to have sold Health Cards to members of their local community (CIMU, 2002a: 17).

A final problem contributing to poor coverage was a direct outcome of the way that service providers were compensated for the workload arising from patients using the Health Card when seeking treatment. This was by a lump sum transfer based on the number of Health Cards allocated to the district, not on the actual use of the Health Cards by the recipients (Pradhan et al., 2002: 15–16). As a result, those responsible for distributing the Health Card – the doctors heading the community health centers and the village midwives – also had a certain financial disincentive that worked to discourage them from distributing the maximum number of Health Cards in their area. Since most doctors and midwives also operated a private practice, the more Health Cards that they distributed, the greater the number of patients looking for free medical treatment, thus reducing demand for their own private health service. Another problem was caused by delays in the disbursement of JPS-BK funds (CIMU, 2002b: 14–15).

In a more detailed and considered study of the Health Card issue, Pradhan et al. (2002) have argued that even though the coverage was relatively low in the initial stages of the JPS-BK program, the 1999 SUSENAS data nevertheless reveals that Health Card recipients were on average not only poorer, but also had lower levels of education. Moreover, there was a high proportion of female-headed households among Health Card recipients, and a higher probability that recipients were working in the agriculture sector compared to non-recipients. Despite the earlier finding of poor coverage and targeting, there is evidence that the distribution of the Health Cards played an important role in maintaining the use of health care services. (Pradhan et al., 2002: 4). Figure 3.2 illustrates that the introduction of Health Cards helped to prevent a further decline in the use of health care services between 1998 and 1999. Without Health Cards, the use of public health services might have declined below 10 per cent in 1999. After the introduction of the Health Card scheme, the utilization rate in 1999 remained at 10.5 per cent.

Poverty targeting in Asia

In fact, the proportion of households using public health care providers increased slightly during this period, while the attendance at private health care services declined. This suggests a substitution from private to public health care induced by the introduction of the Health Card.

Table 3.13 also illustrates that the share of households possessing Health Cards who received outpatient care was 15 per cent, which is greater than the share for households without Health Cards (13 per cent). Health Card owners also appear to have visited public health care providers more often than those without cards. However, a large proportion of those with Health Cards, around 85 per cent, are reported to have sought no health care at all. There was also evidence that some who actually held Health Cards did not use them when seeking medical treatment (4 per cent). There appears to be a number of explanations for both these phenomena: the limited time allocated at some public health facilities for treating those patients holding Health Cards; a lack of access to a nearby public health facility; and the perception on the part of some patients that they would receive a lower standard of service and inferior quality medicines when using Health Cards (Soelaksono et al., 2003: 18–19). Meanwhile, there was also evidence that a very small number of patients from households who had not been allocated Health Cards were reported to have used Health Cards. This seems to have occurred when Health Cards were distributed at a clinic based on perceived need, so that the surveyed head of the household was unaware that a family member had received benefits under this program.

Table 3.13   Utilization of Health Card (percentage seeking health care between December 1998 and February 1999)

	Head of household reported to have received a Health Card	Head of household reported not to have received a Health Card
Received outpatient care	15.10	12.91
Went to public provider	10.61	6.75
Went to public provider and used Health Card	6.74	0.15
Went to public provider and did not use Health Card	3.88	6.60
Went to public provider	4.82	6.48
Did not seek health care	84.57	86.77

Source: Pradhan et al. (2002: Table 2).

Nutrition

The nutrition component of JPS-BK targeted babies, children under five years and pregnant women from poor households, and aimed to improve their nutritional status by providing packages of supplementary foods. The selection criteria for this sub-program were generally similar to the Health Card scheme, drawing on the BKKBN lists to target recipients. The health service posts (*Pos Pelayanan Terpadu*) that had been established at the village level to provide services for children, young mothers and pregnant women were often used as the channel to deliver these packages under the supervision of the village midwife.

The coverage of the nutrition program among the poor appears to have been more effective than the Health Card. The 1999 SUSENAS data reveal that 16.5 per cent of households in the poorest quintile participated in the program. Nevertheless, there was still evidence of a considerable amount of leakage to non-poor families as the participation rate of the richest 80 per cent of the population was 15.8 per cent, almost equal to the coverage of the poor (see Table 3.9). This resulted in close to random targeting, rather than a pro-poor program and implied a high type two error, even if type one problems of undercoverage were less serious than for some of the other targeting measures.

CONCLUSIONS

It is apparent from the above account that the targeting of poverty alleviation programs in Indonesia has been a difficult and frustrating process for central government planners attempting to allocate scarce budgetary resources as efficiently and effectively as possible. Although poor families did benefit to a certain degree, all the programs that we have considered have suffered from two common problems: the type one and type two errors of undercoverage and leakage, respectively. Undercoverage occurred as many poor households were not reached by the program and have therefore not received the assistance that was actually intended for those who were in the disadvantaged section of the community, especially during the immediate Crisis period. At the same time, there has been a significant amount of leakage, with far too many non-poor households – in some instances a disturbingly sizable number from the higher quintiles of income and expenditure, those who are clearly not poor – able to access program benefits. Admittedly, some programs performed far better than others, and there is some evidence, although not conclusive, that the targeting effectiveness of some of the key social safety net programs may have improved after the initial implementation period.

In most cases, the targeting measures that have been adopted in Indonesia have been either geographic targeting or individual and household targeting. Sometimes, these two approaches have been used in tandem for a particular program (see Table 3.5). Yet the effectiveness of both these methods has been limited by the scope and accuracy of the data that have been available.

As far as a regional or spatial perspective on poverty is concerned, reliable and authoritative poverty statistics from BPS have only been accessible as far as the province level. Although useful for revealing the macro picture across the entire archipelago, this is far too broad a level to be really useful for the purposes of budgetary allocation and poverty program targeting. As a result, planners were forced to rely on far more unreliable sources of data to distinguish need in different parts of the country, since detailed, up to date, and accurate information about poverty levels throughout Indonesia – especially in the wake of the economic crisis – was simply unavailable.

We can report, however, on the early results of a major collaborative research program now underway that has been attempting to address this problem. A group of researchers from an independent research institute have been working with BPS staff to test the feasibility of developing detailed 'poverty maps' for the entire country that will provide program planners with a targeting tool to identify poverty incidence disaggregated down to lower levels of administrative authority. The results of a recently published pilot study in three provinces suggest that the methodology will be invaluable for calculating poverty and inequality indicators at least as far as the sub-district (*kecamatan*) level. Work is now underway to extend the methodology to the remaining provinces. Despite the promising nature of this research, some limitations remain. Extending the analysis down to the village level has not proved to be reliable. Nor would these poverty maps necessarily remain useful in the event of a sudden shock – either from environmental or economic causes – as the particular nature of any crisis may render them out of date. Hence, there will be a need for a regular process of revision (Suryahadi et al., 2003b).

Individual or household targeting has presented a separate problem. As we have noted, the annual Core SUSENAS (200 000 households) and the SUSENAS consumption module (65 000 households), which is conducted every three years, only cover a representative sample of the population and so cannot be used for household targeting of a national poverty alleviation program that is delivered throughout the entire country. A complete household survey covering all of Indonesia's urban areas and rural villages, although theoretically feasible, would be extremely expensive and hence an overwhelming additional cost burden on these programs. Consequently, program planners have been forced to rely on the BKKBN registration of family welfare status as the only available source of data covering the entire country. Despite efforts to respond to the criticisms of using these data as a targeting tool (principally the concentration on fixed assets that do not capture transitory shocks and the initial inclusion of non-economic criteria of no relevance for assessing poverty status), problems still remained. At the local level, those charged with the responsibility of allocating program benefits frequently pointed out that the BKKBN registration did not include any reference to factors such as household income levels, source and status of employment, family size and number of dependents. As a result, additional 'local criteria' were sometimes included in the targeting process that was finalized at the grass-roots level.

There has also been some limited use of self-targeting, in particular in the short-lived employment safety net programs. This was achieved by attempting to hold wage rates well below minimum or average rates so that only those who were really desperate for work would be attracted to the program. This would also actively discourage those who are already in paid employment from participation. This was sound in theory, and has reportedly worked in other cases to ensure that the poorest individuals benefited from the program, but as we have noted above, the administration and implementation of the employment programs was poor and rules were often flouted so that wages were not always held to these low levels, thus subverting the original intentions.

From time to time, some have advocated adopting this self-targeting principle as a solution to the problems of excessive leakage in the food security program. It has been argued that a lowering of the quality of the subsidized rice that Bulog distributes would insure that only poor and needy families applied to purchase an allocation. However, this has not been taken up as policy – thankfully in our view – as there are many practical political, administrative and indeed moral objections to attempting such a risky strategy with an essential food staple and a perishable commodity.

In addition to the actual targeting methodology, another factor – or more correctly, a range of factors – exercising a considerable effect on targeting outcomes is the administrative capacity of government agencies to design, plan and implement programs according to a consistent set of objectives. There are many aspects to this problem but it should be stressed that the implementation of the social safety net programs was taking place during a period of immense social and political flux throughout Indonesia. The capacity of central government agencies to deliver programs effectively was under closer scrutiny than ever before. Furthermore, in 1999 Indonesia embarked upon a radical and far-reaching decentralization process, with most major tasks of government rapidly devolved down to the district (*kabupaten* and *kota*) levels. As a result, increased levels of cooperation between the layers of government were required to achieve satisfactory outcomes. This was not always in evidence, especially with tension emerging between the provincial and the district levels of authority.

Nevertheless, the ability of government agencies to overcome some of the logistical problems and organize complex administrative arrangements for some of the social safety nets was an impressive achievement. A prime example was the system put in place so that students who were receiving school scholarships were able to withdraw the funds on a monthly basis through the local post office system. Another was the regular delivery of a significant tonnage of subsidized rice to over 44 000 separate distribution points throughout the archipelago. Delays and administrative problems sometimes occurred but by and large these arrangements made a major contribution to ensuring the relative success of these programs.

The relationship between central levels of administrative authority and the local level, especially in a country as large and complex as Indonesia, nevertheless suggested that a certain amount of flexibility would be required as programs were being implemented. As the social safety net programs got under way, it soon became apparent to central government officials that 'local voice' also had to be taken into account, and that targeting directives that were regarded as unacceptable (for example, program benefits should only be delivered to those on the BKKBN list of KPS families) were likely to be simply ignored or significantly altered at the grass-roots level. Attempts to design programs according to administrative targeting criteria determined in Jakarta were soon revealed to be incapable of being implemented in the field. In some cases, the importance of incorporating some local decision making into the program design had been well understood from the outset (for example, in the targeting approach adopted for the school scholarships program). In other cases, it required a process of trial and error as central government officials came to terms with what was actually occurring during the initial phases of certain programs. As a result, officials then made the required modifications to the official program guidelines. This was certainly what happened with the OPK/Raskin subsidized rice program.

For this reason, it seems quite misleading to draw a distinction between de facto versus de jure targeting as one recent study has characterized the process, since this implies that what was occurring at the local level was in breach of program rules that had been determined by the central government agencies (Pritchett et al., 2002: 31–32). As we have noted above, in the most recent version of the subsidized rice program's official guidelines the final decision about which families were to become beneficiaries was passed down to village-level decision makers for final determination.

Of course, as a number of authors have pointed out, too much local flexibility can lead to undesirable targeting consequences: there is always the risk that program benefits will be shared out among so large a number of recipients that the essential purpose of the program as a poverty alleviation measure is lost. This certainly occurred in many locations in the case of the subsidized rice program. There is also the risk that local elites can divert the benefits of the program to those for whom it was not intended. Corruption remains a widely acknowledged problem in Indonesia and clearly occurs at all levels. The social safety net programs were not free from instances of theft and misappropriation of material benefits, sometimes involving local officials. Dealing with this problem effectively requires a commitment on the part of government that has not always been evident.

Several observers have noted that effective targeting and successful implementation of poverty alleviation programs can be assisted – especially in the special circumstances of crisis-related programs – if there is a relatively simple message that can be easily communicated to the wider public. This was certainly the case with the cheap rice program and the scholarships program, as the essential elements of these measures were easy to comprehend. Some limited publicity through the mass media was attempted, although this can add to the implementation costs of such programs.

Other programs (for example, PDM-DKE and the entirety of the health sector safety net, JPS-BK) were exceedingly complex, and hence the essential purpose of these programs could not be communicated to the general public in a way that made it clear who the recipients really were and what they should expect by way of program benefits.

Admittedly, the importance of the need to persuade and inform – rather than issue directives – is a relatively new concept in the post-New Order environment in Indonesia. Government officials have so far failed to come to grips with the value of effective communication about the essential purposes and aims of government programs. Most of the effort that was spent in this area leading up to the implementation of the poverty alleviation programs was directed at informing local officials at the various layers of government about the details of the administrative procedures that they were required to follow. A far more concerted effort needs to be directed at informing the wider community.

Another element of the implementation of poverty alleviation programs that has not yet received sufficient attention is an effective monitoring and reporting process. In the early stages of the implementation of the Social Safety Net program, monitoring activities were carried out in specific areas by a range of community groups and non-government organizations. Some of these activities were supported by foreign donor agencies through small grants mainly to promote the idea of transparency and public accountability. However, the monitoring that resulted was somewhat ad hoc and often adversarial, with the most controversial social safety net (PDM-DKE) absorbing most public attention. Subsequently, monitoring of many other programs has been quite limited. Certain districts and government agencies have recruited local university students or NGOs to monitor the delivery of subsidized rice to the delivery points, but their responsibilities did not extend to the actual distribution of rice to recipients.

The two programs where a major effort was made to establish a rigorous and effective monitoring process were the education and health social safety nets. In both cases, a central independent monitoring unit was established in Jakarta, with branches also set up at the provincial level throughout the country. In addition to regular monitoring through field visits by staff and an active publications program of reports and newsletters to inform interested parties of program results, investigations were conducted into any reported irregularities in the operation of the program. The education program monitoring and reporting initiative seems to have been especially useful in keeping track of the program and ensuring that targeting effectiveness was maintained at a satisfactory level. Yet such an ambitious operation with specialist staff recruited for lengthy periods was an expensive operation, and was only possible through the financial backing of those donor agencies who wished to ensure that the program that they were supporting was achieving its objectives. It remains unlikely that the Indonesian government would contemplate replicating such an ambitious operation in other programs, no matter how desirable and useful this may have been.

NOTES

1. The official headcount poverty figure is published by the Central Bureau of Statistics (*Badan Pusat Statistik* or BPS). Their poverty rate calculations are based on the annual National Socio-Economic Survey (*Survey Sosial Ekonomi Nasional* or SUSENAS). The full database consists of the core data based on over 200 000 households and several module data, including a consumption module, which is repeated every three years and covers about 65 000 households across Indonesia. We use 1996 as the pre-Crisis benchmark because it was the last of BPS's pre-Crisis socio-economic surveys. In the 1998 survey BPS changed its method for calculating poverty by revising the non-food bundle. For example, the expenditure for schooling was revised to take account of the nine years of compulsory schooling that had been introduced (previously it was only six years). Then it revised the 1996 figure, adjusting to the 1998 methodology. In the table we present both calculations of the 1996 figure.
2. Some observers have argued that the BPS calculation for 1998 was an overestimate, and was not an accurate reflection of the real situation. Several studies of post-Crisis poverty measurements have produced a lower 1998 poverty rate than the BPS calculation; for example, Frankenberg and Beegle (1999). Nevertheless, all agreed that poverty had worsened considerably following the Crisis.
3. A SUSENAS-type survey but covering only around 10 000 households.
4. Excluding the troubled provinces of Aceh and Maluku.
5. Collected also by the BPS with a sample of 12 000 households in several rounds; May 1997, August 1998, December 1998, May 1999 and October 1999.

6. Gardiner (1999) used the SUSENAS core data to make independent poverty estimates for February 1996, 1997 and 1998.

7. Frankenberg and Beegle (1999) used various versions of the Indonesian Family Life Survey carried out by the RAND Institute and local universities.

8. Although the authors used the SUSENAS database, they applied a different technique to make their calculations, so poverty rates for all sectors are different to the official figures. But here we are concerned more about the relative change between 1996–99 in each sector.

9. By contrast, the transient poor are those whose consumption levels are somewhere near or just below the poverty line. Transient poverty is generally the result of an economic shock so that household income is inadequate to meet basic needs. Households in this category still have the capacity to survive, and can improve their condition if the economy strengthens and grows.

10. See also Dhanani and Islam (2002) for further discussion on 'capability poverty' with regard to the post-Crisis situation in Indonesia.

11. This was shown in the results of a rapid survey of local respondents at the sub-district (*kecamatan*) level conducted in October 1998 by BPS and the World Bank; see also Feridhanusetyawan (2000:114–115). Eastern Indonesia, where headcount poverty levels had always been very high, had also been seriously affected by the 1997–98 El Niño-related drought.

12. BKKBN conduct regular workshops to inform their workers about the procedures to be followed during the registration process, and there is an evident sense of pride among those who hold these positions. Typically, these village cadres who may include the wives of prominent local people, schoolteachers and village officials have often been carrying out the task over a number of years, and have the advantage of a close and intimate knowledge of their local community.

13. The other levels, indicative of improving welfare status, were 'prosperous families' level 1, level 2, level 3, and level 3 plus (*keluarga sejahtera* 1, *keluarga sejahtera* 2, *keluarga sejahtera* 3, and *keluarga sejahtera* 3+); see Sumo and Soedjono (1995).

14. ALEK is *alasan ekonomi* (economic reasons).

15. See Daley and Fane (2002: 311) for further details on anti-poverty programs and the amount of government budget expenditure that has been directed to such measures.

16. The second tranche of the World Bank Social Safety Net Adjustment Loan was eventually canceled after field verification and monitoring surveys revealed evidence of gross excesses and poor implementation in several of these programs.

17. The IDT program was run by the National Development Planning Board (BAPPENAS), in coordination with the Ministry of Internal Affairs and the Central Bureau of Statistics (BPS).

18. Using the 1996 exchange rate at Rp 2300 per US$.

19. The Podes survey is carried out by BPS approximately three times in every ten years, usually immediately before one of the major censuses (population, agriculture, the economy). The Podes questionnaires are completed by sub-district (*kecamatan*) officials who rely on information collected from village officials in their area.

20. These variables were divided into three categories: social and economic characteristics, housing and environment, and population. For a list of the variables used for the 1993 and 1994 selection process, see Alatas (1999: Appendix A).

21. For further details on the complexities of the BPS ranking and selection process for IDT, see Alatas (1999: 4–6) and Sumarto et al. (1997: 12).

22. This report was part of an Asian Development Bank study, reviewing poverty alleviation strategies within the agriculture sector for the Ministry of Agriculture and BAPPENAS.

23. The term *padat karya* had been used widely throughout Indonesia since at least the early 1970s for small-scale village infrastructure activities that selected the required labor entirely from within the village community. It probably also draws on both traditional notions of how to conduct communal self-help activities and the corvée labor schemes that were used by colonial and traditional rulers for public works projects.

Poverty targeting in Asia

24. See for example, Suryahadi et al. (1999: 12–14).
25. The program was mostly referred to in the press and by the general public simply by its abbreviation: few outside the government bureaucracy ever really understood what the full name of the program was or the precise nature of the benefits that it was intended to deliver to beneficiaries.
26. See Akhmadi et al. (1999). A brief English language summary of the central findings appears in SMERU (1999: 4–9).
27. The term OPK was adopted to distinguish this program from those market operations (*operasi pasar*) that the National Logistics Agency conducted periodically by 'dropping' rice into the market place as a price stabilization measure. This had been carried out frequently during 1997 in response to perceived shortages in the availability of rice and other foodstuffs because of the El Niño drought.
28. For details of the disbursements of rice during each phase of the subsidized rice program between 1998 and 2002, see Hastuti and Maxwell (2003: 8).
29. See Kusumastuti (1998: 18–19), who suggested a revision of the BKKBN eligibility criteria and the application of some form of local decision-making as part of the targeting process.
30. For an assessment of this program based on a rapid field assessment, see Hastuti et al. (2000). The report includes a brief comparison between this program and the government's OPK program.
31. At the urging of several international agencies, in particular FAO and the World Food Program, serious consideration was given to introducing a technique known as the Vulnerability Analysis and Mapping (VAM) methodology. Using a multivariate statistical approach and drawing on data from a range of sources (household consumption and expenditure, nutrition and poverty levels, in combination with data on food crop production levels), it was argued that this methodology could be used to create a series of digital maps covering the entire country and coded to indicate levels of local vulnerability to food insecurity in specific areas. Those areas at greatest risk of experiencing food insecurity would be selected to receive the subsidized rice. The VAM methodology was outlined and discussed at a Bulog workshop in Jakarta in November 2001, organized to review the targeting issues.
32. See Hastuti and Maxwell (2003: 6–8) for a more detailed account of the determination of quotas at national, province, district and local levels.
33. Jones and Hagul (2001: 217–218) also reveal that trends in enrollment rates have not changed significantly between males and females.
34. Pradhan and Sparrow, as quoted in Sparrow (2003b: 18), have calculated the monthly household expenditure on education per student for primary, lower and upper secondary schools in the 1997/98 academic year. These were Rp 9562, Rp 27 862 and Rp 53 243 (at February 1999 prices) respectively. Average monthly education expenditure of the poorest 20 per cent of the population at these different levels was estimated to be Rp 4826, Rp 15 725 and Rp 31 549 per student in 1998. Hence, the scholarship provided a significant proportion of costs.
35. See the report by CIMU (2000a:12). CIMU stands for Central Independent Monitoring Unit, a body established and funded jointly by several international agencies exclusively to monitor the implementation of the SGP, as well as to investigate reported irregularities in the implementation of the program.
36. This finding was also supported by Sparrow (2003b), while another study by Cameron (2002) using a different data set, the 100 Village Survey, found that the scholarships were received by 8.4, 13.6 and 9.6 per cent of primary, lower and upper secondary level students, respectively.
37. As Sparrow (2003b: 12) argued, the 100 Village Survey contains a large number of relatively poor villages. Thus the survey may not be representative of the actual conditions in Indonesia.
38. The Asian Development Bank provided funding for 8 provinces, distributed in 4 phases beginning in August 1998, while the State Budget funded 19 provinces in 2 phases

beginning October 1998 (Soelaksono et al., 2003: 5). Some of the State Budget allocations were supported by the IMF loan package.

39. A system of community health centers, commonly known as Puskesmas (*Pusat Kesehatan Masyarakat*), had been established during the previous decades, and had made basic health care accessible to both urban and rural villages throughout Indonesia.

REFERENCES

Akhmadi, B. Sulaksono, Hastuti, J. Maxwell, M. Naibu, P. Wibowo, S. Budiati and S. Kusumastutu (1999), 'Tahap Persiapan Pelaksanaan Program PDM-DKE: Hasil Pengamatan Lapangan Kilat Tim SMERU di Empat Propinsi', SMERU Working Paper, May, Jakarta.

Akita, T. and J. Setto (2000), 'Inpres Desa Tertinggal (IDT) Program and Indonesian regional inequality', *Asian Economic Journal*, **14** (2), 167–86.

Alatas, V. (1999), 'Exploiting the left behind villages in Indonesia: exploiting program rules to identify effects on expenditures and employment', mimeo, November.

Badan Pusat Statistik (1999), 'Survey Sosial Ekonomi Nasional Questionnaire', Jakarta.

Badan Pusat Statistik (2000), *Statistik Indonesia*, Jakarta.

Badan Pusat Statistik (2001), *Statistik Indonesia*, Jakarta.

Badan Urusan Logistik (2001), *Pentunjuk Pelaksanaan (Juklak) Program Beras Untuk Keluarga Miskin (RASKIN)*, Jakarta.

Booth, A. (2000), 'Poverty and inequality in the Soeharto era: an assessment', *Bulletin of Indonesian Economic Studies*, **36** (1), 73–104.

Cameron, L. (2001), 'The impact of the Indonesian financial crisis on children: an analysis using the 100 villages data', *Bulletin of Indonesian Economic Studies*, **37** (1), 43–64.

Cameron, L. (2002), 'Did social safety net scholarships reduce drop-out rates during the Indonesian economic crisis?', *Policy Research Working Paper* No. 2800, Washington, DC: World Bank.

CIMU (2000a), 'Special issue: history and overview of the scholarships and grants program', Warta CIMU, September.

CIMU (2000b), 'Special issue: the impact of the scholarships and grants program', Warta CIMU, November.

CIMU (2001a), 'The scholarship and grants program – report to the government of the Netherlands', 30 April 2001.

CIMU (2001b), 'The effects of the scholarship program at the household level', Warta CIMU, November.

CIMU (2002a), 'Sentinal sites survey final report', 28 March 2002, British Council, Jakarta.

CIMU (2002b), 'National survey final report', 11 April 2002, British Council, Jakarta.

Daley, A. and G. Fane (2002), 'Anti-poverty programs in Indonesia', *Bulletin of Indonesian Economic Studies*, **38** (3), 309–31.

Dhanani, S. and I. Islam (2002), 'Poverty, vulnerability and social protection in a period of crisis: the case of Indonesia', *World Development*, **30** (7), 1211–31.

Feridhanusetyawan, T. (2000), 'The social impact of the Indonesian economic crisis', in Thailand Development Research Institute (TDRI), *Social Impacts of the Asian Economic Crisis*, Bangkok.

Frankenberg, T. and K. Beegle (1999), 'The real costs of Indonesia's economic crisis: preliminary findings from the Indonesia family life surveys', mimeo.

Gardiner, P. (1999), 'Poverty estimation during the economic crisis', mimeo.

Hastuti, Akhmadi and J. Maxwell (2003), 'Rice for poor families (RASKIN): did the 2002 program operate effectively? Evidence from Bengkulu and Karawang', SMERU Working Paper, June.

Hastuti, Akhmadi, P. Wibowo, S. Budiyati, W. Munawar and M. Nabiu, (2000), 'Pelaksanaan Operasi Pasar Swadaya (OPSM-WFP) di Tiga Daerah Perkotaan di Jawa', SMERU *Laporan Khusus* (SMERU Working Paper).

Hill, H. (ed.) (1994), *Indonesia's New Order: The Dynamic of Socio-Economic Transformation*, Sydney: Allen and Unwin.

Hill, H. (1996), *The Indonesian Economy Since 1966: Southeast Asia's Emerging Giant*, Cambridge, UK: Cambridge University Press.

Irawan, P. (ed.) (2001), *Anti-Poverty Programs in Indonesia: Analysis, Prospects and Policy Recommendation*, Jakarta: Badan Pusat Statistik.

Jones, G. (2003), 'SMERU's rapid assessment of education problems, JPS scholarship and block grants program in four kabupatens', SMERU Special Report, September.

Jones, G. and P. Hagul (2001), 'Schooling in Indonesia: crisis-related and longer-term issues', *Bulletin of Indonesian Economic Studies*, 37 (2), 207–32.

Kusumastuti, S. (1998), 'Implementation of special market operation (OPK) program: results of a SMERU rapid field appraisal mission in five provinces', SMERU Special Report, Jakarta.

LP3ES and MENPHOR (2000), *Studi Evaluasi JPS-OPK Beras di Daerah Perdesaan Tahun Anggaran 1999/2000*, Jakarta.

Olken, B., M. Nabiu, N. Toyamah and D. Perwira (2001), 'Sharing the wealth: how villages decide to distribute OPK rice', SMERU Working Paper, October.

Pangestu, M. and I. Azis (1994), 'Survey of recent development', *Bulletin of Indonesian Economic Studies*, 30 (2), 3–47.

Pradhan, M., F. Saadah and R. Sparrow (2002), 'Did the healthcard program ensure access to medical care for the poor during Indonesia's economic crisis?', Tinbergen Institute Discussion Paper, Amsterdam.

Pradhan, M., A. Suryahadi, S. Sumarto and L. Pritchett (2000), 'Measurement of poverty in Indonesia: 1996, 1999 and beyond', SMERU Working Paper, June.

Pritchett, L., S. Sumarto and A. Suryahadi (2002), 'Targeted programs in an economic crisis: empirical findings from the experience of Indonesia', SMERU Working Paper, October.

Sen, A.K. (1999), *Development as Freedom*, New York: Alfred A. Knopf.

SMERU (1999), 'Results of a SMERU team rapid assessment of the first phase of the PDM-DKE program', *SMERU Newsletter*, no. 4, March–April.

Soelaksono, B., S. Budiyati, A. Hastuti, M. Naibu, B. Akhmadi, P. Wibowo, S. Kusumastuti and J. Maxwell (2003), 'The impact of the crisis on the use and effectiveness of community health services: Puskesman, Posyandu and Bidan Desa – case studies in three kabupaten', SMERU Special Report.

Sparrow, R. (2003a), 'Protecting education for the poor in times of crisis: an evaluation of the Scholarships and Grants program in Indonesia', mimeo, April.

Sparrow, R. (2003b), 'The JPS scholarship program', *SMERU Newsletter*, no. 6, April–June.

Sumarto, S. and A. Suryahadi (2001), 'Principles and approaches to targeting: with reference to the Indonesian social safety nets programs', SMERU Working Paper.

Sumarto, S., A. Suryahadi and L. Pritchett (2000), 'Safety nets and safety ropes: who benefited from two Indonesian crisis programs – the "poor" or the "shocked"?', Policy Research Working Paper No. 2436, World Bank, Washington DC.

Sumarto, S., A. Suryahadi and W. Widyanti (2001), 'Design and implementation of the Indonesian social safety net programs: evidence from the JPS module in the 1999 SUSENAS', SMERU Working Paper, March.

Sumarto, S., S. Usman and S. Mawardi (1997), 'Agriculture's role in poverty reduction: bringing farmers to the policy formulation process', Agriculture Sector Strategy Review, Ministry of Agriculture, Jakarta, ADB TA 2660-INO, Study B-4 November.

Sumo, B. and S. Soedjono (eds) (1995), *Kamus istilah keluarga berencana, keluarga sejahtera, kependudukan*, Jakarta: Ministry of Population and National Coordinating Board of Family Planning.

Suryahadi, A., and S. Sumarto (2001), 'The chronic poor, the transient poor, and the vulnerable in Indonesia before and after the crisis', SMERU Working Paper, May.

Suryahadi, A., Y. Suharso and S. Sumarto (1999), 'Coverage and targeting in the Indonesian social safety net programs: evidence from 100 Village Survey', SMERU Working Paper, August.

Suryahadi, A., S. Sumarto and L. Pritchett (2003a), 'The evolution of poverty during the crisis in Indonesia', SMERU Working Paper, March.

Suryahadi, A., W. Widyanti, D. Perwira, S. Sumarto, C. Elbers and M. Pradhan (2003b), 'Developing a poverty map for Indonesia: an initiatory work in three provinces', SMERU Working Paper, May.

Swisher, G. (1999), 'Padat Karya Desa: a village-managed labor-intensive drought relief project in Eastern Indonesia', *SMERU Newsletter*, no. 4, March–April.

Tim Dampak Krisis (2000), 'Laporan Perkembangan Pelaksanaan Operasi Pasar Khusus OPK, Januari 1999–Maret 2000', SMERU *Laporan Khusus* (SMERU Working Paper), Jakarta.

World Bank (1995), 'Village infrastructure project for Java', Staff Appraisal Report No. 13776-IND, Republic of Indonesia, April, Washington DC.

World Bank (1996), 'Second village infrastructure project', Staff Appraisal Report No. 15467-IND, Republic of Indonesia, September, Washington DC.

4. Poverty targeting in the People's Republic of China

Wang Sangui

INTRODUCTION

The People's Republic of China (PRC) has achieved remarkable progress in rural poverty reduction since the beginning of the reform period in the late 1970s. Measured by the official poverty line, the poor rural population was reduced from 250 million in 1978 to 80 million in 1993 and further to 28 million in 2002, or from 31 per cent of the rural population to only 3 per cent. This has been made possible by a combination of fast general economic growth and targeted poverty reduction programs. However, the evidence we survey below suggests that, whilst the latter may have played some role, their impact is likely to have been weak at best. Location targeting has been the main instrument of targeting used in PRC and there is surprisingly little evidence on who, within particular targeted areas, received the benefits from such programs. This chapter summarizes the targeting measures used in anti-poverty programs in PRC, with the focus on rural poverty, and considers the evidence on the effectiveness of the various poverty interventions.

POVERTY IN PRC

Despite the magnitude of the reduction in the official estimates of poverty there is still a considerable debate on the scale of poverty in PRC and on the accuracy of official statistics. Further, with the restructuring of state-owned enterprises and consequent unemployment, urban poverty is becoming a sensitive political issue, even though official statistics suggest that the latter is still a trivial phenomenon. The Appendix to this chapter surveys the debate on the poverty line and the alternative national poverty estimates that are available for rural and urban areas. However, there is widespread agreement that today poverty is principally a regional problem with serious pockets of poverty in particular provinces.

PRC is a large country with wide differences in resource endowment, climate, population, and economic and social development. Rural poverty is to a large extent a regional phenomenon with a high concentration in the southwestern, northwestern and central mountainous areas. The problem of poverty is especially serious in the areas inhabited by minority nationalities.

Based on the official poverty line and income data in different provinces collected from household surveys, the National Bureau of Statistics (NBS) have estimated the poor population in each province and autonomous region. Data on the provincial incidence of poverty and the proportion of the provincial poverty-stricken population in the national total for 1985, 1993 and 2001 are given in Table 4.1.

Based on the data from these three years, we can conclude that broadly the provinces or autonomous regions suffering from comparatively serious poverty are Henan, Inner Mongolia, Shanxi, Shaanxi, Gansu, Ningxia, Qinghai, Xinjiang, Guangxi, Sichuan, Guizhou and Yunnan, while the provinces or regions having a comparatively large poverty-stricken population are mainly Henan, Shaanxi, Gansu, Guangxi, Sichuan, Guizhou and Yunnan. All are in the western region, except Henan.

Table 4.1   Poverty incidence by province (headcount ratio) (1985, 1993 and 2001)

Province	Poverty incidence			Percent of national poor population		
	1985	1993	2001	1985	1993	2001
North						
Beijing	0.0	0.55	0.53	0.0	0.03	0.06
Tianjin	0.0	0.14	0.52	0.0	0.01	0.07
Hebei	4.90	13.76	1.81	1.88	9.07	3.33
Henan	24.90	12.59	2.10	13.68	11.92	5.64
Shandong	2.30	5.83	0.70	1.24	5.18	1.56
Northeast						
Liaoning	6.50	3.85	3.22	1.14	1.07	2.55
Jilin	0.0	6.23	3.08	na	1.13	1.51
Heilongjiang	14.10	5.22	4.55	2.08	1.20	2.92

Table 4.1   (continued)

	Poverty incidence			Percent of national poor population		
Province	1985	1993	2001	1985	1993	2001
Northwest						
Inner Mongolia	10.60	10.75	13.30	1.17	1.90	6.28
Shanxi	4.10	11.87	6.62	0.69	3.31	5.25
Shaanxi	41.60	19.19	7.78	8.33	6.50	7.36
Ningxia	53.00	29.53	13.60	1.34	1.31	1.80
Gansu	43.90	26.15	9.60	6.03	6.20	6.64
Qinghai	5.00	16.79	16.90	0.11	0.66	1.95
Xinjiang	0.90	14.10	6.50	0.05	1.48	2.02
Yangtze River						
Shanghai	0.0	0.15	0.0	0.0	0.01	0.00
Jiangsu	0.0	2.42	0.20	na	1.61	0.36
Zhejiang	4.50	3.53	0.18	1.22	1.57	0.23
Anhui	5.10	8.55	1.79	1.83	5.19	3.13
Jiangxi	12.10	3.24	2.76	2.72	1.27	3.02
Hubei	3.70	6.16	1.82	1.16	3.12	2.44
Hunan	12.60	3.14	2.09	4.92	2.06	3.86
South						
Fujian	6.30	1.14	0.24	1.16	0.37	0.22
Guangdong	0.0	0.50	0.06	na	0.34	0.14
Hainan	na	4.67	1.72	na	0.27	0.30
Southwest						
Guangxi	22.20	7.82	3.35	6.08	3.72	4.62
Chongqing	na	na	3.99	na	na	3.33
Sichuan	35.10	10.12	3.31	24.98	11.77	7.83
Guizhou	36.80	21.85	10.40	7.72	7.90	11.12
Yunnan	41.30	23.77	7.89	9.90	9.71	9.34
Tibet	na	5.98	15.20	na	0.15	1.13
National average	14.81	8.83	3.20	100.00	100.00	100.00

Note: na = not available.

Source: Calculated by the author from data supplied by NBS.

Since the poor rural population is mainly concentrated in remote mountainous areas with a fragile ecological system, a harsh climate and underdeveloped infrastructure and social services, the poor are vulnerable to internal and external shocks. The high proportion of transitory poverty found in studies discussed in the Appendix indicates that households around the poverty line frequently move into and out of poverty, due to changes both external and internal to their family environment. Poor households in poor areas commonly suffer from damage to the natural environment, water losses and soil erosion; a shortage of good quality agricultural land (for example, in the southwestern rocky mountain and karst areas and northwest where there is a scarcity of water); a deficiency in infrastructure, such as road and water conservancy facilities, and a lack of basic social services, such as primary education and health care.

The consequences are low agricultural productivity and the underdevelopment of market relationships in the areas in which the poor are clustered. Research has shown that there are notable differences between impoverished families and non-impoverished families in terms of demographic characteristics, resources, assets and ability. Econometric analysis has demonstrated that a rural household's net per capita income depends negatively on family size, and positively on labor availability within the household, the education level of the household head, members' non-agricultural job experience, the quality of the cultivated land at its disposal and the productive assets owned by the household (Li and Wang, 1999; Wang and Li, 2003). In rural areas where grain production, in particular, has grown most rapidly there is a clear tendency to find the greatest reductions in rural poverty (Weiss, 2003).

TARGETING MEASURES IN ANTI-POVERTY PROGRAMS

In 1986 the government put forward a major rural poverty reduction initiative with the objectives of stimulating economic development in poor areas and lifting the bulk of the rural poor out of poverty. This initiative was reinforced in 1994 when the 'Eight-Seven Poverty Reduction Plan' was launched. The aim of this was to bring 80 million rural poor out of poverty in seven years (1994–2000). In this section we discuss the details of the key targeting mechanisms used in PRC to meet these goals, before later considering their effectiveness.

The key characteristic of the poverty reduction program has been its regional targeting; in other words up to relatively recently all poverty reduction funds from the central government were targeted at defined geographical regions and were aimed directly at the poor resident within these units. Counties remained the basic unit for state poverty reduction investments until 2001. The central government first designated poor counties and then channeled all the anti-poverty funds to these poor counties through different government departments and state-owned banks. Four organizations – the Leading Group for Poverty Reduction (LGPR), the Agricultural Bank of China, the National Planning and Development Commission, and the Ministry of Finance – were central in the delivery and management of government poverty reduction funds. Each organization used its own administrative system to channel poverty alleviation funds from the central government to the provincial governments and then to the county governments. The rules and criteria adopted by these organizations for fund distribution and project selection have formed the basis for targeting within poor counties, although these were not always transparent or followed closely.

Sources of Poverty Reduction Funds

The LGPR has categorized three kinds of funds as rural poverty reduction funds; these are subsidized loans, food-for-work and budgetary funds. The total amount spent by the central government since 1986 under these headings is presented in Table 4.2. Total nominal poverty funds increased steadily over 1986 to 2002, from 4.2 billion yuan to 29.1 billion yuan, which is an annual rate of nearly 13 per cent. However, the funds increased much more slowly in real terms at an annual rate of 6 per cent. Because of high inflation in the late 1980s and early 1990s, the funds stagnated in real terms until 1996, after which they increased dramatically. Over the whole period subsidized loans accounted for 59 per cent of the total, food-for-work funds for 24 per cent and budgetary funds for 17 per cent. Total poverty funds were roughly 5 per cent of the central government budget and 0.2 per cent of GDP. Their shares of the government budget were relatively higher in the early and late 1990s and their share of GDP was highest in the mid-1980s.

In addition to these three main funds from central government, several other sources are also important for poor counties. One study estimates that poverty investments by local governments and government departments have been roughly a quarter of the investments from the central government (Li, 2001). In addition international donors, such as the World Bank, the United Nations Development Program (UNDP) and the International Fund for Agricultural Development (IFAD), and bilateral development agencies, such as those of Australia, Japan and the United Kingdom, have also had various poverty reduction projects in PRC for many years.

Table 4.2   Poverty reduction funds from the central government (100 million yuan)

Year	Subsidized loans		Food-for-work		Budgetary funds		Subtotal		Share of government budget	Share of GDP
	Nominal	Real (1986 constant price)	Nominal	Real (1986 constant price)	Nominal	Real (1986 constant price)	Nominal	Real (1986 constant price)	%	%
1986	23.0	23.0	9.0	9.0	10.0	10.0	42.0	42.0	5.0	0.4
1987	23.0	21.4	9.0	8.4	10.0	9.3	42.0	39.1	5.0	0.4
1988	29.0	22.8	0.0	0.0	10.0	7.9	39.0	30.7	4.6	0.3
1989	30.0	20.0	1.0	0.7	10.0	6.7	41.0	27.4	4.6	0.2
1990	30.0	19.6	6.0	3.9	10.0	6.5	46.0	30.1	4.6	0.2
1991	35.0	22.2	18.0	11.4	10.0	6.4	63.0	40.0	5.8	0.3
1992	41.0	24.7	16.0	9.6	10.0	6.0	67.0	40.4	5.7	0.3
1993	35.0	18.6	30.0	16.0	11.0	5.9	76.0	40.5	5.8	0.3
1994	45.0	19.7	40.0	17.5	12.0	5.3	97.0	42.5	5.5	0.2
1995	45.0	17.2	40.0	15.3	13.0	5.0	98.0	37.4	4.9	0.2
1996	55.0	19.8	40.0	14.4	13.0	4.7	108.0	38.8	5.0	0.2
1997	85.0	30.3	40.0	14.3	28.0	10.0	153.0	54.6	6.0	0.2
1998	100.0	36.6	50.0	18.3	33.0	12.1	183.0	67.0	5.9	0.2
1999	150.0	56.6	50.0	18.9	43.0	16.2	243.0	91.7	5.9	0.3
2000	150.0	57.5	50.0	19.2	48.0	18.4	248.0	95.0	4.5	0.3
2001	185.0	71.5	60.0	23.2	40.0	15.4	285.0	110.1	4.9	0.3
2002	185.0	72.4	66.0	25.8	40.0	15.7	291.0	113.9	4.3	0.3
Total	1246.0	554.0	525.0	225.8	351.0	161.3	2122.0	941.1	5.1	0.2

Source: Poverty funds data are from the LGPR; GDP and government budget data are from the *China Statistical Yearbook*, various years.

Designation of Poor Counties

Since almost all of poverty reduction funds had to go to the nationally designated poor counties before they could be used for anti-poverty projects or by poor households, the process and accuracy of poor county designation had a critical effect on targeting effectiveness. Poor county designation began in 1986 when the newly established Leading Group for Poverty Reduction (LGPR) under the State Council designated 258 poor counties in 17 provinces and autonomous regions. The original criteria for being selected as a national poor county was that the average net income per capita of all rural residents within the county should be less than 150 yuan. However, different treatment was given to different counties. Revolutionary bases, where the Communist Party and its army were active in the revolutionary era, minority counties and pastoral areas, received preferential treatment. In some of these areas per capita net income could be as high as 300 yuan and they still received poor county designation. Of the original 258 poor counties, in only 83 was the per capita net income of rural households below 150 yuan, in 82 it was between 150 and 200 yuan and in a further 93 it was between 200 and 300 yuan. The fact that per capita incomes in only a third of the counties were under the original LGPR income line of 150 yuan showed that the selection of poor counties was highly political. In 1987 an additional 13 counties in old revolutionary areas and two other counties were added to the list of poor counties. In 1988 27 pastoral and semi-pastoral counties were also designated as national poor counties to give a total of 328 counties.[1] Shaanxi, Gansu, Yunnan, Guangxi and Sichuan had the greatest number of poor counties, while Gansu, Ningxia, Shaanxi, Qinghai and Guangxi had the highest proportion of their population designated as poor (see Table 4.3).

The central government also required that all provinces and autonomous regions designate their own poor counties and that these counties be supported with provincial funds. By 1988 370 counties had been designated as provincial poor counties. In 1989, Hainan was made a separate province from Guangdong and three counties in Hainan province were added to the list of national poor counties. Subsequently, there were no major changes in the list of poor counties until 1993.

In 1993, as part of the preparation for the Eight-Seven Poverty Reduction Plan, adjustments were made to the list of state-designated poor counties. Despite the estimated decrease in the national rural poor (using the official poverty line) from 125 million in 1985 to 80 million in 1993, the number of state-designated poor counties was increased from 331 to 592 (see Table 4.4). The LGPR defined a per capita net income for rural households of less than 300 yuan in 1990 as the standard for selecting new poor counties.

Table 4.3   National and provincial poor counties, 1988

Province	National poor counties		Provincial poor counties	
	Number	Percent of rural population	Number	Percent of provincial rural population
North				
Hebei	14	9.4	35	21.5
Henan	15	11.7	9	7.8
Shandong	9	9.9	5	4.4
Northeast				
Liaoning	3	6.9	8	13.4
Jilin	–	–	11	15.2
Heilongjiang	–	–	6	9.0
Northwest				
Inner Mongolia	16	23.9	24	34.8
Shanxi	14	13.8	21	11.6
Shaanxi	34	27.4	12	13.9
Ningxia	8	53.5	–	–
Gansu	31	47.5	12	16.0
Qinghai	10	36.3	10	48.7
Xinjiang	17	20.1	13	26.3
Yangtze River				
Zhejiang	3	2.3	–	–
Anhui	9	14.8	8	11.2
Jiangxi	17	23.4	39	44.6
Hubei	13	15.1	24	20.6
Hunan	8	5.4	20	17.7
South				
Fujian	14	19.1	2	1.1
Guangdong	4	4.5	27	20.6
Hainan	–	–	–	–
Southwest				
Guangxi	23	18.0	25	19.5
Sichuan	21	12.3	30	18.0
Guizhou	19	29.6	12	12.5
Yunnan	26	20.5	15	11.9
Tibet	–	–	–	–
Total	328	12.6	370	13.9

Source: Calculated from data in Office of the Leading Group for Economic Development in Poor Areas (1989); and SSB (1989).

Table 4.4 National poor counties, 1993 and 2001

Province	National poor counties 1993				National poor counties 2001			
	Number	Rural pop. in poor counties (million)	Percent of provincial rural pop.	Percent of pop. in poor counties	Number	Rural pop. in poor counties (million)	Percent of provincial rural pop.	Percent of pop. in poor counties
North								
Hebei	39	16.6	31.2	8.3	39	11.6	21.5	5.8
Henan	28	16.8	22.0	8.4	31	20.9	26.6	10.6
Shandong	10	6.8	9.4	3.4	–	–	–	–
Northeast								
Liaoning	9	3.5	15.4	1.7	–	–	–	–
Jilin	5	0.9	5.8	0.4	8	1.1	7.6	0.5
Heilongjiang	11	2.2	12.1	1.1	14	2.7	14.2	1.4
Northwest								
Inner Mongolia	31	6.8	47.9	3.4	31	6.0	44.0	3.0
Shanxi	35	5.9	26.2	3.0	35	5.4	23.2	2.7
Shaanxi	50	12.0	43.77	6.0	50	11.8	43.0	6.0
Ningxia	8	2.0	55.8	1.0	8	2.2	55.0	1.1
Gansu	41	11.9	62.1	6.0	43	13.1	64.4	6.6
Qinghai	14	1.4	43.5	0.7	15	2.0	59.8	1.0
Xinjiang	25	3.0	35.8	1.5	27	4.1	44.0	2.1

Yangtze River								
Zhejiang	3	0.8	2.3	0.4	–	–	–	–
Anhui	17	15.6	31.8	7.8	19	16.4	32.2	8.3
Jiangxi	18	7.9	25.1	4.0	21	9.1	28.4	5.0
Hubei	25	11.5	28.3	5.8	25	11.0	27.9	5.6
Hunan	10	6.1	11.5	3.1	20	9.7	17.9	4.9
South								
Fujian	8	2.1	8.0	1.0	–	–	–	–
Guangdong	3	0.8	1.4	0.4	–	–	–	–
Hainan	5	0.6	13.8	0.3	5	0.6	11.5	0.3
Southwest								
Guangxi	28	7.7	20.0	3.9	28	8.2	20.4	4.1
Sichuan	43	19.3	20.6	9.7	36	13.1	18.9	6.6
Chongqing	–	–	–	–	14	9.6	39.4	4.8
Guizhou	48	16.8	57.5	8.4	50	19.1	60.5	9.7
Yunnan	73	20.1	61.1	10.1	73	20.5	59.3	10.4
Tibet	5	0.2	10.6	0.1	–	–	–	–
Total	592	199.2	23.49	100.0	592	198.22	30.53	100.0

Note: pop. is population.

Source: Calculated from SSB (1994) and NBS (2003b).

145

Now 326 counties conformed to this standard. At that time as poor counties enjoyed various allowances and preferential access to resources, the idea of dropping counties from the new list met with strong opposition. The result was that few were removed from the list, while many new ones were added.

The revision of the list of poor counties in 1993 must be considered progressive, since it was made on the basis of the poverty line recommended by the National Bureau of Statistics, with the result that many previously neglected poor counties were added. In some poor provinces and autonomous regions, previously province-designated poor counties were changed into state-designated national ones, and no additional provincial poor counties were selected. The readjustment created the greatest benefit for Yunnan, Guizhou, Hebei provinces and the Inner Mongolian Autonomous Region. The proportion of the total rural population living in poor counties in the three latter areas rose by 20 per cent, and in Yunnan by 40 per cent. Coastal provinces, such as Fujian, Guangdong, Shandong and Zhejiang saw a falling share of their population covered as a result of the readjustment. The proportion of poor county rural population in Fujian, for example, was reduced by 11 per cent.

After the government announced in early 2001, when the Eight-Seven Poverty Reduction Plan was completed, that basically the problem of absolute poverty had been resolved, the national poverty reduction strategy entered a new stage.[2] To reflect the changes in the poverty situation in different regions and to focus on poverty problems of inland provinces and autonomous regions, the LGPR readjusted the poor county list once again in 2001, renaming these as 'key poverty reduction counties'. The total number of national poor counties was still kept at 592, while the distribution of poor counties further shifted to the central and western provinces. All the poor counties in the coastal region designated in 1993 were eliminated from the new national poor county list, as the provincial governments in the coastal regions were assumed to take full responsibility for poverty reduction within their jurisdiction.

Designation of Poor Villages

With the decrease in the rural poor, it was judged that the county was no longer the appropriate targeting unit. The government issued a new Poverty Reduction Compendium for the next 10 years in 2001, in which village targeting was proposed, although, as we have seen, key poverty reduction counties were still designated and the counties would still exercise overall administration of poverty reduction funds targeted at villages. With the financial and technical help of the Asian Development Bank and the United Nations Development Program, LGPR developed a methodology and indicators for identifying poor villages. Now it is a requirement that most poverty reduction funds go to poor villages. Non-poor villages in key poverty reduction counties are no longer eligible for poverty funds, while poor villages in non-key poverty reduction counties qualify for such funds. County governments must take the responsibility to identify poor villages within an overall quota for each county set by the provincial government.

A weighted poverty index is used for village ranking. The index is generated from the score of eight indicators, namely: livelihood indicators (grain production per person-year, cash income per person-year, and percentage of bad quality houses); infrastructure indicators (percentage of households having difficulty in accessing potable water, percentage of villages with access to reliable electricity supply, percentage of villages with an all-weather road access to the county town); and human resource indicators (percentage of women with long-term health problems, percentage of eligible children not attending school). Except for the first two indicators that are continuous, the rest are proportions and are relatively easy to collect. For cross-village comparison the same indicators are required for all villages. In practice, LGPR has allowed local governments to change some of the indicators and their weights according to the local situation. This decision has made the identification process more flexible, but at the same time makes it more difficult to compare poverty between counties and provinces. In practice, in some instances, the weights on the different indicators have been assigned by groups of villagers in a few sample villages in each county using participatory approaches. This means that villages in different counties will have different weights for the same indicators.

Since the weighted index calculated from the above procedure is only valid for village ranking within a county, county governments (that is the LGPR at the county level) are assigned responsibility for poor village identification. Working teams have been organized to help villages select indicators and collect relevant data. The county LGPR then calculates the weighted index and identifies poor villages by ranking them on their index score, so the higher the index, the poorer the village. The county LGPR must suggest a list of poor villages to the provincial LGPR and the latter adjusts the number of poor villages in each county according to the total number of poor villages the provincial government has agreed to support within the planned time period. The list of all poor villages identified in this way must be publicized within the county for monitoring purposes. Poverty funds allocated to villages can be used for purposes identified by the communities themselves.

Measures for Urban Poverty Reduction

Urban poverty has come to be discussed as an important policy issue since the mid-1990s, particularly with the retrenchment in the state-owned enterprise sector. The task of urban poverty reduction is assigned to municipal and township governments. The central government provides subsidies for the local governments to establish a minimum living standard system. Criteria for selecting urban residents who are eligible for receiving subsidies, and the amount of subsidies, are determined by municipal and township governments. No official urban poverty line based on income or consumption has been developed for any city. Instead a set of mixed indicators, including employment status, housing, illness and disability have usually been used to identify the subsidy recipients. The amount of subsidy received by each recipient differs according to their income and living conditions. Unlike rural poverty reduction, the Ministry of Civil Affairs is the only government organization that is assigned responsibility for the administration of the urban minimum living standard system. City and county bureaus of the Ministry are the implementation agencies of the system, and they rely on urban residents' committees at the community level to provide the necessary information to identify beneficiaries.

By the end of September 2003, 21.8 million urban residents in 8.9 million households were deemed eligible to receive subsidies, and a monthly subsidy of 56 yuan was distributed to each recipient on average. (The exchange rate at the time was approximately 8 yuan to the US dollar.) However, the minimum living standard and average subsidies provided differ between cities and provinces, usually determined in line with their financial strength and the coverage of the program (see Table 4.5).

Table 4.5   Urban minimum living standard program (2003)

Province/city	Recipients (1000)	Households (1000)	Monthly subsidy (yuan)
Total	**21 800**	**8950**	**56**
North			
Beijing	155	69	230
Tianjing	249	103	71
Hebei	745	299	38
Henan	1241	534	44
Shandong	740	272	51

Table 4.5   (continued)

Province/city	Recipients (1000)	Households (1000)	Monthly subsidy (yuan)
Northeast			
Liaoning	1531	573	59
Jilin	1467	578	53
Heilongjiang	1570	619	46
Northwest			
Inner Mongolia	701	291	45
Shanxi	752	327	45
Shaanxi	784	271	63
Ningxia	152	57	73
Gansu	568	232	48
Qinghai	194	75	70
Xinjiang	795	315	60
Yangtze River			
Shanghai	447	206	139
Zhejiang	76	39	117
Jiangsu	324	135	81
Anhui	1048	429	47
Jiangxi	1013	383	56
Hubei	1615	644	50
Hunan	1441	600	42
South			
Fujian	191	76	54
Guangdong	345	126	74
Hainan	84	35	49
Southwest			
Guangxi	516	213	46
Sichuan	1394	647	51
Chongqing	704	343	74
Guizhou	412	180	51
Yunnan	622	317	60
Tibet	38	12	70

Source: Ministry of Civil Affairs (2003).

TARGETING MEASURES AT THE PROJECT LEVEL

Under the terms of the implementation of the poor county targeting system poverty reduction funds were delivered to counties through different channels. The county governments and the Agricultural Bank of China county branches played key roles in project selection and community targeting. Here we discuss the use of the main categories of poverty funds disbursed through this system and some of the limited evidence on their impact. Due to lack of data, little empirical work has been done on the effectiveness of poverty targeting at the community and household levels. Much of the evidence is anecdotal and here we draw on field interviews with local officials, households and other anecdotal evidence.

Subsidized Loans

The main objective of the subsidized loan program was to provide low-cost credit (typically at nominal interest rates of 2 to 3 per cent) to support productive activities in poor areas. Subsidized loans were managed mainly by LGPR county offices and the Agricultural Bank of China county branches. The choice of projects and households to be supported was left mainly to LGPR county offices, whilst loan recovery was left to the bank county branches. However, with the commercialization of the state-owned banking system in recent years, the branches of the Agricultural Bank of China have been given more independence in deciding the use of subsidized loans.

When the subsidized loan program began in 1986, the government believed that a key constraint facing poor farmers was the lack of available capital and an inability to gain access to the formal credit system. The government also felt it was important to provide technical assistance and other services. With this premise, priority in the first phase of lending was given to distributing subsidized loans directly to poor households selected by poverty officials to develop cropping, animal husbandry, and agricultural processing. An official survey at the end of 1987 showed that in the first year of the program, 92 per cent of subsidized loans were distributed directly or indirectly to farm households, rather than to county, township or village enterprises.

This pattern of loan distribution ended in 1989, when the LGPR opted to encourage the development of economic entities (*jingji shiti*), as a means of assisting the poor. These economic entities were enterprises engaged in some kind of productive or service activity that helped poor households to escape from poverty. The new policy stipulated that in order to qualify for subsidized loans at least half of the employees of the economic entities had to be from poor households. This change in lending priorities was based on the view that most poor households could not make good use of subsidized loans on their own, because they lacked the necessary technical and management ability and could not achieve economies of scale in operation. In contrast, the view was that economic entities, such as collectively managed orchards or companies selling agricultural products, were managed by professional personnel, who could coordinate activities on a larger scale. An important goal of the reform was to improve the productivity of loans and achieve higher repayment rates. Evidence from some poor counties and provinces revealed that since 1989, over 70 per cent of subsidized loans had been distributed to economic entities.

The main problem with lending to economic entities was that the connection to poor households was much less direct, which compromised the original targeting goals of the program. Many of the loans were given to township and village enterprises or county-owned enterprises, increasing the revenue base for local governments, but not necessarily benefiting poor households. What was more serious was that most of the industrial projects built with subsidized loans failed due to technical, management and market limitations; hence, there was no clear improvement in the repayment rate of the loans. At a national conference on poverty in September 1996, the government decided to return the focus of lending to providing direct loans to poor households for cropping and animal production.

Impact of subsidized loans
The subsidized loan scheme has been widely criticized for failing to target the poor effectively. To a large extent the problem has been due to the political and economic environment in which local government institutions operate and to conflicting goals. First, to provide incentives for effective loan use and repayment, local poverty officials often used past performance as a criterion in awarding new loans, even when the objective was poverty reduction. Many local officials believed that the poor are incapable of managing projects successfully and preferred to promote economic development (and indirectly poverty reduction) by lending to enterprises, economic entities and large farms.

Even more important sources of poor targeting arise because of factors motivating local officials. There are three local players with a stake in the use of subsidized loans; the local office of the LGPR, the local government, and the local branches of the Agricultural Bank of China. Local government officials have been concerned with generating revenues and furthering economic development in general, not just in poor areas and for poor households. This may have led them to support the diversion of funds to enterprises or investment in more promising areas. This is especially true given the acute fiscal woes of many local governments in poor areas.

Agricultural Bank officials are interested in profit and so care about loan repayment above all else. As the transaction costs of small loans to poor households are relatively high and loan use is difficult to supervise, both the Agricultural Bank of China and the Agricultural Development Bank[3] were unwilling to grant loans to poor farmers in the absence of stringent supervising mechanisms. Because they disbursed the funds, they could veto projects proposed by the local LGPR if they felt the likelihood of repayment was low. This has led to numerous conflicts between bank officials and poverty officials. Even when loans were approved, Agricultural Bank officials had an incentive to shorten the period of the loan (so that funds could be relent quickly at higher rates), delay loan disbursement, or divert loans outright. Finally it is argued frequently in the media that misappropriation and corruption led to the diversion of subsidized loans to non-poor groups.

The diversion of subsidized loans to non-poverty reduction activities has become more serious in recent years with the commercialization of the Agricultural Bank of China and the closure of many local branches. A survey by the Ministry of Finance found that a majority of subsidized loans were made either to large-scale enterprises or for infrastructure construction, such as highways. In 2002 of 750 million yuan in subsidized loans made in Jiangxi province, only 150 million were household loans and these did not necessarily go to poor households. Similarly the same study found that Pingjiang county in Hunan province and Sichuan and Le An county in Jiangxi province had not made any loans to poor households in recent years (Wen, 2003).

Even when loans were lent directly to households in poor villages, in many cases they were not given to the poorest households. Evidence from a nationwide survey of villages conducted in 1996 provides some evidence on the limited targeting effectiveness of subsidized loans within villages. Of the 184 villages in six provinces that were surveyed, 32 had received poverty loans a total of 58 times in the past. Of these 58 times, data on the average wealth of households exist in 33 cases. Village leaders were asked whether most loans went to better-off farmers, average farmers, or poorer farmers. Fifty-eight per cent of the time the loans went mostly to farmers of average wealth, while 43 per cent of the time they went to farmers of below average wealth. In no cases did village leaders report that the loans went mainly to better-off farmers. However, the relative frequency of the allocation of loans to average rather than poor farmers appeared to have increased in the 1990s. Loans received before 1990 went to poor households 45 per cent of the time. Loans received in 1990 and after went to such households only 36 per cent of the time, indicating a weakening of targeting effectiveness (Rozelle et al., 1999).

Micro-credit schemes were introduced in 1997 as an important measure to improve targeting accuracy, as well as loan recovery. Their use spread rapidly, so that by the end of 2001, the amount of micro-credit issued by the Agricultural Bank of China through the use of subsidized loans totaled 3.8 billion yuan, covering 2.3 million poor households and a poor population of 10.6 million (Cao, 2003). In assessing some of the early efforts at micro-finance in PRC, Park and Ren (2001) find mixed success between types of program, with those by non-governmental organizations performing considerably better in terms of excluding richer borrowers than government programs.

Food-for-Work

The main aim of food-for-work was to make use of surplus labor in poor areas to build infrastructure, such as roads, water conservancy and drinking water facilities, whilst at the same time providing poor farmers with job opportunities and income sources, thus raising both short-term income and longer-term development prospects. The central feature of the scheme was the payment of project costs in kind. The relevant project implementation institutions (such as the traffic bureau for roads or the water conservancy bureau for water projects) received coupons to be exchanged for grain, cloth and daily necessities. These project agencies would make the exchange and obtain the goods that would be made available to project participants. Materials to be used on the projects were allocated by state-run commercial departments. In some cases food coupons could be exchanged for cash through the banking system and this allowed some direct cash payment to participants.

Initially, poor areas were required to secure state-allocated materials from coastal and other more developed areas and then distribute them to the project implementation agencies, which in turn would sell the materials in local markets or give them directly to the project participants. Due to the cost of transporting materials from coastal to poor areas, in the 1990s such materials began to be sold in their places of origin and the cash thus obtained was remitted to the poor areas, where the relevant planning committee office would distribute it among project implementation units. Beginning in 1997, however, all the funds used for such schemes came from the government budget rather than from the sale of grain or industrial goods. Official policy dictated that the resources provided by the central government for the food-for-work scheme were to be augmented by the provincial, prefecture and county governments. But in reality, due to the strain on local financial resources, the matching funds from local governments were often very limited.

Implementation procedures depended on the scale and nature of the projects. Large-scale projects, such as roads connecting counties and townships, were usually implemented by specialized county government bureaus (such as the traffic bureau), while small-scale, community-based projects were usually implemented by village committees and township governments. Specialized construction teams were hired for the construction work of large-scale projects, and wages or lump sum construction fees were paid to workers on construction teams. For community-based, small-scale projects, village committees and township governments usually mobilized compulsory labor to carry out the construction; wages in kind or in cash might or might not be paid to these workers depending on the budget of the projects. Where no wages were paid, the involvement of workers became a form of informal tax in kind.

An argument in favor of food-for-work programs has been that because the funds bypass local budget bureaus, to date relatively few funds have been diverted for other uses, which has been common for many earmarked budgetary items, especially in poor counties (Park et al., 1996). However, there was also a concern that expanding the scope of food-for-work would make it more difficult to monitor and would increase the incentives for local governments to divert the funds to other uses, by substituting food-for-work projects for other funds that would have gone towards infrastructure construction.

Provincial poverty officials have reported that in addition to poverty status, other criteria used in allocating these funds have included the quality of project design, the ability of local leaders, and past performance. In some provinces, such as Henan, before 1994 some projects were awarded to non-poor counties (though often with poor townships), but since then all funds have been allocated to national or provincial poor counties. Some county officials, however, report that amounts awarded to different counties depend more on project feasibility and quality than on poverty status. This is likely to be even more true within counties. Zhu and Jiang (1995) report that villages that have greater population, favorable environmental conditions, more surplus labor, and are more remotely located are more likely to be involved in these projects, which, if accurate, suggests not unreasonable targeting.

One important issue in assessing the poverty alleviation role of food-for-work projects is the cost borne by local residents in the form of uncompensated labor effort. Because funds are limited, in many areas funds are used to pay for material supplies, while as we have noted labor is supplied through *yiwugong* (essentially a labor tax). In some areas with these projects, the amount of *yiwugong* may surpass regulated limits (usually a maximum of 30 labor days per year). These costs to the poor in the form of foregone leisure or other income-earning activities must be weighed in assessing how well the programs were targeted and how much they benefited the poor. Zhu and Jiang (1995) report that 40 per cent of households in their sample (in Sichuan, Ningxia and Shandong) worked without receiving any pay. Older, male workers with less land and more education were more likely to participate in such projects. They also found that for most workers (78 per cent), time spent working on these projects did not detract from income-earning activities, but rather decreased leisure only, which suggests a high degree of labor surplus.

Budgetary Development Funds

The low level of economic development in poor areas made it impossible for most poor counties to be self-sufficient financially, as their expenditures on poverty projects exceeded revenues. It was the purpose of the budgetary development funds to support productive construction projects and other investments in poor areas by means of special funds. These funds could be used to support promising activities in industry, infrastructure or agriculture. In addition a small proportion of the funds have also been used for primary education and basic health care, for example for the construction of schools and health clinics.

All budgetary development funds came from the Ministry of Finance, although as noted above there is a requirement that local governments (at the province, prefecture and county level) provide matching funds, which were rarely forthcoming. Project identification and implementation procedures were much the same as for the food-for-work funds, except that some funds could be used in the area of social and human development, and the project scale was smaller. For these projects wages were not usually paid to project participants, except where skilled workers or specialized construction teams were needed.

Of the three main poverty programs, least is known about the distribution and use of budgetary development funds because of the classified nature of budgetary data. Nonetheless a number of targeting concerns warrant mention. First, because the development fund program began before the designation of poor counties in 1986, many of these funds were given to counties not officially designated as poor, which increased coverage but also increased leakage. Second, just as for food-for-work funds, there is the risk that poor counties will substitute development funds for other budgetary resources that would have been allocated for similar purposes, reducing the impact of such funds on realized investment. Assuming perfect fungibility, development funds at worst act as a pure budget subsidy, and so should help local governments in poor counties meet their own fiscal needs, even if these lack a poverty focus. However, if these transfers also affect their poverty-focused activity, there could be a crowding out problem.

Regulations stipulating that development funds be used to benefit poor households through development projects probably prevented full crowding out. However, as local governments had a much stronger influence on the use of these funds than subsidized loans or food-for-work funds, the danger of bias toward revenue-producing investments was greater. Another concern is that when development funds were used in education activity for the construction of schools, this usually required that villages collected supplementary fees from households to finance any funding gaps, which might have had adverse poverty consequences, at least in the short term.

EMPIRICAL ASSESSMENT OF TARGETING MEASURES

Here we consider the evidence on the effectiveness of these various targeting programs, first looking at the accuracy of poor county designation and the equity of poverty fund distribution, and then considering how these funds have impacted on poor counties. We draw extensively on empirical work by the author.

Accuracy of Poor County Designation

We have noted above that many counties were designated as poor on the basis of broadly political criteria. Initial evidence on targeting accuracy can be found in the frequency distributions of poor and non-poor counties across income levels. In 1986, only half of the counties in the lowest income decile were designated as poor, even though there were even more counties designated as poor in the next income group (see Figure 4.1). By 1993, far fewer counties in the lowest income groups were being excluded, implying better coverage, but there were many more counties designated as poor in the middle-income groups, implying greater leakage (see Figure 4.2).

Overall targeting effectiveness can be evaluated more formally by defining 'targeting gaps' and 'targeting errors' (Park et al., 2002). Targeting gaps describe mis-targeting in the full sample with respect to a reference poverty line, while targeting errors describe mis-targeting given a set number of targeted beneficiaries. Similar to poverty measures, gaps and errors can be aggregated using different weights.

Two types of targeting gaps can be calculated: the targeting count gap (TCG_t) and the targeting income gap (TIG_t). The targeting count gap is defined as

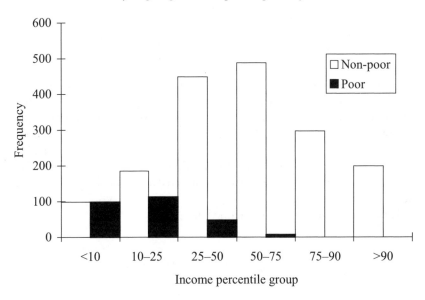

*Figure 4.1   Income per capita distribution in poor and non-poor counties,
1986*

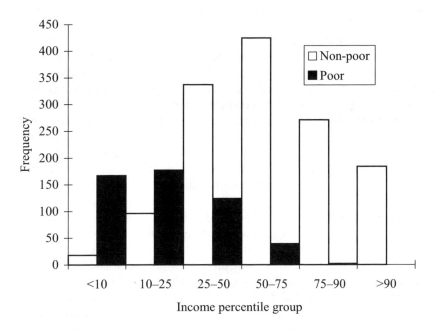

*Figure 4.2   Income per capita distribution in poor and non-poor counties,
1993*

$$TCG_t = \frac{1}{N}\sum_{i=1}^{N}\{I_{it1}(P_{it}=0,Y_{it}<Z_t)+I_{it2}(P_{it}=1,Y_{it}>Z_t)\}$$

Here N is the total sample of counties, indexed by i. I_{it1} is an indicator variable for type one error (or incomplete coverage) that equals one if a county is not designated as poor ($P_{it}=0$), but its income per capita (Y_{it}) is below the poverty line (Z_t). I_{it2} is an indicator variable for type two error (or leakage) that equals one if a county is designated as poor ($P_{it}=1$), but its income per capita is above the poverty line.[4] TCG_t can be interpreted as the percentage of counties that are mis-targeted and is easily disaggregated into type one and type two error.

The targeting income gap is defined as

$$TIG_t = \frac{1}{N}\sum_{i=1}^{N}\{(Z_t-Y_{it})I_{it1}+(Y_{it}-Z_t)I_{it2}\}$$

where the indicator variables are as defined above. TIG is similar to TCG except that mis-targeting is weighted by the magnitude of mis-targeting, measured as the difference between county income and the poverty line.[5]

Yearly TCG and TIG measures for poor county designation are presented in Tables 4.6 and 4.7. Both measures are sensitive to the chosen poverty line; as the line is increased, type one error increases and type two error decreases. The tables give the TCG and TIG for each year from 1986–1995 for two different lines, the official poverty line and a relative poverty line equal to 60 per cent of mean income per capita.

The results show that targeting effectiveness has deteriorated steadily over time, that incomplete coverage or omission of the poor has fallen, while leakage has increased, and that using the official poverty line, targeting gaps jumped noticeably after the new poor county designations in 1993. As seen in Table 4.6, the percentage of counties that were mis-targeted increased from 14 to 22 per cent using the official poverty line and from 15 to 19 per cent using the relative poverty line. While failure to designate a poor county as poor was nearly twice as likely as designating a non-poor county as poor in 1986 (using either the official or relative poverty lines), by 1995 the opposite was true using the relative line, and using the official line virtually all mis-targeting was due to leakage. Considering that about one fifth of counties are mis-targeted, the TIG of 77 yuan in 1995 for the official line implies that the average magnitude of mis-targeting in mis-targeted counties is about 385 yuan, or nearly two thirds of the poverty line.[6] Only part of the targeting gaps can be explained by preferential treatment towards minority and revolutionary base counties. In 1986, 25 per cent of leakage in the TCG (using the official poverty line) was due to minority counties and 35 per cent to revolutionary base counties. By 1995, the comparable figures were 35 per cent and 19 per cent, respectively.

Table 4.6   Targeting count gap, 1986 to 1995

	Official poverty line			Relative poverty line (60% of average income per capita)			
	Type I	Type II	Total	Line	Type I	Type II	Total
1986	0.094	0.050	0.144	598	0.099	0.050	0.149
1987	0.082	0.065	0.146	611	0.097	0.061	0.158
1988	0.044	0.101	0.144	586	0.086	0.073	0.159
1989	0.056	0.096	0.152	538	0.096	0.079	0.175
1990	0.078	0.093	0.171	570	0.093	0.085	0.178
1991	0.058	0.101	0.158	590	0.093	0.084	0.177
1992	0.038	0.107	0.145	628	0.087	0.083	0.171
1993	–	–	–	655	0.028	0.150	0.178
1994	0.005	0.232	0.237	703	0.047	0.137	0.185
1995	0.004	0.218	0.222	793	0.065	0.120	0.185

Note: Calculations based on sample of 1837 counties with complete data for all years.

Source: Park et al. (2002).

One problem with the targeting gap measure is that it is sensitive to the number of poor counties designated. If the number of designations is less than the number of truly poor counties, type one error is unavoidable, and if designations exceed the number of poor counties, type two error is unavoidable, even when targeting is perfect in that designations go to the poorest counties. Another way to assess targeting, then, is to compare outcomes with the perfect targeting case given the number of poor county designations. The targeting count error (TCE) is the percentage of designations not given to counties that would be targeted under this definition of perfect targeting, or

$$TCE_t = \frac{1}{D} \sum_{i=1}^{N} I_{it}(Y_{it} < Z_t^*, P_{it} = 0)$$

Here Z_t^* is the income level of the marginal, or threshold, county when targeting is perfect given the number of available designations (D). Similar to targeting gaps, the indicator functions can be weighted by income differences with counties that were mistakenly targeted to calculate targeting income error (TIE_t) or by rank differences to calculate targeting rank error (TRE_t).[7] These statistics are reported in Table 4.8, and show that by any measure, targeting error was substantial in the original designations (in fact a majority of designations were mis-targeted), increased steadily over time, fell dramatically after new designations in 1993 to levels even below that of the original designations, and then began increasing once again. Thus, the 1993 designations reduced targeting error, but through a strategy of expanded coverage beneficial to counties above the absolute or relative poverty thresholds.

Table 4.7   *Targeting income gap, 1986 to 1995*

	Official poverty line			Relative poverty line (60% of average income per capita)			
	Type I	Type II	Total	Line	Type I	Type II	Total
1986	9.6	6.2	15.8	598	11.6	6.1	17.7
1987	8.2	9.1	17.3	611	11.1	7.5	18.6
1988	3.3	16.4	19.7	586	8.5	9.6	18.1
1989	4.3	17.3	21.7	538	9.6	11.1	20.7
1990	6.5	16.2	22.7	570	9.7	13.0	22.7
1991	4.5	21.9	26.5	590	9.9	15.9	25.8
1992	2.9	29.9	32.9	628	9.7	19.1	28.8
1993	–	–	–	655	1.9	26.0	27.8
1994	0.3	65.8	66.1	703	4.6	29.6	34.2
1995	0.2	76.4	76.5	793	7.8	31.2	39.0

Note: Calculations based on sample of 1837 counties with complete data for all years.

Source: Park et al. (2002).

However, even if poor county designation was perfect, there would still be mis-targeting due to the existence of the non-poor in poor counties and of the poor in non-poor counties. Both of these phenomena have been important. In 2002 the total rural population in the 592 poor counties was around 200 million, while the poor population was only 28 million by the official poverty line or a little less than 100 million measured by the US $1 a day purchasing power parity standard. Even if all of the poor were resident in poor counties, the majority of households in poor counties would still not be poor.

Table 4.8   National targeting error, 1986 to 1995

	Targeting count error	Targeting rank error	Targeting income error
1986	0.524	363	242
1987	0.504	381	265
1988	0.574	447	264
1989	0.625	532	302
1990	0.649	564	332
1991	0.629	621	378
1992	0.618	682	422
1993	0.280	260	153
1994	0.319	313	212
1995	0.334	323	267

Note: Calculations based on sample of 1837 counties with complete data for all years.

Source: Park et al. (2002).

Data from the National Bureau of Statistics indicate that of the 80 million rural poor in 1992, only 23 million lived in non-poor counties, accounting for 29 per cent. However, this proportion has increased. An estimate from the same source suggests that the poor living in non-poor counties accounted for 38 per cent of the total poor population in 2001. Rural household data provide evidence that an even larger percentage of the poor live in non-poor counties. For example, one study indicated that about half of the poor in four southern provinces did not live in poor counties (Ravallion and Jalan, 1999).

Determinants of Poor County Designation

Having quantified the degree of targeting error, we now turn to a formal analysis of the determinants of poor county designation. As we have seen, status as a minority or revolutionary base county has had a significant effect on poor county designation. In 1990, 637 counties were minority counties (33 per cent) and 195 were revolutionary base areas (10 per cent). Twenty per cent of minority counties and 44 per cent of revolutionary base counties were designated as poor in 1986, accounting for 38 per cent and 30 per cent, respectively, of all poor counties. In 1993, the number of minority counties designated as poor more than doubled (to 46 per cent of all minority counties), but the number of revolutionary base counties designated as poor increased only slightly. As a share of all poor counties, however, the number of minority and revolutionary base counties fell to

30 per cent and 16 per cent, respectively, in 1993 because the total number of poor counties increased substantially.

Using county-level economic data from the Ministry of Agriculture, which were the basis for poor county designations in 1986,[8] Park et al. (2002) studied the determination of poor county status by estimating probit functions for poor county designations in 1986 and 1993. Explanatory variables include income per capita, grain production per capita, industrial share of total income in the year preceding the designations, status as a minority county or revolutionary base county, and provincial dummy variables. All explanatory variables have estimated coefficients that are statistically significant. The fitted probabilities correctly predict the status of 92 per cent of county designations in 1986 and 88 per cent in 1993.

The marginal effects on the probability of poor county designation at the sample means for poor counties are presented in Table 4.9. In 1986 a 1 per cent increase in income per capita reduces the probability of being designated a poor county by 1.3 per cent, a 1 per cent increase in grain output per capita decreases the probability by 0.2 per cent, and an increase in the industrial share of income of 1 per cent reduces the probability by 0.7 per cent. Designations are less responsive to per capita income and grain production in 1993 (1.1 per cent and 0.1 per cent, respectively) and slightly more responsive to industrial share of income (0.8 per cent). Being a minority or revolutionary base county increases the probability of designation by 15 per cent and 45 per cent, respectively, in 1986, and by 17 per cent and 18 per cent, respectively, in 1993. Overall the responsiveness of poor county designation to both economic and political variables decreases in 1993, mainly because of the larger number of countries designated as poor.

Table 4.9 Marginal effects on probability of poor county designation (from probits evaluated at poor county means)

	1986	1993
Log (income per capita) (t–1)	–1.31	–1.13
	(0.0749)	(0.0526)
Log (grain output per capita) (t–1)	–0.216	–0.124
	(0.0509)	(0.0270)
Industrial share of income (t–1)	–0.705	–0.769
	(0.308)	(0.135)
Minority	0.146	0.166
	(0.0633)	(0.0377)
Revolutionary base	0.441	0.180
	(0.0411)	(0.0255)

Table 4.9   (continued)

	1986	1993
Provincial dummies:		
North		
Henan	–0.240	–0.138
Shandong	0.392	–0.111
Northeast		
Liaoning	0.175	0.0882
Jilin	–	0.0309
Heilongjiang	–	0.0381
Northwest		
Inner Mongolia	–0.136	0.0140
Shanxi	0.282	–0.00751
Shaanxi	0.126	0.00762
Ningxia	–	–0.369
Gansu	–0.302	0.00431
Qinghai	0.343	–0.297
Xinjiang	0.363	–0.0626
Yangtze River		
Zhejiang	0.0834	–0.194
Anhui	0.244	–0.212
Jiangxi	–0.0426	–0.0474
Hubei	0.347	0.0533
Hunan	–0.182	–0.391
South		
Fujian	0.443	0.0613
Guangdong	0.143	–0.00769
Southwest		
Guangxi	0.0600	–0.129
Sichuan	–0.231	–0.46
Guizhou	–0.219	–0.341
Yunnan	–0.119	–0.320

Notes: Sample sizes are 1908 and 1953 and pseudo R-squared is 0.49 and 0.54. Marginal effects for minority and revolutionary base status as well as provincial effects are the effect of change from 0 to 1. Provincial effects are with respect to Hebei. Marginal effects evaluated at full sample means in 1986 and 1993 are the following: income –0.129 and –0.704, grain –0.0212 and –0.0773, industrial share –0.0689 and –0.481, minority 0.181 and 0.130, and revolutionary base 0.143 and 0.216 (all statistically significant at the 1 per cent level).

Source: Park et al. (2002).

Many provincial dummies have large and significant coefficients, suggesting that there was considerable discrimination against specific provinces. In the 1986 designations, some poor provinces in the southwest (Sichuan, Guizhou, Yunnan), center, (Henan, Hunan) and northwest (Inner Mongolia, Gansu) were at a severe disadvantage, while a county was much more likely to be designated as poor if it was in the wealthier provinces of Fujian, Shandong, Hubei, or Xinjiang. The starkest contrast is between Gansu and Fujian; other things being equal, a county in Gansu was 70 per cent less likely to be designated as poor than a county in Fujian. In 1993, despite a large number of newly designated counties in relatively disadvantaged provinces, such as Yunnan and Guizhou, southwest provinces remained at a distinct disadvantage, along with Qinghai and Ningxia in the northwest and Anhui and Hunan in central PRC.[9] Many provinces favored in 1986 no longer appeared favored in 1993.

Distribution of Poverty Funds between and within Poor Counties

Having considered errors in designation of poor counties we now turn to evidence on the allocation of the various poverty funds described above, both between and within counties. Using the National Bureau of Statistics county level data collected from the Rural Poverty Monitoring Survey in a regression model, we test the extent to which county poverty funding amounts from different sources for the period 1998–2001 can be explained by county characteristics for the sample of poor counties where data exist.[10] The variables used and the regression results are presented in Table 4.10.

The results suggest that, apart from investment from 'other sources', poverty fund allocations across poor counties are significantly and positively related to the level of poverty incidence, as measured by the headcount ratio (the proportion of the poor in the total population). A one percentage point increase in poverty incidence will increase the total poverty fund allocation per capita by 0.76 yuan. For central government funds the increase will be 0.85 yuan and for subsidized loans 0.46 yuan. The size of the rural population has a significantly negative impact on the per capita allocation of all poverty funds, indicating that large counties are at a disadvantage. Interestingly, although revolutionary base counties are favored in poor county designation, they are discriminated against in fund allocation between counties, as other things being equal, revolutionary base counties receive 26 yuan per capita less than non-revolutionary counties. Minority counties are still at an advantage, as they receive 14 yuan per capita more than non-minority counties, again allowing for other factors. Inland border counties are also favored in poverty fund allocation. Compared with

Table 4.10   Determinants of poverty fund allocation (1998–2001)

Independent variables	Total poverty funds	Central government funds	Other funds	Subsidized loans	Budgetary funds	Food-for-work
Poverty incidence	0.76***	0.85***	–0.16	0.46***	0.18***	0.21***
	(3.57)	(5.34)	(–0.41)	(4.01)	(4.17)	(3.67)
Rural pop.	–2.44***	–1.89***	–0.74***	–1.06***	–0.30***	–0.52***
	(–18.29)	(–18.84)	(–3.03)	(–14.63)	(–11.24)	(–14.56)
Revolutionary base	–25.83***	–26.07***	–5.70	–15.85***	–2.55	–7.68***
	(–3.02)	(–4.05)	(–0.37)	(–3.40)	(–1.48)	(–3.32)
Minority	13.65*	9.75*	13.33	10.06**	0.85	–1.16
	(1.84)	(1.74)	(0.98)	(2.48)	(0.57)	(–0.57)
Border	66.96***	45.27***	–16.68	16.87***	13.21***	15.19***
	(6.24)	(5.61)	(–0.85)	(2.89)	(6.11)	(5.23)
Highland	0.11	2.67	–4.81	1.44	0.58	0.65
	(0.01)	(0.38)	(–0.28)	(0.28)	(0.31)	(0.25)
Mountainous area	6.64	9.66	4.46	2.51	2.55	4.60*
	(0.76)	(1.47)	(0.28)	(0.53)	(1.45)	(1.95)
Year	3.18	7.82***	–7.47**	3.79***	3.03***	1.00*
	(1.57)	(5.12)	(–2.01)	(3.42)	(7.40)	(1.83)
Shanxi	–27.53**	–20.42**	–6.50	–28.93***	2.99	5.53
	(–2.09)	(–2.05)	(–0.27)	(–4.01)	(1.12)	(1.54)
Inner Mongolia	–6.53	–12.01	–5.35	–24.95***	4.38	8.56**
	(–0.43)	(–1.04)	(–0.19)	(–2.99)	(1.42)	(2.07)
Liaoning	–56.69***	–54.87***	–13.07	–41.95***	–6.22	–6.70
	(–2.86)	(–3.66)	(–0.36)	(–3.86)	(–1.55)	(–1.24)
Jilin	49.52*	79.27***	26.73	44.00***	4.82	30.45***
	(1.96)	(4.15)	(0.58)	(3.18)	(0.94)	(4.43)
Heilongjiang	103.35***	70.60***	54.32	14.92	17.58***	38.10***
	(5.56)	(5.06)	(1.60)	(1.48)	(4.70)	(7.59)
Anhui	143.74***	115.36***	37.44	59.85***	17.98***	37.54***
	(7.29)	(7.76)	(1.04)	(5.56)	(4.52)	(7.03)
Fujian	5.49	–39.03**	67.17*	–31.91***	–7.50*	0.38
	(0.26)	(–2.41)	(1.71)	(–2.72)	(–1.73)	(0.07)
Jiangxi	37.09**	37.36***	2.38	15.17	2.88	19.31***
	(2.18)	(2.90)	(0.08)	(1.63)	(0.84)	(4.17)
Shandong	–10.45	–2.81	0.10	–4.12	0.37	0.93
	(–0.53)	(–0.19)	(0.00)	(–0.39)	(0.10)	(0.18)
Henan	53.63***	52.53***	12.99	27.08***	9.43***	16.02***
	(3.93)	(5.10)	(0.52)	(3.63)	(3.41)	(4.32)

Poverty targeting in Asia

Table 4.10   (continued)

Independent variables	Total poverty funds	Central government funds	Other funds	Subsidized loans	Budgetary funds	Food-for-work
Hubei	34.42**	34.28***	–6.27	20.51**	3.34	10.43**
	(2.15)	(2.84)	(–0.21)	(2.34)	(1.03)	(2.40)
Hunan	122.77***	90.44***	19.59	53.72***	14.51***	22.21***
	(5.39)	(5.26)	(0.47)	(4.32)	(3.15)	(3.60)
Guangxi	14.43	33.75***	–22.45	18.29**	5.52*	9.94**
	(0.97)	(3.00)	(–0.82)	(2.24)	(1.83)	(2.46)
Hainan	–27.86	54.38***	–35.73	–1.71	10.26**	45.83***
	(–1.10)	(2.85)	(–0.77)	(–0.12)	(2.01)	(6.67)
Chongqing	65.01***	56.85***	–3.13	24.58**	12.24***	20.04***
	(3.29)	(3.82)	(–0.09)	(2.28)	(3.07)	(3.74)
Sichuan	163.53***	152.04***	–15.40	91.14***	21.49***	39.41***
	(9.85)	(12.27)	(–0.51)	(10.16)	(6.47)	(8.85)
Guizhou	3.35	8.34	–15.79	8.10	–0.40	0.65
	(0.25)	(0.83)	(–0.65)	(1.11)	(–0.15)	(0.18)
Yunnan	–11.93	–22.04 **	38.48*	–9.06	–5.77**	–7.21**
	(–0.98)	(–2.40)	(1.72)	(–1.36)	(–2.34)	(–2.18)
Shaanxi	3.64	9.12	–4.69	11.70*	–0.79	–1.78
	(0.29)	(0.96)	(–0.20)	(1.69)	(–0.31)	(–0.52)
Gansu	7.39	20.18**	–10.29	1.06	16.40***	2.72
	(0.59)	(2.15)	(–0.45)	(0.16)	(6.53)	(0.81)
Qinghai	211.25***	215.78***	6.26	162.21***	7.71**	45.86***
	(12.09)	(16.34)	(0.20)	(16.96)	(2.18)	(9.66)
Ningxi	117.41***	99.54***	25.53	44.82***	36.12***	18.60***
	(5.41)	(6.07)	(0.64)	(3.77)	(8.22)	(3.15)
Xinjiang	25.151	79.18***	3.22	8.46	23.15***	47.58***
	(1.55)	(6.45)	(0.11)	(0.95)	(7.04)	(10.79)
No. of obs.	2121	2128	2128	2128	2128	2128
Adjusted R^2	0.38	0.47	0.01	0.38	0.29	0.37

Notes:
*** significant at 0.01 level.
** significant at 0.05 level.
* significant at 0.10 level.

Source: Calculated by the author.

counties on the plains, counties in highland and mountainous areas have no special advantage in allocation.

Many provincial dummies have large and significant coefficients, indicating some provinces are at an advantage, while others are discriminated against. Compared with counties in Hebei province, which is the reference point for the analysis, those in Shanxi, Inner Mongolia, Liaoning, Fujian and Yunnan are at a disadvantage, while those in Jilin, Heilongjiang, Anhui, Jiangxi, Henan, Hubei, Hunan, Guangxi, Hainan, Chongqing, Sichuan, Gansu, Qinghai, Ningxia and Xingjiang have an advantage. Qinghai has the most favored treatment as its poor counties receive 211 yuan per capita more than expected from the central government, after controlling for characteristics like poverty incidence, population size and minority status.

The anomalies found here confirm the view that regional targeting may be a rather 'blunt instrument' for reaching the poor (Ravallion and Lipton, 1995). Even when funds are targeted at the poorest regions, there is considerable leakage to the non-poor in poor regions and lack of coverage of the poor in non-poor regions. Further, even between poor counties there are important anomalies in the per capita allocation of funding. In PRC political factors have strongly influenced poverty targeting from the outset. Entrenchment of political interests to maintain poor county status has made removal of poor county designation difficult, leading to a tendency to expand coverage and increase leakage, thus widening targeting errors over time. The evidence presented here suggests that political constraints are likely to undermine regionally targeted programs, when targeting is at the county level or higher.

OVERALL EFFECTIVENESS OF POVERTY TARGETING

To date there is limited evidence on the overall effectiveness of poverty reduction programs in PRC and here we survey the main contributions. The challenge of such assessments is to isolate the effect of poverty programs, since progress or lack of progress in reducing poverty may reflect factors other than the targeting programs themselves. Some have argued, for instance, that poor areas stood to gain more from market and commercialization reforms since the planning system forced them into production patterns that went against their comparative advantage to a greater extent than in richer areas (Lardy, 1983). To back this up there is some evidence that income growth in poor counties was greater than in non-poor counties in some regions, allowing for other factors (Park et al., 1996; Tong et al., 1995). A number of studies have looked specifically at the impact of poor county targeting and we survey the more important of these.

Jalan and Ravallion (1998b) assess whether being located in an officially designated poor county affects growth in household expenditures, controlling for geographic externalities and other community variables that are likely to determine income growth. Utilizing National Bureau of Statistics panel data (1985 to 1990) on households in four southwest provinces (Guizhou, Yunnan, Guangxi and Guangdong), they find that living in a national poor county increases consumption by 1.1 per cent per year above what would be expected, although this gain is offset by a growing divergence in consumption relative to non-poor counties, due to the unfavorable characteristics of poor counties. Using this consumption growth as a measure of benefits the rate of return on poverty investments is estimated to be 12 per cent.[11] The authors themselves point out that this may overestimate the poor county program's effect, since some public expenditure may not be included, funds may be used for consumption rather than investment purposes, and the variables used to control for area characteristics may omit factors that give poor counties an advantage in growth.

Rozelle et al. (1998) examine the effectiveness of targeted poverty interventions across economic sectors in 43 poor program counties of Shaanxi province during 1986–91. The authors adopt three separate sectoral growth models in which the rate of growth of output per capita is a function of current-year poverty expenditures, poverty expenditures lagged one year, government expenditures per capita (to control for other investments), rural income per capita (to control for private investment), human capital (represented by the share of the labor force that had graduated from middle school in 1985), lagged output (to control for the initial size of the sectors), and county and time dummy variables (to control for county characteristics and time-related effects), as well as population density (as a proxy for the relative abundance of labor). In the agricultural growth equation they also include as a regressor changes in the availability of agricultural land, while in the growth equation for state-owned industry, they include as regressors fixed investment in enterprise assets in both current and lagged form.

The results reveal that for the sample of national and provincial poor area counties, targeted poverty funds allocated directly to households for agricultural activities have a significant and positive effect on growth. In contrast, investments in township and village enterprises or county state-owned enterprises do not have a discernible effect on growth. In a more disaggregated part of the study, investments in agricultural infrastructure (such as terracing or soil leveling) do not by themselves positively affect growth in agricultural output. These results suggest that the poverty funds targeted directly at households have a positive growth effect. The study is based on data from only one province, and similar work using data from other provinces is necessary to have confidence that the results for Shaanxi can be generalized to other parts of the country. Also an important source of poverty funds, namely the food-for-work funds, are excluded from the estimation, which is most likely to affect the impact of infrastructure investment.

For another province, Sichuan, Zhang et al. (2002) analyze the impact of participation in national and provincial poor county programs on income growth. They classify all counties in Sichuan into poor program counties, non-program poor counties and non-poor counties. Growth of income per capita in poor program counties was positive and exceeded the very small rise for non-program poor counties; however, it did not keep pace with the increase in the non-poor counties. In terms of statistical significance, growth rates of poor program counties were statistically indistinguishable from those of non-poor counties, whilst non-program poor counties had significantly slower growth than either of the other groups.

The authors use a regression model to identify the determinants of growth and examine the impact of the poverty programs using data from 1990 to 1996 for 177 counties. The growth of income is regressed on independent variables representing resource endowment, the economic structure of the county, investment (by type) made through the fiscal system (which includes some but not all of poor area expenditures) and program participation. They find investment in agriculture, health, education and electrification positively affects growth, though the effect on growth of other investments (in 'other infrastructure') is not apparent. The presence of a poverty program positively impacts on growth, keeping the relative growth of poor program counties from falling as much as that of poor, non-designated counties. After accounting for endowments, structure, and initial level of income, poor program counties grew more slowly than non-poor counties (by about 3 per cent per year). However, this slower income growth was still faster than growth for non-program poor counties, which, allowing for the county characteristics captured here, experienced growth nearly 5 per cent slower than non-poor counties. An important difference between Zhang et al. (2002) and Rozelle et al. (1998) is that the former uses data from all counties in Sichuan, while the latter only works with designated poor counties. This allows the use of non-designated poor counties as a comparator group, although incomplete coverage of poverty expenditures is a limitation common to both studies.

Using a different methodology, Fan et al. (2002) develop a simultaneous equation model to estimate the effects of government expenditure on output and poverty through different channels. They conclude that poverty funds matter for growth and poverty alleviation, but not nearly as much as investments in other sectors. The study, using provincial data for the past 26 years between 1970 and 1995, shows that government spending on production-enhancing investments, such as agricultural R&D, irrigation, rural education and infrastructure (including roads, electricity and communications) have all contributed not only to growth, but also to poverty reduction. One of the most striking results is that large parts of the poverty effect are realized through improved access to rural non-farm employment. Government anti-poverty loans specifically targeted for poverty alleviation have the smallest impact on poverty reduction of any of the investment programs considered. The strength of the study lies in its adoption of a simultaneous equation model and the use of a provincial panel data set. However, of the poverty-targeting funds only subsidized loans are taken into consideration. Also methodologically there may be a bias against the impact of poverty loans, as they do not enter into the simultaneous 'production equations' and therefore do not generate feedbacks in the way that infrastructure and other non-poverty investments do.

One of the most detailed and disaggregate approaches is provided by the author and others using Ministry of Agriculture county level data, for all counties where relevant data exist (Park et al., 2002). To estimate the impact of poverty reduction policy on average income growth in poor counties, growth in a county's rural income per capita from one period to another is modeled as a function of the county's status as a designated poor county at the beginning of the period, initial income per capita, other initial characteristics (principally grain production per capita), county time-invariant characteristics, and prefecture time-varying factors. A panel is constructed from data for each county for four time periods: 1981–85, 1985–89, 1989–92, and 1992–95. The first period pre-dates the poor county programs, and the first poor county designations occurred during the second and third periods, with additional designations being made during the fourth period. Information on growth rates before the poverty program began makes it possible to identify the effects of poor county status while also controlling, through a county dummy variable, for unobservable characteristics that have persistent effects on growth. The coefficients on the poverty status variable can be interpreted as the program effect allowing for all other factors. The results suggest that poverty designation and the funds that come with it have a positive growth effect, allowing for other factors. Rural household net income per capita is found to increase 2.2 per cent faster annually in poor counties than in non-poor counties over 1986–92, and 0.9 per cent faster over 1992–95, other things held equal.[12] This means that although growth was nonetheless lower in poor areas, their relative disadvantage due to their starting point and characteristics was reduced by the poverty funds. The effects are larger than those found by Jalan and

Ravallion (1998b) for the period of 1985–90 in four southwest provinces, discussed above. Furthermore, these figures are based on national data, not, as with earlier studies, on data from one province alone.

Using this estimate of program impact on rural income growth, it is possible to estimate the rate of return on poverty investment. In real terms, the poverty spending included here fell during 1985–92 and then recovered to about its initial level, averaging 9.5 billion yuan per year (in 1995 yuan), equivalent to 89 yuan per person or 14 per cent of rural income. Based on the 2.2 per cent impact on incomes, the poverty program on average increased rural income by 13.8 yuan per person per year. This suggests a rate of return of 15.5 per cent, somewhat higher than the 12 per cent estimated by Jalan and Ravallion (1998b). For the 1992–95 period, the approximate doubling of the program's coverage reduced spending per capita to 55 yuan and the implied rate of return is 11.6 per cent.

These results of Park et al. (2002) are open to different interpretations. Total poverty expenditure may be considerably greater than the central government funds included in this study, which do not cover items like the administrative costs of programs, matching or supplementary funds provided by local governments and international donor funds. Some argue that the total of such spending is much greater than official central government poverty alleviation funds (Xie, 1994). Indirect evidence of low repayment rates on subsidized loans and suspected substitution effects, discussed above, may make the relatively high rate of return surprising. Most critically the results provide no evidence on the distribution of benefits within counties, so high impacts do not necessarily benefit the poor within poor counties. Other factors, however, may bias the estimates downward, particularly if targeted programs also benefit poor counties not officially designated as poor, as leakage will dilute the measured impact on targeted counties. This will be reinforced if provincial governments shift other budgetary allocations away from counties supported by national poverty alleviation funds.

Evidence from all of the above studies surveyed here suggests that poverty programs in PRC have had a positive impact on household income and poverty reduction in poor areas, although there is also evidence that the impact from other non-poverty focused investment has been even greater. There is also some evidence that during the 1990s the impact of targeted poverty funds on poverty reduction decreased with the decrease of the rural poor population and the increase in such funds, possibly because of the worsening targeting problems and the diversion of some poverty funds. Nonetheless a major omission of all studies is that due to the lack of reliable poverty data at the disaggregate level within counties, none of the above has managed to disaggregate gains to poor counties into those to the poor and to the non-poor within the counties. It is clear that this requires further research.

CONCLUSIONS

PRC has made enormous strides in poverty reduction over the last 25 years, despite the continuing disputes in the literature on the precise magnitude of remaining poverty and the extent of its decline over time. Since the mid-1980s there has been a consistent targeted poverty reduction program, although central government expenditures, which are the only component for which there is comprehensive data, have never exceeded 6 per cent of total government expenditure. The central focus of targeting has been location targeting, based on poor counties, and the within-county allocations have been determined in a variety of ways, not all of which have been based on objective need. There is also substantial evidence of errors in poor county designations, which appear to have increased in the early 1990s with the addition of new counties to the list. There was competition for access to these funds and the ensuing political pressures worsened targeting accuracy at this time. The limited evidence available implies that access to poverty funds did have a positive effect in counteracting the unfavorable geographic and social conditions faced by many poor areas. Their incomes may have grown more slowly than in higher income areas, but their relative disadvantage was reduced modestly by the availability of poverty funds. Despite this positive conclusion we still know very little about how such funds affected intra-county distribution between poor and non-poor and hence have little conclusive evidence on their net effect on poverty reduction. There is in fact substantial anecdotal evidence on the misuse of poverty funds. Finally, we also know fairly conclusively that the main driver of poverty reduction has been very rapid economic growth and through their growth effect other non-poverty investments have in fact had a major poverty reduction impact.

APPENDIX: POVERTY IN PRC

Though there are disagreements on the magnitude of the absolute poor in rural PRC and even on the trends in change in poverty over different time periods, all can agree that the numbers of rural poor have been reduced very substantially with the fast growth of the economy and of household income in the past 25 years.

Official Poverty Estimates

The official estimate of the rural poor population is based on the poverty line defined by the National Bureau of Statistics (NBS). Rural poverty is defined by NBS as 'difficulty in material well-being so great that a person or a family cannot reach the socially acceptable minimum standard of living.' Therefore a fundamental principle in defining the poverty line is 'the minimum expense required to meet people's basic living needs for necessary goods and services under the specific conditions of time, place and social development' (Tang, 1994a). The NBS divides basic personal consumption expenditures into two categories, food consumption expenditures and non-food consumption expenditures (clothing, housing, communications, fuel, health and medical care, education, entertainment and so forth). Food consumption to meet minimum calorie requirements is the most important factor for setting the poverty line. To determine the poverty line requires; first, an estimate of minimum calorific intake based on nutritional standards; second, a food consumption bundle to meet this; third, the monetary value of the minimum food consumption expenditure based on the prices of the different foods in this bundle; and finally, the Engel coefficient (food consumption as a proportion of total consumption by the poor), which can be used to calculate non-food consumption expenditures and the poverty line.

Based on the recommendations of the China Nutrition Association, the NBS adopted a daily intake of 2400 calories per person as the minimum nutritional standard (Wang et al., 1996). The following principles were applied in defining the food bundle that met this nutritional standard. First, all food in the bundle should be necessities, excluding what were deemed 'harmful and extravagant' consumption (such as cigarettes, alcoholic beverages and sweets). Second, the food bundle should reflect the real consumption pattern in rural areas. NBS estimated rural household consumption of essential goods using the 1984 sample survey statistics on rural households. Table A.4.1 shows the food bundle and the corresponding calorific intake adopted by the NBS. The prices used by the NBS in calculating food consumption expenditures are the weighted average prices of the various foods. An Engel coefficient of 60 per cent was used in computing the non-food consumption expenditure before 1998, on the grounds that 60 per cent was usually employed internationally, and furthermore the cost of food constituted about 60 per cent of the average total living expenses of Chinese rural households in 1984 (Tang, 1994a).

Following this approach, the NBS calculated the 1984 rural poverty line as 200 yuan per person per year.

Table A.4.1   Food consumption bundle adopted by the NBS

Consumption item	Unit calories (Cal./Kg)	Amount consumed (kg)	Calorific intake (Cal./day)	Proportion of total calories
Grain	3150	220.00	2115.6	88.0
Vegetable oil	8990	2.45	60.34	2.5
Vegetables	204	100.00	56.0	2.3
Pork	3950	8.70	94.0	4.0
Eggs	1635	1.30	5.8	0.2
Animal oil	8960	1.36	33.4	
Mutton and beef	1746	0.54	2.6	
Milk	1522	0.75	3.13	3.0[*]
Poultry	1845	0.74	3.74	
Fish, shrimp	1091	0.96	2.87	
Sugar	3970	1.00	10.9	
Fruit	604	3.00	4.96	

Note: * The combined proportion of animal oil, mutton and beef, milk, poultry, fish and shrimp, sugar and fruit.

Over the years, the NBS adjusted the poverty line established for 1984, initially in line with the changes in the rural retail price index and later with those in the rural consumer price index. In 1990 the prices of households' self-consumed agricultural and other products used in the calculations changed from controlled state-planned purchase prices to an average of state-planned purchase prices and the above-quota purchase prices in contract purchases. Table A.4.2 shows the NBS poverty line in different years.

In 1999 the NBS conducted a new set of poverty line calculations using the 1998 national rural sample survey data (NBS, 2000). A standard food bundle of 27 items in 15 categories was established from the mean consumption pattern of households with income per capita less than 800 yuan, adjusted to meet a lower calorific standard of 2100 calories. The income necessary to purchase the standard bundle of food items was estimated at 527 yuan.

The non-food expenditure share was calculated using a regression method.[13] The estimated non-food expenditures at the poverty line were 108 yuan, giving a poverty line of 635 yuan. However the non-food expenditure share of 17 per cent from this approach was substantially lower than the 40 per cent share assumed in the earlier calculations.

Table A.4.2   Per capita income and the official poverty line for rural areas

Year	Average annual net income per capita (yuan)	Poverty line (yuan)	Poverty line / net income (%)
1978	134	100	74.6
1984	355	200	56.3
1985	398	206	51.8
1986	424	213	50.0
1987	463	227	49.0
1988	545	236	43.3
1989	602	259	43.0
1990[a]	686	300	43.7
1991	709	304	42.9
1992	784	320	40.8
1993	922	n.a.	n.a.
1994	1221	440	36.0
1995	1578	530	34.2
1996	1926	580	30.1
1997	2090	630	30.1
1998	2165	635	29.3
1999	2210	625	28.3
2000	2253	625	27.7
2001	2366	635	26.8
2002	2476	627	25.3

Notes:
n.a.: not available.
[a]   In 1990, the NBS changed the pricing of rural households' self-consumed products.

Source: Tang (1994b) and other data provided by the NBS.

After setting the poverty line in different years, using the household survey system it set up in one third of counties in the early 1980s and the income data from more than 60 000 sampled rural households, the NBS estimated the proportion of rural households and the rural population whose net per capita income was below the poverty line. Table A.4.3 gives the NBS estimates of the poor population in rural areas. According to these figures the rural poor have decreased dramatically over the past 25 years. The absolute poor population decreased from 250 million in 1978 to 28 million in 2002, and the poverty-stricken population as a proportion of the total rural population decreased from 31 per cent to 3 per cent.

Table A.4.3   Official rural poverty headcount (1978–2002)

Year	Rural population (million persons)	Poor population (million persons)	Percentage of poor
1978	803	250	30.7
1984	843	128	15.1
1985	844	125	14.8
1986	850	131	15.5
1987	857	122	14.3
1988	867	96	11.1
1989	878	106	12.1
1990	896	85	9.5
1991	905	94	10.4
1992	912	80	8.8
1993	913	75	8.2
1994	915	70	7.6
1995	917	65	7.1
1996	919	58	6.3
1997	915	49	5.4
1998	920	42	4.6
1999	922	34	3.7
2000	928	32	3.4
2001	934	29	3.1
2002	935	28	3.0

Source: NBS (2000, 2001, 2002, 2003).

Potential Bias of the Official Estimates

Criticisms of official poverty estimates focus on the methodology used by the NBS to calculate the official poverty line (Park and Wang, 2001). The calculation may be subject to a number of potential biases that may work in opposite directions, although mainly towards underestimating poverty. First, an arguably unrealistic food bundle was adopted, in which consumption items viewed to be non-necessities were excluded (for example alcohol and sweets). As a result grain accounted for 88 per cent of expenditures, even though grain comprises only around 70 per cent of actual food expenditures by poor households. Over-weighting of grain in the standard bundle leads to the under-pricing of calories, since grain is a relatively cheap source of calories. This gives a downward bias to the poverty line and leads to an underestimation of poverty. Second, as we have seen, planned prices rather than market prices were used to value own-produced consumption goods before 1990. Insofar as market prices were higher and insofar as the rural poor had to purchase their marginal needs on open markets, this will bias downward estimates of food consumption. Third, the reduction in the share of non-food expenditure in the poverty line estimate was controversial and appeared to contradict known expenditure patterns.[14] Fourth, some have criticized the NBS sample for under-representing households in remote and minority areas, and those with illiterate household heads. Fifth, despite the availability of expenditure data, NSB has always calculated poverty rates using income data, even though for poverty calculations expenditures are considered to be a better measure of both current and long-term welfare, and since individuals try to smooth consumption over time, expenditures tend to vary less from year to year than incomes. In PRC average incomes are 10 per cent to 20 per cent higher than average expenditures, so that using income data results in lower poverty rates.[15] Finally, and perhaps most critically, the implicit inflation rates evident in the official poverty lines appear much lower than the actual change in the rural consumer price index and do not allow for regional price differences.

There has been considerable debate on this latter point. For example, Khan and Riskin (2001) point out that even the rural consumer price index is likely to underestimate the growth in living costs of the poor, because their budget shares for food are higher than the average and food prices have grown faster than other prices.[16] In the initial years the official poverty lines are consistent with the rural retail price index, and in the final years of Table A.4.2 they are consistent with the rural consumer price index. However in the intervening years, there are large discrepancies. Most notably the poverty line increases only modestly during the high inflation years of 1988 and 1989, and there is a sharp increase in the poverty line in 1997 that is far in excess of inflation. This helps explain why official statistics show a steady reduction in poverty in the late 1980s, while other estimates show little change. If the 1985 line is inflated by the rural consumer price index, the 2000 poverty line reaches 721 yuan compared with the official line of 625 yuan. This suggests that poverty reduction over time may be exaggerated significantly.

Like poverty lines in many countries the NBS national poverty line does not allow for regional price differences in calculating the required food expenditures, nor does it allow for regional differences in the food bundle. Food prices vary greatly between different provinces due to transport costs and imperfect market integration. For example, Chen and Ravallion (1996) estimate that the cost of purchasing the NBS food bundle was 23 per cent higher in Guangdong than in Guangxi in the late 1980s. Similarly in 1992 and 1995, the local NBS of Jiangxi province calculated provincial poverty lines of 400 and 750 yuan using local prices and the national food bundle, which were well above the official national poverty lines of 320 and 530 yuan, respectively (see Table A.4.2). Failure to account for regional price differences may exaggerate the concentration of poverty in poor regions.

Alternative Estimates of Rural Poverty

Because of these sources of bias in the official poverty estimates, other estimates have been made using different methods and data sources. The main alternative estimates of rural poverty are presented in Table A.4.4.

Because of the potential arbitrariness of choosing any one poverty line, arguably it is more important to examine trends in poverty over time. All estimates agree that there was a spectacular reduction in poverty in the early 1980s. Again all estimates other than the official poverty count show little or no progress in poverty reduction in the late 1980s. Reductions in the

Table A.4.4   Alternative estimates of rural poverty headcount (proportion of poor in total population)

Source	Sample data	Survey	1978	1984	1985
NSB Official	National (income groups and household income)[a]	NBS	30.7	15.1	14.8
World Bank (1992)	National (income groups)	NBS	33.0	11.0	11.9
World Bank (2001)	National (income groups)	NBS			
World Bank (2001)	National (expenditure groups)[b]	NBS			
Khan (1996)	National (income groups)	NBS			14.0
Khan and Riskin (2001)	19 provinces (household income)	Own survey			
Riskin and Li (2001)	19 provinces (household income)	Own survey			
Jalan and Ravallion (1998b)	5 provinces (household expenditures)	NBS			28.4

Notes:
[a]   Income groups before 1995, household data from 1995 onwards.
[b]   Expenditure groups constructed from national mean expenditure and income group distributions.

Source: Park and Wang (2001), World Bank (2001), Wang et al. (2004).

official count are almost certainly due to insufficient inflation of the poverty line in 1988 and 1989. In the early 1990s, Khan (1996) and the World Bank (2001) show little change until after 1993. The official poverty count falls steadily throughout the 1990s. Khan and Riskin (2001) and Riskin and Li (2001) emphasize the small magnitude of poverty reduction from 1988 to 1995. Riskin and Li (2001) report that using NBS's own income definition and poverty line, they estimate a poverty headcount of 9.4 per cent, which is higher than the official figure of 7.1 per cent. As mean incomes are the same in their 19 province sample and the NBS's national sample, the only plausible explanation is differences in the distribution of incomes.[17]

World Bank (2001) uses a constant price US $1 per day poverty line. The purchasing power parity dollar per day standard was established to facilitate inter-country comparisons, and is not based on nutritional standards, consumption patterns, or social norms specific to PRC. The official poverty line is broadly equivalent to 0.67 cents per day and hence the World Bank poverty estimates are considerably above the official ones. However, what is striking is the rapid fall in poverty in the mid-1990s reported both by World Bank (2001) and the official estimates, although they vary in both the numbers of poor and the headcount.

A further limitation of official poverty estimates is that they draw no distinction between chronic and transitory poverty. Other estimates suggest

1986	1987	1988	1989	1990	1991	1992	1993	1994	1995	1996	1997	1998	1999	2000	2001	2002
15.5	14.3	11.1	12.1	9.5	10.4	8.8	8.2	7.6	7.1	6.3	5.4	4.6	3.7	3.4	3.1	3.0
11.9	11.1	10.4	12.3	11.5												
				29.1	28.2	27.7	27.1	24.0	20.3	14.0	12.7	10.8	10.5	12.0	10.6	9.4
	35.4			40.0	38.0	37.7	37.9	32.3	28.8	22.6	22.7	22.8	23.5	21.0	19.5	17.2
			16.1			13.9		13.6	14.1	13.6						
32.7								28.6								
	12.7								12.4							
27.5	23.0	22.8	25.3	28.3												

that in PRC transitory poverty, those who move above or below the poverty line, is a significant proportion of the total poor. For example, using panel data for households in four provinces from 1985–1990, Jalan and Ravallion (1998a) find that the share of the poor who are not chronically poor varies from 30 per cent to 46 per cent. McCulloch and Calandrino (2001) find that in 1991 and 1995, 57 per cent and 46 per cent of the poor in Sichuan were experiencing transitory poverty. Using data from six poor counties for 1997 and 2000, Wang and Li (2003) find that around 30 per cent of the poor are transitory. Given these proportions it is clear that if the goal is to measure chronic poverty, annual poverty headcounts are likely to overstate the extent of such poverty substantially.

Nutritional Outcomes

The poverty headcount is conceptually a nutrition-based standard of welfare, since the poverty line is constructed to reflect the expenditure necessary to purchase a food bundle that provides a minimum acceptable number of calories per day. One way to validate official poverty statistics is to look directly at nutritional outcomes in the population. In general these also support the pattern of a rapid fall in poverty during the 1990s. For example, Zhu (2001) analyzes 1995 rural household data from 19 provinces and finds that 17 per cent of the rural population had a calorific intake below 2100 calories and 28 per cent had a calorific intake below 2400 calories, which at different times were the standards used in constructing the official poverty line. She also finds that the prevalence of inadequate calorie consumption is only weakly correlated with income, casting doubt on exclusive use of income as a poverty indicator. Similarly using aggregate production, trade and demographic data, and a minimum energy requirement of 1920 calories, the FAO (2000) estimated that the share of the population with insufficient calorie intake fell from 30 per cent in 1979–1981 to 17 per cent in 1990–1992 and to 11 per cent in 1996–1998.

A common indicator of long-term nutrition is the prevalence of stunting in children. A national survey by WHO/UNICEF in 1992 found a stunting rate in children of 31.4 per cent (FAO, 2000). A series of national surveys conducted by the Ministry of Health found stunting rates of 41 per cent in 1990, 39 per cent in 1995, and 23 per cent in 1997.[18] In officially designated poor counties, the stunting rate was much higher. A 1995 Ministry of Health survey found a stunting rate of 43 per cent in poor counties and the China Rural Poverty Survey directed by the author found a stunting rate of 46 per cent among children in 6 poor counties. These stunting rates compare with a stunting rate of 36 per cent in all developing countries, 37 per cent in Africa and 13 per cent in Latin America (ACC/SCN, 2000). These statistics suggest high rates of malnutrition in the poorer parts of rural PRC. They also suggest little progress in poverty reduction in the early 1990s, but substantial progress beginning in the mid-1990s. This pattern is consistent with the poverty headcount estimates.

Health indicators published by the Ministry of Health show steady progress in the quality of life in the 1990s. Interestingly, the trends in indicators like infant, under-5 and maternal mortality rates suggest rapid progress in the early 1990s, but less progress in the late 1990s, somewhat contradicting the nutritional findings noted above. Again, however, progress is evident over the decade.

Urban Poverty

Urban poverty was not an issue for the government until the mid-1990s, because urban residents were covered by a wide range of welfare programs from the government or state-owned enterprises. Up to then the government treated poverty exclusively as a rural problem. To date the government has released no official poverty lines or poverty counts for the urban population. State guarantees of jobs, pensions, housing and health care for all urban workers under socialism, along with a strict residence permit system, created a large urban–rural income gap that has been widened rather than reversed by market reforms. Early estimates of urban poverty by the World Bank (1992) found insignificant poverty incidence up to 1990. However, since the mid-1990s, restructuring of state-owned enterprises and substantial layoffs of workers have created significant dislocation for many workers. Growing urban poverty thus has become a real prospect.

Table A.4.5   Recent trends in urban poverty

Poverty headcount rate at $1/day income	1990	1992	1996	1998	1999	2000
National	23.1	21.6	10.6	7.9	7.8	8.8
Rural	31.0	30.0	14.9	11.4	11.2	13.7
Urban	0.9	0.0	0.2	0.0	0.25	0.3
Poverty headcount rate at $1/day consumption						
National	32.9	30.2	17.4	17.8	17.8	16.1
Rural	44.4	41.4	24.8	26.2	27.0	25.0
Urban	1.0	0.8	0.4	1.0	0.5	0.5

Source: World Bank (2003).

Using grouped income data, Khan (1996) estimates that the urban poverty headcount fell from 20 per cent in 1981 to 13 per cent in 1985 and to only 5 per cent in 1991. Khan and Riskin (2001) estimate an urban poverty rate of 6.8 per cent in 1988 and 8.0 per cent in 1995. Using urban household survey data collected by the NBS and the US $1 a day poverty line, the World Bank (2003) estimated that the urban poverty headcount rate in the 1990s was equal to or below 1 per cent, measured either with income or consumption data (see Table A.4.5). Compared with rural poverty, urban poverty appears much less of a problem from these estimates. However, Khan and Riskin (2001) argue that the World Bank's urban poverty line is too small a percentage (23 per cent) of average income to be realistic. However, many of the potential biases in constructing rural poverty lines and poverty counts also characterize urban poverty statistics. Valuation of non-wage benefits is particularly difficult.

NOTES

1. These included the poor counties in the 'three Xi' prefectures that had been given state financial aid since the early 1980s, namely, Dingxi and Hexi prefectures in Gansu province and Xihaigu prefecture in Ningxia Autonomous Region.
2. See the Appendix for a discussion of national poverty trends.
3. Agricultural Development Bank was set up in 1994 to manage policy loans for the agricultural sector, and took charge of subsidized loans for four years. In 1998 the responsibility for subsidized loans was assigned back to the Agricultural Bank of China.
4. Chapter 1 discusses these two types of targeting error.
5. TCG and TIG are analogous to the widely used poverty headcount and poverty gap measures, but are two-sided rather than one-sided.
6. Since the targeting income gap for all counties is 77 yuan and all the income gaps are from one fifth of the mis-targeted counties, the average magnitude of mis-targeting in mis-targeted counties is 385 yuan.
7. The targeting income error formula is the same as for targeting income gap except the poverty line Z is now the income of the threshold county and the summation is divided by D, instead of N. Targeting rank error replaces income difference with income rank difference.
8. The Ministry of Agriculture data is known to show more poverty in China's southwest and less in the northwest in comparison with the National Bureau of Statistics data (World Bank, 1992). Both data are available for poor counties in 1994 and 1995. The two series have a rank correlation of 0.89 and 0.92 in the two years.
9. Part of the measured bias against southwest provinces may be due to biases in the Ministry of Agriculture versus National Bureau of Statistics data. However, officials in Beijing confirmed that the number of poor counties in the poorest provinces was limited to preserve balance among provinces.
10. Among 592 poor counties, 532 counties have complete data for all four years.
11. The authors find that living in an area with poor natural conditions reduces consumption growth; namely poor areas tend to grow slower because of geographic externalities. Without allowing for geographic externalities, the estimated rate of return from poverty programs is zero.

12. The specification implicitly assumes that poor county designation is not endogenous to time-varying unobservables that differ within prefectures and are not correlated with initial characteristics. The authors estimate three equations in first differences simultaneously, using an iterative 3SLS procedure, imposing appropriate cross-equation restrictions and using different instruments for the three equations. The instruments are lagged variables for income, grain production and poverty status. The coefficients on the poverty status variables should be interpreted as the effect of the poverty program on counties in the same prefecture in the same period with the same starting income and grain production levels and controlling for time-invariant unobservables. Without allowing for fixed effects, the effect of the poverty program is negative in both periods, although not statistically significant in the second period.
13. This involves estimating non-food expenditures based on a regression of food share on a constant and the log of total expenditures/food poverty line.
14. As we have noted, the non-food expenditure share of 40 per cent used prior to 1998 dropped sharply to 17 per cent in 1998 due to the change from a fixed share to regression estimation. Data made available to the author by the NBS show that in 1999, the non-food expenditure shares of the poor, defined as those with incomes below 850 yuan per capita, in Guizhou, Gansu and Henan province were 27 per cent, 33 per cent and 49 per cent, respectively.
15. The poverty headcounts of the World Bank (2001) are about ten percentage points higher using expenditure rather than income data (see Table A.4.4).
16. Chen and Ravallion (1996) calculate price indices for the poor that grow significantly faster than the overall consumer price index in two of four provinces. Khan and Riskin (2001) find that the growth of the consumer price index for the poor is four percentage points higher than that for the overall consumer price index for the period 1988 to 1995.
17. Riskin and Li (2001) use a national poverty line while deflating incomes by provincial price indices, which will produce an unpredictable bias in the change in the poverty headcount.
18. Personal communication with China Centre of Preventive Medicine, Ministry of Health.

REFERENCES

Administrative Committee on Coordination, Subcommittee on Nutrition (ACC/SCN) (2000), 'The fourth report on the world nutrition situation', ACC/SCN in collaboration with IFPRI, Geneva.
Cao, Hongmin (2003), 'Study on development-oriented poverty reduction model in rural China', Ph.D. Dissertation, China Agricultural University, Beijing.
Chen, Shaohua and M. Ravallion (1996), 'Data in transition: assessing rural living standards in Southern China', *China Economic Review*, **7** (1).
Fan, Shenggen, Zhang Linxiu and Zhang Xiaobo (2002), 'Growth, inequality, and poverty in rural China: the role of public investments', International Food Policy Research Institute, Research Report No. 125, Washington, DC.
Food and Agriculture Organization (FAO) (2000), *The State of Food Insecurity in the World, 2000*, Rome: FAO.
Jalan, J. and M. Ravallion (1998a), 'Transient poverty in post reform rural China', *Journal of Comparative Economics*, vol. 26, pp. 338–57.
Jalan, J. and M. Ravallion (1998b), 'Are there dynamic gains from a poor-area development program?', *Journal of Public Economics*, vol. 67, pp. 65–85.
Khan, A. (1996), *The Impact of Recent Macroeconomic and Sectoral Changes on the Poor and Women in China*, New Delhi: International Labor Organization.

Khan, A. and C. Riskin (2001), *Inequality and Poverty in China in the Age of Globalization*, New York: Oxford University Press.

Lardy, N. (1983), *Agriculture in China's Modern Economic Development*, New York: Cambridge University Press.

Li, Wen and Wang Sangui (1999), 'Sources of income inequality in China's poor counties', in *Annual Report on Economic and Technological Development in Agriculture*, Beijing: China Agricultural Press.

Li, Zhou (2001), 'Poverty reduction efforts by government departments in China', paper presented at the International Conference on Poverty Reduction and NGO Development in China, Beijing.

McCulloch, N. and M. Calandrino (2001), 'Poverty dynamics in rural Sichuan between 1991 and 1995', Working Paper, Institute of Development Studies, University of Sussex, Brighton.

Ministry of Civil Affairs (MCA) (2003), 'Statistics of the minimum living standard program for urban residents in cities above the county seat'.

National Bureau of Statistics (NBS) (2000), *Monitoring Report of Rural Poverty in China*, Beijing: China Statistical Press.

National Bureau of Statistics (NBS) (2001), *Monitoring Report of Rural Poverty in China*, Beijing: China Statistical Press.

National Bureau of Statistics (NBS) (2002), *Monitoring Report of Rural Poverty in China*, Beijing: China Statistical Press.

National Bureau of Statistics (NBS) (2003a), *Monitoring Report of Rural Poverty in China*, Beijing: China Statistical Press.

National Bureau of Statistics (NBS) (2003b), *China Rural Economic Statistics by County 2002*, Beijing: China Statistical Press.

Office of the Leading Group for Economic Development in Poor Areas (1989), *Outlines of Economic Development in China's Poor Areas*, Beijing: China Agricultural Press.

Park, A. and Ren Changqing (2001), 'Microfinance with Chinese characteristics', *World Development*, **29** (1), 39–62.

Park, A. and Wang Sangui (2001), 'China's poverty statistics', *China Economic Review*, vol. 12, pp. 384–98.

Park, A., Wang Sangui and Wu Guobao (2002), 'Regional poverty targeting in China', *Journal of Public Economics*, vol. 86, pp. 123–53.

Park, A., S. Rozelle, C. Wong and Ren Changqing (1996), 'Distributional consequences of reforming local public finance in China', *China Quarterly*, vol. 147, pp. 751–78.

Ravallion, M. and J. Jalan (1999), 'China's lagging poor areas', *American Economic Review*, **89** (2), 301–5.

Ravallion, M. and M. Lipton (1995), 'Poverty and policy', in J. Behrman and T. Srinivasan (eds), *Handbook of Development Economics*, volume III, Amsterdam: North Holland.

Riskin, C. and S. Li (2001), 'Chinese poverty inside and outside the poor regions', in C. Riskin, R. Zhao and S. Li (eds), *China's Retreat from Equality: Income Distribution and Economic Transition*, Armonk, New York: M.E. Sharpe.

Rozelle, S., A. Park, V. Bezinger and Ren Changqing (1998), 'Targeted poverty investments and economic growth in China', *World Development*, **26** (12), 2153–67.

Rozelle, S., Li Guo, Shen Minggao, A. Hughart and J. Giles (1999), 'Leaving China's farms: survey results of new paths and remaining hurdles to rural migration', *China Quarterly*, vol. 158, pp. 367–93.

State Statistical Bureau (SSB) (1989), *China Rural Economics Statistics by County, 1980–1987*, Beijing: Statistical Press.

State Statistical Bureau (SSB) (1994), *China Rural Economic Statistics by County 1993*, Beijing: Statistical Press.

Tang, Ping (1994a), 'Research on poverty criteria and poverty situation in China', *Economic Research Materials*, vol. 52, pp. 2–13.

Tang, Ping (1994b), 'Preliminary study of the poverty standard and poverty conditions in China's rural areas', *China Rural Economy*, No. 8.

Tong, Zhong, S. Rozelle, B. Stone, Dehua Jiang, Jiyuan Chen and Zhikang Xu (1995), 'China's experience with market reform for commercialization of agriculture in poor areas', in J. von Braun and E. Kennedy (eds), *Agricultural Commercialization, Economic Development, and Nutrition*, Baltimore: Johns Hopkins Press.

Wang, Sangui and Wen Li (2003), 'Changes and their causes of household income in poor counties', *Issues in Agricultural Economy*, vol. 3, pp. 19–24. Also in *Poverty Reduction and Development*, No. 2, pp. 17–24.

Wang, Sangui, Ying Xia and Liu Xiaozhan (1996), 'Criteria to measure poverty in China', in Institute of Agricultural Economics, Chinese Academy of Social Sciences, *Research on Economic and Technological Development in Agriculture*, Beijing: China Agricultural Technology Press.

Wang, Sangui, Zhou Li and Yanshun Ren (2004), '8–7 National poverty reduction program in China: the national strategy and its impact', China country case study for Shanghai Poverty Conference, Shanghai, May.

Weiss, J. (2003), 'Explaining trends in regional poverty in the People's Republic of China', ADB Institute Discussion Paper No. 1, ADB Institute, Tokyo; available at www.adbi.org.

Wen, Qiuliang (2003), 'Real situation of rural poverty reduction and adjustments to poverty reduction policy', mimeo, Ministry of Finance, Beijing.

World Bank (1992), *China: Strategies for Reducing Poverty in the 1990s*, Washington, DC: World Bank.

World Bank (2001), *China: Overcoming Rural Poverty*, Washington, DC: World Bank.

World Bank (2003), *China: Promoting Growth with Equity, World Bank Country Study*, Report No. 24169-CHA, Washington, DC: World Bank.

Xie, Yang (1994), 'Description of the capacity for mobilizing social forces to alleviate poverty', *(shehui fuping gongneng de yige telie)*, *Tribune of Economic Development (kaifa luntan)*, No. 6.

Zhang, Linxiu, Huang Jikun and S. Rozelle (2002), 'Growth or policy? Which is winning China's war on poverty?', University of California, Department of Economics, Working Paper.

Zhu, Ling (2001), 'Food security of low-income groups in rural China', in C. Riskin, R. Zhao and S. Li (eds), *China's Retreat from Equality: Income Distribution and Economic Transition*, Armonk, New York: M.E. Sharpe.

Zhu, Ling and Zhongyi Jiang (1995), '*Yigong-Daizhen* in China: a new experience with labor-intensive public works in poor areas', in J. von Braun (ed.), *Employment for Poverty Reduction and Food Security*, Washington, DC: International Food Policy Research Institute.

5. Poverty targeting in Thailand

Peter Warr and Isra Sarntisart

INTRODUCTION

This chapter examines the efforts of the Thai government to direct particular categories of government expenditures preferentially towards the poor. The government professes an interest in doing this and the chapter aims to determine empirically whether this is being achieved by focusing on the geographic distribution of this expenditure across provinces. We begin with a review of the characteristics of poverty in Thailand. We then summarize government policies with respect to poverty reduction and present estimates of the magnitude of poverty-related expenditures. The overall distributional effects of general categories of government expenditures are reviewed first, before we consider the effects of the specific category of poverty reduction expenditures. The focus is geographic targeting, in the sense of allocation of expenditures between provinces, as there is insufficient data to allow an assessment of intra-provincial allocations.

POVERTY IN THAILAND

In Thailand, as elsewhere, the measurement of poverty and the analysis of its causes are controversial. Nevertheless, all major studies of poverty incidence in Thailand agree on some basic points:

- Absolute poverty has declined dramatically in recent decades, with the exception of a recession in the early 1980s and the period following the Crisis of 1997–98.
- Poverty is concentrated in rural areas, especially in the northeastern and northern regions of the country.
- Large families are more likely to be poor than smaller families.
- Farming families operating small areas of land are more likely to be poor than those operating larger areas.
- Households headed by persons with low levels of education are more likely to be poor than others.

The following discussion draws upon the official poverty estimates produced by the Thai government's National Economic and Social Development Board, which, like all other available poverty estimates, are based upon the household incomes collected in the household Socio-Economic Survey data. Despite their imperfections, these are the only data available covering a long time period. These survey data have been collected since 1962. The early data were based on small samples, but their reliability has improved steadily, especially since 1975. Table 5.1 shows all of the available official data for the four decades from 1962 to 2002.

Table 5.1   Thailand: poverty incidence,[a] 1962 to 2002 (headcount measure, per cent of total population)

	Aggregate	Rural	Urban
1962	88.3	96.4	78.5
1969	63.1	69.6	53.7
1975	48.6	57.2	25.8
1981	35.5	43.1	15.5
1986	44.9	56.3	12.1
1988	32.6	40.3	12.6
1990	27.2	33.8	1.6
1992	23.2	29.7	6.6
1994	16.3	21.2	4.8
1996	11.4	14.9	3.0
1998	12.9	17.2	3.4
2000	14.2	21.5	3.1
2002	9.8	12.6	3.0
Poverty share[b] 2000	100.0	92.6	7.4
Population share[c] 2000	100.0	68.4	31.6

Notes:

[a]   Poverty incidence means the number of poor within a reference population group expressed as a proportion of the total population of that group. The headcount measure of aggregate poverty incidence is the percentage of the total population whose incomes fall below a poverty line held constant over time in real terms; rural poverty is the percentage of the rural population whose incomes fall below a poverty line held constant over time in real terms, and so forth.

[b]   Poverty share means the number of poor within a reference population group expressed as a proportion of the total number of poor within the whole population.

[c]   Population share means the population of a reference group expressed as a proportion of the total population.

Source: Data obtained from Development Evaluation Division, National Economic and Social Development Board, Bangkok and Medhi (1993).

Table 5.1 focuses on the familiar headcount measure of poverty incidence: the percentage of a particular population whose household incomes per person fall below the poverty line.[1] The table confirms that most of Thailand's poor people reside in rural areas. The household survey data are classified according to residential location in the categories 'municipal areas', 'sanitary districts' and 'villages'. These correspond to inner urban (historical urban boundaries), outer urban (newly established urban areas) and rural areas, respectively. Poverty incidence is highest in the rural areas, followed by outer urban, and lowest in the inner urban areas. When these data are recalculated in terms of the share of each of these residential areas in the total number of poor people and then the share of the total population, as in the last two rows of the table, respectively, a striking point emerges. In the year 2000 rural areas accounted for 93 per cent of the total number of poor people but only 68 per cent of the total population.

Table 5.2 shows estimates of three measures of poverty incidence, covering the years 1988 to 2002. The first and fourth columns are based upon the headcount measure of absolute poverty incidence. This measures the proportion of the population (column 1) or the absolute number of people (column 4) whose incomes fall below a poverty line established by the National Economic and Social Development Board. Because minimum needs vary with household size and location, the poverty lines corresponding to households of particular sizes also vary according to household characteristics. The second column (poverty gap ratio) measures the average difference between the incomes of those below the poverty line and the poverty line itself, expressed as a proportion of the poverty line, while the third column is the average value of the square of this difference (the squared poverty gap: see also Chapter 1). The three measures capture different aspects of poverty, but because all three move in exactly the same direction over time our discussion will focus on the first, the headcount measure.

The data reveal a very considerable decline in poverty incidence up to 1996, a moderate increase to 1998 and a further increase over the following two years. Over the eight years from 1988 to 1996, measured poverty incidence declined by an enormous 21.4 per cent of the population, an average rate of decline in poverty incidence of 2.7 percentage points per year. That is, each year, on average 2.7 per cent of the population moved from incomes below the poverty line to incomes above it. Over the ensuing two years ending in 1998 poverty incidence increased by 1.5 per cent of the population. Alternatively, over the eight years ending in 1996 the absolute number of persons in poverty declined by 11.1 million (from 17.9 million to 6.8 million); over the following two years the number increased by 1.1 million (from 6.8 to 7.9 million). By this calculation, measured in terms of absolute numbers of people in poverty, the Crisis reversed one tenth of the poverty reduction that had occurred during the eight-year period of economic boom immediately preceding it.

Table 5.2   Thailand: poverty incidence by different measures

Period	Headcount measure (%)	Poverty gap ratio	Squared poverty gap	Number of poor (in millions)
1988	32.6	10.4	4.6	17.9
1990	27.2	8.0	3.3	15.3
1992	23.2	6.8	2.8	13.5
1994	16.3	4.3	1.7	9.7
1996	11.4	2.8	1.1	6.8
1998	12.9	3.2	1.2	7.9
2000	14.2	4.1	1.7	8.9
2002	9.8	2.4	1.4	6.2

Source: As in Table 5.1.

During periods when incomes are steadily increasing, lags in reporting changes in household incomes may not be important. But during periods when past trends are suddenly reversed, as with the Crisis of 1997 and beyond, these reporting lags can be very significant. For this reason, for assessment of the impact that the economic crisis had on poverty incidence, the 1996 data are best compared with the 2000 data, not those of 1998. This comparison roughly doubles the poverty impact of the Crisis – from 1.1 million additional poor to 2.1 million. The post-Crisis economic recovery subsequently erased all of this increase in the absolute number of the poor, so that by 2002 there were 6.2 million poor Thais, about half a million fewer than in 1996.

From Table 5.3, it is apparent that one region, the northeast, accounted for 61 per cent of the poor in 2000, but only 34 per cent of the total population. Every other region's share of the total number of poor is smaller than its share of the total population. Combining Tables 5.1 and 5.3, it is clear that poverty is an issue for rural people, especially in the northeast. In 2000 rural people in the northeast accounted for 63 per cent of all poor people in Thailand, but only 29 per cent of the total population.

Table 5.4 confirms that poverty incidence is highest among households with larger numbers of members. Combining the largest three household size categories shown in the table (5 persons and over), this group represents only 62 per cent of the total number of poor people compared with 44 per cent of the total population. From Table 5.5, it is apparent that age of household head is also related to poverty incidence, but the relationship is less dramatic. Households headed by persons over 60 years are more likely to be poor than households headed by younger persons, accounting for 42 per cent of all poor people in 1999 but only 27 per cent of the population. Households headed by persons in their twenties are least likely to be poor.

Table 5.3   Thailand: poverty incidence by region (headcount ratio, %)

Period	North	Northeast	Central	South	Bangkok and vicinity
1988	32.0	48.4	26.6	32.5	6.1
1990	23.2	43.1	22.3	27.6	3.5
1992	22.6	39.9	13.3	19.7	1.9
1994	13.2	28.6	9.2	17.3	0.9
1996	11.2	19.4	6.3	11.5	0.6
1998	9.0	23.2	7.7	14.8	0.6
2000	12.2	28.1	5.4	11.0	0.71
2002	9.8	18.9	4.3	8.7	1.4
Poverty share 2000	17.8	60.6	8.3	11.9	0.6
Population share 2000	18.8	34.2	23.3	13.3	10.4

Source: As in Table 5.1.

Table 5.4   Thailand: poverty incidence by household size (headcount ratio, %)

Period	1 person	2 persons	3 persons	4 persons	5 persons	6 persons	7 persons
1988	3.4	10.6	20.2	29.1	34.9	41.2	50.4
1990	3.7	9.2	16.1	23.0	28.3	34.3	43.2
1992	2.9	6.5	14.3	20.9	27.4	32.2	33.5
1994	1.0	3.2	8.6	16.4	19.4	23.7	27.9
1996	1.0	2.5	6.2	10.9	13.8	19.5	18.3
1998	1.2	3.0	6.6	10.7	17.1	20.2	22.0
2000	0.8	4.2	9.5	15.1	20.6	19.7	27.4
2002	0.2	3.4	11.1	24.1	21.4	20.4	19.1
Poverty share 2000	0.11	2.34	10.72	24.96	24.85	14.76	22.26
Population share 2000	2.24	8.91	18.07	26.47	19.31	11.99	13.01

Source: As in Table 5.1.

Table 5. 5   Thailand: poverty incidence by age of household head (headcount ratio, %)

	20–29	30–39	40–49	50–59	60–69	70 +
1988	26.4	33.0	35.1	32.4	32.4	33.8
1990	23.0	27.4	28.3	26.9	26.6	30.6
1992	17.3	23.2	24.3	23.3	22.3	27.5
1994	12.0	16.7	16.0	16.6	14.7	22.9
1996	7.7	12.0	11.7	10.5	11.6	14.0
1998	8.7	13.1	12.0	13.6	12.7	16.3
2000	7.8	16.7	16.6	16.3	14.8	17.9
2002	4.0	24.9	25.9	17.4	16.0	11.7
Poverty share 2000	0.29	19.52	21.94	16.05	42.19 *	
Population share 2000	0.77	24.34	27.52	20.50	26.86 *	

Note: * Data relate to '60 and over' age category.

Source: As in Table 5.1.

Finally, Table 5.6 focuses on farm land-owning households. In 2000 these households accounted for 26 per cent of the total population of Thailand, but 56 per cent of all poor people. It is therefore not the case that poor people are necessarily landless, or even with very small land holdings. The table shows that among farming households, those with small land holdings (less

Table 5.6   Thailand: poverty among farm owners' households by size of holdings (headcount ratio, %)

	Less than 5 *rai*	5 to 19 *rai*	20 *rai* or more
1988	67.7	56.2	32.9
1990	52.9	52.1	26.9
1992	41.2	46.3	31.2
1994	28.9	36.0	21.0
1996	37.2	29.9	12.1
1998	41.9	29.3	13.5
2000	45.4	43.6	20.8
2002	34.5	37.0	16.7
Poverty share 2000	10.76	62.48	26.76
Population share 2000	8.02	48.47	43.51

Source: As in Table 5.1.

than 5 *rai*) are the most likely to be poor, but poverty incidence in this group is only marginally higher than for those with intermediate sized holdings (5 to 19 *rai*).[2] The reason is that those with very small land holdings obtain significant off-farm incomes, as well as on-farm incomes. As a proportion of the total number of poor land holders, those with intermediate sized land holdings are a more significant group, accounting for more than one third of all poor households.

More dramatic than any of these data, however, are recently released data on the relationship between poverty incidence and education. According to the National Economic and Social Development Board's data, of the total number of poor people in 2002, 94.7 per cent had received primary or less education. A further 2.8 per cent had lower secondary education, 1.7 per cent had upper secondary education, 0.48 per cent had vocational qualifications and 0.31 per cent had graduated from universities. Thailand's poor are overwhelmingly uneducated, rural and living in large families. But they are not necessarily landless.

What caused the long-term decline in poverty? Long-term improvements in education have undoubtedly been important, but despite the limitations of the underlying household survey data, a reasonably clear statistical picture emerges on the relationship between poverty reductions and the rate of economic growth. The data are summarized in Table 5.7, which divides the periods shown into high, medium and low growth categories. During periods of rapid growth there was a dramatic decline in the incidence of absolute poverty. As Table 5.1 shows, decline was not confined to the capital, Bangkok, or its immediate environs, but occurred in rural areas as well. Since 1988, the largest absolute decline in poverty incidence occurred in the poorest region of the country, the northeast.

It is obvious that over the long term, sustained economic growth is a necessary condition for large-scale poverty alleviation. No amount of redistribution could turn a poor country into a rich one. Moderately rapid growth from 1962 to 1981 coincided with steadily declining poverty incidence. Reduced growth in Thailand caused by the world recession in the early to mid-1980s coincided with worsening poverty incidence in the years 1981 to 1986. Then, Thailand's economic boom of the late 1980s and early 1990s coincided with dramatically reduced poverty incidence. Finally, the contraction following the Crisis of 1997–98 led to increased poverty incidence. The recovery since the Crisis has been associated with significant poverty reductions.

In summary, the evidence from Thailand indicates that the rate of aggregate growth is an important determinant of the rate at which absolute poverty declines, even in the short run. However, the statistical relationship is far from perfect. Reduction of poverty incidence must depend on more than just the aggregate rate of growth.

Table 5.7   Thailand: GDP growth, poverty and inequality, 1962 to 2002

Year	Annual GDP growth (%)	Annual change in poverty incidence (headcount ratio)	Annual change in Gini coefficient
Rapid growth periods			
1986–88	9.75	−6.15	0.00
1988–90	10.27	−2.70	1.95
1992–94	7.01	−3.45	−0.45
Average	*9.01*	*−4.10*	*0.50*
Medium growth periods			
1962–69	5.08	−3.60	0.20
1975–81	4.86	−2.18	0.23
1990–92	6.47	−2.00	0.60
1994–96	6.44	−2.45	−0.60
2000–02	5.58	−2.21	n.a.
Average	*5.69*	*−2.49*	*0.11**
Slow growth periods			
1969–75	4.15	−2.42	−0.15
1981–86	3.67	1.88	0.88
1996–98	−6.50	0.80	−0.20
1998–00	4.16	0.60	n.a.
Average	*1.37*	*0.22*	*0.18**

Note: n.a. = not applicable.

Source: Poverty and GDP data from National Economic and Social Development Board, Bangkok.

POVERTY REDUCTION PHILOSOPHY

In governments' policy documents relating to poverty reduction, three perceived dimensions of poverty itself, and three dimensions of a strategy for reducing it, can be identified. These dimensions are 'opportunity', 'security' and 'community'. Opportunity refers to the capacity to participate in economically rewarding activity. When opportunity is improving, average incomes of poor people and average levels of their economic well-being, narrowly conceived, will increase. Security refers to the existence of mechanisms to maintain well-being in the face of unexpected short-term reductions in incomes. Improved security means reducing over time the variance of the economic well-being of poor people. Community refers to social capital. Community can be a means to achievement of the other two dimensions of poverty reduction, but it is also an end in itself because the extent to which it is present – the extent to which people feel themselves part of a larger social whole – affects the well-being people enjoy, given the levels of the other two dimensions.

Thai thinking on poverty reduction has some distinctive features. Central to these is the desire to use decentralized local community approaches, which minimize the dependency on the central government. At its present stage of development, Thailand does not wish to develop a developed country welfare state apparatus. The fear is that this could lead to perceived permanent entitlements and waste and may not serve the best long-term interests of the society, even including those who are presently poor. The intention is to utilize those features of the existing social infrastructure to assist the poor and not to undermine them.

The meaning of the above three categories may be illustrated through stylized examples of government programs and policies directed towards them.

Opportunity

- *promoting economic growth of a quality consistent with economic advancement of the poor*

The macroeconomic recovery program will have effects on the poor by affecting their opportunities to participate in the market economy and on what terms.

- *targeting the poor through government programs which build human capital, including education and health care*

Programs are in place for improving the targeting of education and public health spending towards the poor. We analyze the effectiveness of these programs in this chapter.

- *overcoming social exclusion*

The government is making attempts to overcome the social isolation of some of the poorest groups. This category overlaps strongly with 'Community', above.

- *raising agricultural productivity*

This item refers to the provision of support services to agricultural smallholders to raise productivity and enhance diversification.

Security

- *social safety net measures for groups and families, who fall into or risk falling into destitution*

The government is attempting to reach social groups presently outside the safety net provided by existing institutions (principally non-government), especially the aged, children, unemployed and marginalized or excluded minorities.

- *social protection measures to help the poor (and the non-poor) sustain consumption during and following sudden loss of income or high emergency expenditures through risk management type savings and insurance schemes*

This refers to the government's short-term and long-term measures, some introduced after the 1997 Crisis, to deal with income insecurity in the form of a pension program, health insurance, severance pay, an unemployment welfare fund and other programs.

Community

- *strengthening the resources and capabilities of local communities to promote self-reliant development of the poor*

Various Thai government programs are aimed at strengthening the capacity of local communities to assist the poor and develop local self-reliance, rather than using direct transfers from the central government as the principal instrument of assisting poor people.

- *ensuring that governance issues are addressed in the context of decentralization measures*

Local communities require not only resources, but also training in accounting and reporting skills to support the monitoring requirements of the central government. Systems of local accountability are also under development.

Decentralization

Thailand's new Constitution promulgated in 1997 and the Decentralization Act, which followed it, specify an ambitious program of decentralization of government expenditures. The share of total government expenditures outlaid by local government authorities is scheduled to increase from around

8 per cent in 2000 to 35 per cent in 2006. The program involves both transfers of revenue from the central government to the local level and the transfer of some taxing powers to the local level as well. Because some forms of expenditure cannot be decentralized, obvious examples of which include defense and foreign affairs, the level of decentralization in the remaining areas, including education, health and social security, will necessarily be well in excess of the overall target of 35 per cent.

The declared purpose of the decentralization is to increase the extent to which local communities have control over the way revenues are appropriated and thus to increase the degree of local accountability for public expenditures. Despite this laudable goal, preliminary indications suggest that the program may be too ambitious in the degree of decentralization that is planned. If so, this will have serious implications for the capacity of the government to deliver sustained social safety net programs in the future, as well as other forms of expenditure that are important for the poor.

The nature of Thailand's decentralization process is made clearer by comparison with Indonesia, which is also embarked on an ambitious decentralization program. In Indonesia, a high proportion of government expenditure is to be reallocated to the provincial (*kabupaten*) level. This means decentralization to about 350 local level government authorities, with an average population size of over half a million. Considering that Thailand's population is one quarter of Indonesia's, a similar degree of decentralization would mean devolving a large proportion of expenditures to around 80 local administrative units, corresponding roughly to the number of provinces (*changwat*).

But Thailand's 76 provincial governments are not democratically elected (provincial governors are appointed from Bangkok) and the decentralization program has not been aimed at increasing expenditure significantly at this level, but rather at the *tambon* level, meaning the 7000 or so *Tambon* Administrative Councils. In rural areas, the average population size of these authorities is about 5000. They are seemingly too small; the average *tambon* cannot support a high school or the professional administrative staff needed to account properly for the way a large increase in funds is actually being spent.

Wastage of public expenditures will result if the *Tambon* Administrative Councils are unable to manage large increases in expenditures well. Local level corruption will also increase in many areas if effective programs of monitoring cannot be implemented in time. The basic problem, of low levels of participation in secondary education among Thailand's rural population, will not be addressed by the decentralization program, unless local Tambon Administrative Councils are able to group themselves into larger units. This will probably happen if the program proceeds, but it will take time, and meanwhile serious disruption could result. As the central government transfers revenue to the local level it necessarily transfers functions as well. The education, health and other services now provided by the central government and which are crucial for poor people may not be forthcoming from the *tambon* level if the Tambon Administrative Councils are inadequately prepared.

Thailand's current Prime Minister, Dr Thaksin Shinawatra, has a background in corporate business. He is a centralizer, not a decentralizer. The decentralization program is mandated by the constitutional changes of 1997 but they are not necessarily to the liking of the current government. Not surprisingly, in view of the above discussion, recent statements by the Prime Minister and others have suggested the intention to focus resources at the provincial level and not simply at the *tambon* level. For the reasons set out above, this makes ample sense in terms of efficient management. Constitutional problems may arise, but if so, the parliamentary majority of the present government is large enough to push through any desired constitutional changes. There would be a political cost, however, with elections due in 2005.

Poverty goals
Reflecting the Prime Minister's enthusiasm for introducing business managerial practices and thinking into government, the post of provincial governor has been renamed 'CEO Provincial Governor'. Under the poverty reduction strategy recently outlined by the National Economic and Social Development Board, each CEO Provincial Governor will be responsible for developing benchmarks against ten specified 'Living Standard Measurement Criteria'.

The Living Standard Measurement Criteria specify that all Thais must have access to:

1. Lifelong training opportunities giving the opportunity to acquire the skills needed to earn a living.
2. Affordable universal health insurance.
3. A decent standard of living for indigent and elderly people.
4. An adequate diet, especially for school-age children.
5. Adequate shelter.
6. Adequate, clean drinking water (five liters per person per day) and water supply (45 liters per person per day).
7. Electricity supply.
8. Information necessary for their profession.
9. Capital and other resources for starting their own businesses.
10. A livable environment.

These ten goals can be seen as a compromise between the Prime Minister's thinking in favor of business approaches to solving social problems, on the one hand, and the conceptual framework of opportunity, security and community outlined above. Responsibility for monitoring achievement of these provincial benchmarks will lie with the National Economic and Social Development Board, and it will report the results publicly. It is clear that the role of the provincial governors has been significantly upgraded. It is not yet clear to what extent this will be matched by resource flows to the provincial level or to what extent the results of the official monitoring will influence these flows.

POVERTY-FOCUSED EXPENDITURE

Having noted these broad principles we now consider the type and magnitude of poverty-targeted expenditures. Because of changes in policy following the election of the government of Thaksin Shinawatra in March 2001, along with changes in the format and availability of data, is it necessary to consider the pre-2001 and post-2001 periods separately.

Prior to 2001 and the Election of the Thaksin Government

Until the year 2000, the government ran targeted poverty-oriented programs of four basic types:

- Cash transfers to poor families and the elderly administered by the Department of Public Welfare of the Ministry of Labor and Social Welfare.
- In-kind transfers, of which the major example is the means tested low-income Health Card aimed at providing for medical services run by the Ministry of Public Health. Other examples are the School Lunch Program (Ministry of Education) and subsidies for housing.
- Income generation programs such as the Poverty Alleviation Program, run by the Community Development Department of the Ministry of Interior, which gives interest-free loans to low-income households for income generation activities and the Student Loan Scheme, by the Ministry of Finance, for students of low-income families at upper secondary and tertiary levels of the education system.
- Special off-budget programs, often begun at the initiative of incoming governments or ministers.

These poverty-oriented programs expanded sevenfold in baht terms or from 1.1 per cent to 4.6 per cent of central government expenditure between the fiscal years 1993 to 2000 (see Table 5.8). One component of this increase is controversial – the Education Loans Program, which began operation in 1997. There is dispute as to whether this program is poverty-targeted or not. Although it was officially said to be directed at poorer students, the implementation of this targeting is left to the educational institutions themselves. These institutions report that they lack the resources to determine whether a student is or is not from a 'poorer' household and therefore are unable to target the program to the poor in any meaningful way. If this category is excluded, the increase in poverty-related expenditures is from 1.1 per cent to 3.3 per cent of total expenditures. Because of changes in the format of available data, instituted after 2000, this table cannot be extended beyond that year.

The World Bank's Public Expenditure Review for Thailand, completed in 2001 and covering the period ending in 2000, drew three main conclusions from these data. First, contrary to popular impressions (perhaps due to the number of programs), the level of government expenditure on poverty-related activities was quite small and the likely impact on poverty was, correspondingly, also small. This assessment is supported by data from the Bureau of the Budget (Table 5.8), discussed above. According to these data, in the year 2000 poverty-related expenditures represented between 3.3 and 4.6 per cent of total government expenditures, depending on whether the Education Loans Program is considered 'poverty-related'.

The World Bank's second conclusion was that targeting needs to be drastically improved since many non-poor seemed to be receiving benefit (for example, for Health Cards) and since funds for cash and in-kind transfer were seemingly allocated across provinces roughly by population, whereas the incidence of poverty varied substantially by province and the greatest proportions and numbers of poor were in the north and northeast. Thirdly, there was a proliferation of programs to assist the poor, but coordination between them was inadequate and there was little systematic effort to evaluate the effects of the programs. Since fiscal year 1996, there have been some attempts at rationalization with the Poverty Alleviation Program, job creation program and some housing support receiving smaller allocations and the rise in overall funds for poverty assistance in the two succeeding years being driven by the Education Loans Program.

Contrary to the contraction in many parts of the budget following the Crisis in 1997 and budget tightening agreed with the IMF, actual expenditure for assistance to the poor rose from 25.6 billion baht to 34 billion baht (a 33 per cent increase in nominal terms and a 23 per cent increase in real terms) between fiscal years 1997 and 1998, or from 2.8 to 4.1 per cent of

Table 5.8 Thailand: poverty reduction programs, 1993 to 2000 (millions of baht)

Program	1993	1994	1995	1996	1997	1998	1999	2000
Income Generation	**315**	**602**	**1,911**	**2456**	**9147**	**18301**	**20587**	**11772**
Poverty alleviation program	0	0	923	1342	564	1	587	172
Job creation (road construction)	315	602	988	1114	133	0	0	0
Education loans program	0	0	0	0	8450	18300	20000	11600
In-kind transfers	**5422**	**7926**	**8629**	**11007**	**7396**	**4947**	**12538**	**14943**
School lunch programs	820	1833	2570	2633	3765	2425	2365	2546
Housing programs	1132	1648	1831	3388	1484	503	353	1150
Health Programme for the needy	3470	4445	4228	4986	5768	8418	9821	11246
Cash transfers	**0**	**612**	**914**	**1226**	**1787**	**1821**	**1688**	**2339**
Nominal Total								
(millions of baht, current prices, total above items)	**5737**	**9140**	**11454**	**14689**	**25582**	**33989**	**44987**	**41449**
As % of total expenditure	*1.1*	*1.5*	*1.8*	*1.9*	*2.8*	*4.1*	*5.5*	*4.6*
Nominal Total less education loans	**5737**	**9140**	**11454**	**14689**	**17132**	**15689**	**24987**	**29849**
As % of total expenditure	*1.1*	*1.5*	*1.8*	*1.9*	*1.9*	*1.9*	*3.0*	*3.3*
Real Total								
(millions of baht, constant 2003 prices, CPI deflator)	**8170**	**12401**	**14677**	**17791**	**29343**	**36062**	**47588**	**43158**

Source: Bureau of the Budget, Bangkok.

total government expenditures (Table 5.8). The increase in the Education Loans Program accounted for more than the total increase. The sum of all other categories of expenditure, taken together, therefore contracted in nominal and real terms, even though cash transfers and the Health Card expenditures increased somewhat. Expenditures on school lunches, housing assistance and job creation contracted sharply. A particularly significant change was the discontinuation of the Job Creation Program, which was essentially for rural roads and which might have helped mitigate some of the worst impacts of the Crisis on the rural areas.

After the 2001 Election of the Thaksin Government

With the election of the new government of the *Thai Rak Thai* Party in early 2001, led by Dr Thaksin Shinawatra, six new programs were initiated, with the stated objective of assisting the poor. Together, these programs were called the Grass Roots Economic and Social Security Program. The six component programs are:

- The Debt Moratorium for Smallholding Farmers program
- The Village Fund program
- The One Tambon One Product program
- The People's Bank program
- The New Entrepreneur Promotion program
- The Health Security for All program (30 baht Health Card scheme)

Table 5.9 shows the budgets of each of these programs since their inception. The second and sixth are by far the most significant. Both involve large fiscal outlays. For example, the Village Fund scheme injects one million baht per village. Since there are around 75 000 villages in Thailand, this amounts to 75 billion baht, or close to US $2 billion. Although it was first thought that the funds would be grants, it was subsequently announced that they would be loans. None of these six programs is explicitly targeted towards poor people. Because the services offered under the 30 baht Health Card are very basic, according to media reports a significant element of self-targeting is almost certainly involved. Many of the non-poor will elect to pay for better treatment than is available with the 30 baht card.

None of these programs is explicitly poverty-targeted, in that it is specifically designed to favor poor over non-poor households. Nevertheless, because of their magnitude they are significant. Data on the allocation of these funds by province or by income category of recipient households are not available and it is therefore not yet possible to analyze their distributional effects. These programs are additional to the regular poverty reduction budget of the government, which is larger and for which disaggregated provincial level data have been obtained for the purposes of this study.

Table 5.9   Grass roots economic and social security project: 2001–2003, budget (millions of baht)

Project	2001	2002	2003	Total	Share (%)
Debt Moratorium for Smallholding Farmers	2371	9325	6718	18414	9.0
One Tambon One Product	–	–	800	800	0.4
Village Fund	66071	8218	–	74286	36.3
Health Security for All	1910	53094	55709	110713	54.2
New Entrepreneur Promotion	–	182	–	182	0.1
Nominal Total (millions of baht, current prices)	**70352**	**70816**	**63227**	**204395**	**100.0**
Real Total (millions of baht, 2003 prices)	**72117**	**72107**	**63227**	**207451**	**100.0**

Note: The People's Bank Project uses the operating budget of the Government Saving Bank, which provided about 10191 million baht of credit in 2001–2002.

Source: National Economic and Social Development Board, Bangkok.

The pre-existing poverty-related programs of the government and new programs which do not fall within the five categories identified within Table 5.9 plus the additional People's Bank category have been reclassified by the Bureau of the Budget for statistical reporting purposes covering the years 2000 onwards. The new data are summarized in Tables 5.10 (number of projects) and 5.11 (budgets of the major categories). Fortunately, in its reclassification of poverty-related expenditures the Bureau of the Budget has provided retrospective data for one year, 2000, for which data are also available under the former classification shown in Table 5.8. Comparing the two data sets for that year (Tables 5.11 and 5.8), it is clear that the new classification is significantly broader, approximately doubling the size of the 'poverty-related' category, so that in 2002 it reached 13 per cent of total government expenditures.

Clearly, the reclassification of government expenditures reflects a definitional change, and an element of arbitrariness necessarily enters these classifications. However, in the one year for which data are available under both classifications, 2000, the definitional change increased 'poverty-related' expenditures by 5.8 per cent of total government spending (from 4.6 to 10.4 per cent). The question is whether the new classification accurately reflects the true size of poverty-targeted expenditures. That is, we wish to know the extent to which these expenditures really are 'poverty-related'. We take up this question below.

Table 5.10 Thailand: poverty reduction expenditures, number of projects – 2000 to 2002

Category	2000	2001	2002
Poor and low-income people	3	3	1
Infrastructure	23	63	18
Agriculture and natural resources	36	32	17
Health and social welfare	28	32	91
Education and training	11	10	32
Others	69	19	26
Total	**125**	**118**	**104**

Source: Bureau of the Budget, Bangkok.

Table 5.11 Thailand: Poverty reduction expenditures, budgets – 2000 to 2002

Category	2000	2001	2002
Poor and low-income people	8.9	9.4	1.0
Infrastructure	25.8	15.9	23.5
Agriculture and natural resources	6.1	8.4	14.7
Health and social welfare	23.5	27.0	44.2
Education and training	3.3	3.3	4.5
Others	20.8	28.8	45.2
Nominal Total (billions of baht, current prices, total above items)	**88.0**	**92.8**	**133.1**
As % of total government expenditure	*10.4*	*10.6*	*13.0*
Real Total (billions of baht, constant 2003 prices, CPI deflator)	**92.0**	**96.9**	**135.5**

Note: Actual expenditures for FY 2003 were not yet available under this classification at the time of writing, but budgeted expenditures were 133.6 billion baht, current prices.

DISTRIBUTIONAL EFFECTS OF GENERAL GOVERNMENT EXPENDITURE

Before turning to the examination of government expenditures directed towards the poor, it is helpful to review the distributional effects of government expenditures as a whole. Studies of the distributional effects of government activity in Thailand have focused heavily on the tax system. Many studies have addressed the question of tax incidence, including Medhi (1976), Pichit (1985), Chalongphob, Pranee and Tienchai (1988) and Chalongphob and Direk (1999). The general conclusion has been that the tax system is roughly distributionally neutral, with the exception of the personal income tax and the corporate income tax, which are progressive, but which represent only a small part of government revenue. Most studies have recommended that the proportion of revenue collected from these two taxes be increased. It has not happened.

Surprisingly little attention has been given to identifying the manner in which government expenditures in Thailand generate differential benefits among households of varying incomes. Only one study appears to have addressed the issue systematically. Chalongphob and Direk (1999) analyze the distributional effects of the major components of government expenditure, including education, public health and basic infrastructure, divided in each case into operational expenditures, investment expenditures and loans. Although the methodology is open to criticism, the strength of the study is that it attempts to do this within a comprehensive framework, which permits direct comparison with its results on the tax system, summarized above.[3]

Table 5.12 summarizes the results on expenditure benefits by taking the estimated expenditure benefits by income decile and computing simple linear regressions which relate the total benefit from public expenditure received by each income group (the dependent variable) to its income (the independent variable), with the results classified by type of expenditure. The final column of the table presents these results in terms of elasticities, evaluated at the mean of the distribution. An elasticity of exactly one would mean that as incomes increase, the percentage increase in total benefit received is the same as the percentage increase in income. An elasticity which is positive but less (greater) than one, means that as income increases the benefit received increases by a proportion smaller (larger) than the proportional increase in income.

The final column, reporting elasticities of expenditure benefit with respect to income, indicates that as incomes increase, the benefit received also increases, but with an elasticity of 0.4. A 10 per cent increase in income corresponds to a 4 per cent increase in the total benefit received from public expenditure, overall. For transportation expenditure, this elasticity is 1.1, indicating that benefits received by richer groups increase even more rapidly with rising incomes than do incomes themselves. For education expenditures the elasticity is 0.32 and significantly different from zero. For health care it is only 0.02 (but still significantly different from zero) and for agriculture it is –0.09 (and again significantly different from zero). In interpreting these results the methodological shortcomings of the study need to be borne in mind.

Table 5.12   Thailand: results of regressions of expenditure benefit against income

Types of expenditures	Intercept	*t*-statistic	Coefficient	*t*-statistic	R-squared	Elasticity
Total	18577.500	34.963	0.048	36.648	0.994	0.412
Education	7850.853	17.514	0.014	12.741	0.953	0.327
Health care	4833.409	63.110	0.000	2.135	0.363	0.022
Agriculture	6706.751	25.157	–0.002	–2.980	0.526	–0.086
Transportation	–813.468	–3.743	0.035	66.222	0.998	1.092

Source: Calculations by authors based on data in Chalongphob and Direk (1999).

The geographical incidence of public expenditures is very relevant when evaluating their distribution and poverty impact. Regional disparities in incomes per capita are very significant, as are the disparities in poverty incidence (see Table 5.3 above). Bangkok, central, and east regions have per capita incomes well above the average for the country, with Bangkok over three times the national average. The other four regions are sharply below the average, with mean incomes per capita in the northeast and north being one tenth and one seventh that of Bangkok, respectively. These data are consistent with findings from other sources that the lowest income and highest poverty levels in Thailand are to be found in the northeast, north and south. Other sources show that these regions are relatively deprived of economic and social infrastructure. Moreover, while the Crisis of 1997–98 had a severe adverse impact on all regions, the poorer regions seem to have suffered the most, in terms of the size of the decline in their real incomes and the increase in their unemployment rates.

The Comptroller General's Office accounting system allows the breakdown of central government expenditure by location of the office from which the expenditures took place; some 85 to 90 per cent of central government expenditure can be broken down in this fashion. The major problem with such a breakdown is that government debt service and the salary payments of many ministries and agencies are distributed centrally, not locally and hence are attributed to the Bangkok region. To circumvent these problems, these items are deleted from the data set used in the analysis that follows.

An important study undertaken by a British consulting firm (Mokoro, 1999) reviewed Thailand's public expenditure system. The Mokoro report deals only with the expenditure system, but covers a wide range of issues relating to expenditures, of which the distributional effect is only one. The Mokoro report covers the role of public expenditure policy in macroeconomic stabilization and national resource allocation and contains detailed descriptions of the expenditure programs in education, health, agriculture and road-building. The study also reviews expenditures related to poverty incidence. The data assembled in the report include a new data set on the distribution of government expenditures by region, of which there are seven, and by province, of which there are 77, including the Bangkok metropolis.

The full distributional effects of government expenditure policy may be thought of at two levels. First, there is the distribution of expenditures between provinces, and second there is the distribution among households within provinces. If the distribution of incomes between provinces was relatively equal, the first of these distributional issues would be of minor significance. In Thailand, this is far from the case. The distributional effects of government expenditure policy among households within a province are unquestionably important, but extremely difficult to study using available data. The distribution among provinces of widely varying incomes is also important, but much more tractable using available information. We shall investigate this issue below, but it must be kept in mind that the question being asked: how the distribution of expenditures per person varies among provinces according to their incomes per person, is at most only one component of the broader question of how the distribution of expenditures varies among households of varying incomes.

If expenditures were allocated in a manner that at a national level favored poorer households relative to richer households, then, in the context where intra-regional inequality is a significant component of total inequality, we would expect to find that poorer provinces would also be favored relative to richer provinces. If, on the other hand, it were found that the allocation of expenditures per person favored richer over poorer provinces, this contrary finding would be partial (but not necessarily conclusive) evidence that, at a national level, the system of expenditures did not favor the poor.

To investigate these issues, average annual expenditures per person from fiscal years 1997 to 1999 (dependent variables) have been regressed on average incomes per person (independent variable). The latter variable is available for 1996. Table 5.13 reports the regression coefficient between these two variables and its *t*-statistic, the latter shown below the estimated coefficient to which it refers.[4]

Table 5.13   Thailand: distribution of government expenditures by province, 1997 to 1999, total, current and capital

		Bangkok included	Bangkok excluded
Part 1:	Independent variable:	Mean provincial incomes per capita, 1996	
Dependent variable			
Total expenditure	coefficient	64.18	43.43
	t-value	3.52	2.27
Current expenditure	coefficient	34.68	17.35
	t-value	2.74	1.34
Capital expenditure	coefficient	29.51	26.08
	t-value	4.64	3.77
Part 2:	Independent variable:	Poverty incidence (headcount) 1996	
Dependent variable			
Total expenditure	coefficient	−40.17	0.61
	t-value	−0.51	0.008
Current expenditure	coefficient	−25.17	4.44
	t-value	−0.47	0.09
Capital expenditure	coefficient	−15.00	−3.83
	t-value	−0.52	−0.14
Part 3:	Independent variable:	Rural population share 1996	
Dependent variable			
Total expenditure	coefficient	−184.86	−58.24
	t-value	−2.72	−0.72
Current expenditure	coefficient	−108.39	−3.27
	t-value	−2.34	−0.06
Capital expenditure	coefficient	−76.47	−54.97
	t-value	−3.11	−1.81

Source: Calculations by authors using data from Mokoro (1999), with supplementary data from the Comptroller General's Office, Bangkok.

The section of Table 5.13 labeled 'Part 2' shows a similar set of calculations, but with poverty incidence at the provincial level used as the independent variable in place of the income variable. In this table, if higher levels of expenditure per person were associated with higher levels of poverty incidence, a positive coefficient would be observed. A negative coefficient would indicate that high levels of poverty incidence in a province were associated with lower levels of expenditure per person. In 'Part 3' the independent variable is the rural population share of the province.

The results indicate that total expenditures per person by province are significantly related to provincial income per person, and the relationship is positive: provinces with higher incomes per person receive higher expenditures per person. The relationship continues to apply when Bangkok is excluded from the data set, but not quite as strongly. It is possible to conduct these analyses separately for different public expenditure categories; education spending, health spending and so forth. The results, in Table 5.14, indicate that both education and health spending by province were positively related to income per person in both 1997 and 1998, but this relationship is statistically significant only for 1997. The data are weakly indicative that adjustments to education spending from fiscal years 1997 to 1998 were negatively related to provincial incomes, but the reverse applied to adjustments to health spending.

When poverty incidence is substituted as the explanatory variable (Part 2 of these tables), the explanatory power declines markedly. Surprisingly, poverty incidence by province, as measured officially, is weakly correlated with provincial income. Similarly, when rural population share is used as the explanatory variable, the explanatory power is only slightly lower than income. Expenditures per person are higher in richer provinces, which implies that they are higher in urban-dominated provinces than rural provinces.

Tables 5.15 and 5.16 convert these results into elasticity format. First, these tables repeat the estimated coefficients from Part 1 of Tables 5.13 and 5.14, respectively. These coefficients, labeled 'estimated coefficient' can be interpreted as the estimated change in expenditure by region resulting from a unit increase in provincial income. The tables then convert this marginal effect into an elasticity, which may be interpreted as the estimated proportional change in expenditure by region resulting from a unit proportional increase in provincial income. These elasticities have the convenient properties described above. An elasticity between zero and unity means that as provincial incomes (per person) increase, provincial expenditures (per person) also increase, but in a smaller proportion.

From Table 5.15, the estimated elasticity of total expenditures with respect to income is approximately 0.4, a similar result to that derived from estimates of the household distribution of expenditures, discussed above. When Bangkok is excluded from the data set the relationship between provincial expenditures and provincial incomes declines, but does not vanish. Finally, Table 5.16 summarizes, in a similar way, the estimated relationship

Table 5.14   *Thailand: distribution of government expenditures by province, 1997 to 1999, sectoral components*

		Bangkok included	Bangkok excluded
Part 1:	Independent variable:	Mean provincial incomes per capita, 1996	
Dependent variable			
Education	coefficient	5.15	1.92
	t-value	1.77	0.63
Health	coefficient	2.34	2.13
	t-value	1.44	1.19
Social services	coefficient	2.45	1.26
	t-value	0.46	0.22
Agriculture	coefficient	14.90	15.91
	t-value	5.04	4.90
Part 2:	Independent variable:	Poverty incidence (headcount) 1996	
Dependent variable			
Education	coefficient	–11.5633	–6.52
	t-value	–0.97	–0.057
Health	coefficient	–3.91	–3.15
	t-value	–0.59	–0.47
Social services	coefficient	23.60	26.21
	t-value	1.12	1.22
Agriculture	coefficient	–7.94	–5.73
	t-value	–0.58	–0.41
Part 3:	Independent variable:	Rural population share 1996	
Dependent variable			
Education	coefficient	–25.47	–10.43
	t-value	–2.46	–0.83
Health	coefficient	–10.47	–11.50
	t-value	–1.80	–1.59
Social services	coefficient	5.40	19.50
	t-value	0.28	0.82
Agriculture	coefficient	2.42	16.55
	t-value	0.19	1.09

Source: Calculations by authors using data from Mokoro (1999), with supplementary data from the Comptroller General's Office, Bangkok.

Poverty targeting in Asia

Table 5.15   *Thailand: government expenditures by province, 1997 to 1999, estimated coefficients and elasticities with respect to provincial incomes*

	Estimated coefficient	
	Bangkok included	Bangkok excluded
Total expenditure	64.18	43.43
Current	34.68	17.35
Capital	29.51	26.08
	Implied elasticity	
	Bangkok included	Bangkok excluded
Total expenditure	0.421	0.287
Current	0.386	0.195
Capital	0.471	0.420

Source: Calculated by authors from results in Table 5.13 and data on which they are based.

Table 5.16   *Thailand: government expenditures by province, 1997 to 1999, sectoral components; estimated coefficients and elasticities with respect to provincial incomes*

	Estimated coefficient	
	Bangkok included	Bangkok excluded
Education	5.15	1.92
Health	2.34	2.13
Social	2.45	1.26
Agriculture	14.90	15.91
	Implied elasticity	
	Bangkok included	Bangkok excluded
Education	0.236	0.087
Health	0.166	0.146
Social	0.078	0.038
Agriculture	1.598	1.677

Source: Calculated by authors from results in Table 5.14 and data on which they are based.

between the provincial expenditures by sector and provincial incomes. The estimated elasticities are all positive and between zero and unity for all sectors except agriculture. For education, the estimated elasticities are substantially higher when Bangkok is included in the data set, indicating that educational expenditures favor Bangkok heavily, but that among provinces outside Bangkok, richer provinces are not significantly favored.

In the case of health expenditures, there is a positive and significant relationship between per capita expenditures and incomes whether Bangkok is included in the data or not. Social services expenditures are positively related to incomes, but this relationship is not statistically significant. What these results do indicate, however, is that the claim that social services expenditures favor poorer provinces is unsupported by these data.

Agricultural expenditures are the most strongly related to provincial incomes. Agricultural expenditures apparently favor richer provinces and this relationship is the strongest (estimated elasticity over one) of all of the forms of expenditure covered by the data. This surprising result is unchanged by the removal of Bangkok from the data set. While it is true that Thailand's rural populations tend to be the poorest, Table 5.14 shows that agricultural expenditures per person are not significantly related to the rural population share.

These results are, in general, strikingly supportive of the results reported by Chalongphob and Direk (1999) and summarized in Table 5.12. The strong exception relates to agriculture. Chalongphob and Direk's estimates imply a negative relationship with household incomes. This could be reconciled with the strongly positive relationship between provincial expenditure and provincial income, shown in Table 5.13, only if it were supposed that agricultural expenditures within provinces were allocated in a manner which very strongly favored lower income groups. This seems improbable. Future research may illuminate this matter further.

In summary, in so far as total expenditures, education spending and health spending are concerned, the data suggest that the provinces with higher incomes per person receive higher levels of expenditure per person, with elasticities between zero and one. This is even more true of spending on agriculture, where the elasticity is between one and two.

DISTRIBUTIONAL EFFECTS OF GOVERNMENT POVERTY-RELATED EXPENDITURE

Having considered the allocation of general categories of government expenditure we now focus on our main concern: the impact of those programs targeted at the poor. Given a lack of information on intra-provincial allocations our focus is on the allocation between provinces and the extent to which poorer provinces are favored or not. In particular, we ask whether the level of expenditure per person in a given province is related to:

(a) the level of poverty incidence (P) in that province;
(b) the level of household income per household member (Y) in that province;
(c) the size of the rural population relative to the size of the total population (n_R) in that province; and
(d) the overall size of the province, as measured by its total population (N).

The statistical analysis which follows is based on the provincial allocation of the cumulative total of expenditures for the years 2000 to 2002, as summarized in Table 5.11 above. Four models are estimated:

$$E_j^i = \alpha_0^i + \alpha_1^i \ln P_j + \alpha_2 \ln N_j \tag{1}$$

$$E_j^i = \alpha_0^i + \alpha_1^i \ln Y_j + \alpha_2^i \ln N_j \tag{2}$$

$$E_j^i = \alpha_0^i + \alpha_1^i \ln P_j + \alpha_2^i \ln N_j + \alpha_3^i n_j^R \tag{3}$$

$$E_j^i = \alpha_0^i + \alpha_1^i \ln Y_j + \alpha_2^i \ln N_j + \alpha_3^i n_j^R \tag{4}$$

where E_j^i denotes expenditure per person of type i in province j, Y_j denotes average income per person in province j in the year 2000, P_j denotes the official estimate of poverty incidence (percentage of the population with incomes per head below the official poverty line) in province j in the year 2000, N_j denotes total population of province j in the year 2000, and n_j^R denotes the share of the population of province j residing in rural areas in the year 2000.

Models 3 and 4 were discarded because the rural share of the total provincial population (n_j^R) was strongly correlated with poverty incidence at the provincial level. As noted above, poverty in Thailand is a strongly rural phenomenon. The inclusion of both poverty incidence and rural population share thus introduces strong multicollinearity into the regressions. The subsequent discussion will therefore focus on models 1 and 2, which exclude the variable n_j^R.

The regression results are summarized in Tables 5.17 to 5.23. First, Table 5.17 indicates that the total 'poverty-related' budget is positively related to poverty incidence and negatively related to income per person – poorer provinces receive larger budgets per person, but that these statistical relationships are insignificant. The significant explanatory variable is the size of the province. Large provinces receive smaller allocations per person. In terms of the allocation of 'poverty-related' expenditures, it pays to be small. It makes little difference whether the province is rich or poor.

Tables 5.18 to 5.23 now perform a similar exercise for each of the six components of 'poverty related' expenditures summarized in Table 5.11.

- Poor and low-income people
- Infrastructure
- Agriculture and natural resources
- Health and social welfare
- Education and training
- Others

The coefficient on poverty is positive in four of the six components and negative in two (Agriculture and natural resources, and Health and social welfare) but the relationships are far from being statistically significant. Poverty incidence has little to do with the allocation of these expenditures across provinces. Income per capita similarly has little relationship to the allocation of expenditures in all categories except 'Poor and low-income people', where the expected negative coefficient is observed. For this category at least, corresponding to just under 6 per cent of the total 'poverty-related' expenditures reported in Table 5.11, expenditures are seemingly poverty targeted.[5]

The Poor and Low-income People Program had three component categories in 2000. These were:

- Assistance to farmers and the poor
- Health care loan for low-income people
- Health care for low-income people

The first category is assistance to farmers – supposedly poor farmers – who rent land. In some documents this category is called 'Agricultural land rent control for farmer and assistance to farmer and the poor'. Expenditure in this sub-category is positively related to provincial income per capita in each year 2000 to 2002, but the relationship is not statistically significant in any one of these years. The second category is loans for health care. It was negatively related to income per person in 2000 and 2001 (coefficients marginally insignificant at the 90 per cent level), but was discontinued in 2002. The third category is grants for health care and it was negatively and significantly related to income per person in 2000 and 2001 (at the 95 per cent level), but it was also discontinued in 2002. That is, there appears to have been a lessening of the poverty-targeting feature of these expenditures in 2002.

Table 5.17   *Thailand: regression results on relationship between poverty-related expenditure, poverty and income: total budget allocation*

Intercept	$\ln P$	$\ln N$	R^2
16372.910	95.008	−929.764	0.242
(6.050*)	(0.871)	(−4.623*)	
Intercept	$\ln Y$	$\ln N$	R^2
18215.220	−106.248	−989.278	0.256
(4.904*)	(−0.316)	(−4.997*)	

Note: *t* values are in brackets and * indicates statistically significant at 95 per cent level.

Source: Authors' calculations using data from Bureau of the Budget, Bangkok.

Table 5.18   *Thailand: regression results on relationship between poverty-related expenditure, poverty and income: poor and low-income people program*

Intercept	$\ln P$	$\ln N$	R^2
277.368	11.868	−0.860	0.025
(1.249)	(1.325)	(−0.052)	
Intercept	$\ln Y$	$\ln N$	R^2
797.152	−61.206	−1.789	0.066
(2.681*)	(−2.274*)	(−0.113)	

Note: *t* values are in brackets and * indicates statistically significant at 95 per cent level.

Source: Authors' calculations, using data from Bureau of the Budget, Bangkok.

Table 5.19   *Thailand: regression results on relationship between poverty-related expenditure, poverty and income: infrastructure program*

Intercept	$\ln P$	$\ln N$	R^2
4621.135	48.768	−266.062	0.101
(3.397*)	(0.889)	(−2.632*)	
Intercept	$\ln Y$	$\ln N$	R^2
5911.286	−167.805	−256.272	0.098
(3.200*)	(−1.004)	(−2.603*)	

Note: *t* values are in brackets and * indicates statistically significant at 95 per cent level.

Source: Authors' calculations, using data from Bureau of the Budget, Bangkok.

Table 5.20 Thailand: regression results on relationship between poverty-related expenditure, poverty and income: agriculture and natural resources program

Intercept	ln$P$	ln$N$	R^2
748.956	−7.558	−32.593	0.034
(2.503*)	(−0.626)	(−1.466)	
Intercept	ln$Y$	ln$N$	R^2
511.407	27.167	−32.520	0.036
(1.243)	−0.730	(−1.483)	

Note: *t* values are in brackets and * indicates statistically significant at 95 per cent level.

Source: Authors' calculations, using data from Bureau of the Budget, Bangkok.

Table 5.21 Thailand: regression results on relationship between poverty-related expenditure, poverty and income: health and social welfare program

Intercept	ln$P$	ln$N$	R^2
1476.924	−3.503	−64.324	0.022
(2.121*)	(−0.125)	(−1.243)	
Intercept	ln$Y$	ln$N$	R^2
1071.784	62.793	−71.742	0.034
(1.141)	(0.739)	(−1.433)	

Note: *t* values are in brackets and * indicates statistically significant at 95 per cent level.

Source: Authors' calculations, using data from Bureau of the Budget, Bangkok.

Table 5.22 Thailand: regression results on relationship between poverty-related expenditure, poverty and income: education and training program

Intercept	ln$P$	ln$N$	R^2
667.284	13.281	−38.145	0.038
(1.795)	(0.886)	(−1.381)	
Intercept	ln$Y$	ln$N$	R^2
1010.139	−33.265	−41.814	0.040
(2.020*)	(−0.735)	(−1.569)	

Note: *t* values are in brackets and * indicates statistically significant at 95 per cent level.

Source: Authors' calculations, using data from Bureau of the Budget, Bangkok.

Table 5.23   *Thailand: regression results on relationship between poverty-*
             related expenditure, poverty and income: other programs

Intercept	ln$P$	ln$N$	R^2
8581.245	32.150	−527.780	0.485
(9.719*)	(0.903)	(−8.043*)	
Intercept	ln$Y$	ln$N$	R^2
8913.450	66.067	−585.141	0.465
(6.455*)	(0.529)	(−7.950*)	

Note: *t* values are in brackets and * indicates statistically significant at 95 per cent level.
Source: Authors' calculations, using data from Bureau of the Budget, Bangkok.

To test this proposition, data are assembled in Table 5.24 based on the results of regression analyses for all project components of the expenditures summarized in Tables 5.10 and 5.11. This was done separately for each year 2000, 2001 and 2002. The regressions performed were the same as Model 2 above, except that the population size variable (N_j) was deleted. For each of these years, the projects were then classified into three categories:

- *Pro-poor*, meaning that expenditure was negatively related to income per person, significant at 90 per cent level or better.
- *Neutral*, meaning that expenditure was not related to income per person, at 90 per cent level or better.
- *Pro-rich*, meaning that expenditure was positively related to income per person, significant at 90 per cent level or better.[6]

The expenditures corresponding to each project, so classified, were then added and the results are summarized in Table 5.24.

Table 5.24   *Thailand: poverty reduction expenditures classified by relationship*
             to income per person, 2000 to 2002

Type of Project	2000	2001	2002
Pro–poor (significant 90%)	25 664.33	38 245.60	20 964.64
Neutral (insignificant)	21 707.07	17 349.39	15 432.76
Pro–rich (significant 90%)	26 365.57	24 692.97	41 127.00
Total	**73 736.97**	**80 287.96**	**77 524.40**

Source: Authors' calculations, using data from Bureau of the Budget, Bangkok.

In 2000 these three categories were of similar size. The net effect of the 'poverty-related' expenditures was approximately neutral between poor and non-poor provinces. However, the expenditures corresponding to the *pro-poor* and *neutral* categories have contracted over the three years, while those corresponding to the *pro-rich* category have expanded, especially in 2002. By 2002 the 'poverty-related' expenditures were, on balance, positively related to provincial incomes per person – richer provinces received greater benefits per person.

CONCLUSIONS

Thailand's outstanding record of poverty reduction is mainly attributable to the effects of economic growth rather than the government's efforts to assist the poor. The latter are small in magnitude and are not well targeted towards the poor. According to official data, in recent years expenditures directed at assisting the poor have become a substantially more important component of total government spending. The evidence presented here, however, suggests that most of these expenditures are not genuinely focused on the poor. Indeed, the poverty-targeted component of government expenditures seems to have declined rather than increased.

Based on data on the provincial allocation of expenditures, non-poor provinces currently receive somewhat higher levels of 'poverty-related' expenditure per person than poor provinces. Thailand's poor benefit from the government's 'poverty-related' expenditures, but not significantly more than they do from other forms of government expenditures, which are not intended to be poverty-targeted. Government expenditures in the poverty-related categories are not well targeted towards the poor.

More systematic efforts to monitor the distributional effects of these poverty-targeted expenditures is a first step towards a more effective set of policies. A good instrument for this would be an enhanced form of the Socio-Economic Survey, already conducted every two years by the National Statistical Office. In its present form, the survey does not record the benefits received by households from public expenditures. The second step will then be the design of more effective targeting mechanisms than those currently in place.

It must be emphasized that these conclusions are based primarily upon one component of the overall distribution of government expenditures: their allocation between provinces. Because of limitations in the available data, we have not studied the allocation of expenditures within provinces. If these data were available, there is a possibility that the strong conclusions stated above would require amendment.

NOTES

1. The data shown are identical to the most recent data from the National Economic and Social Development Board (NESDB) for the years 1988 to 1998. The data for the earlier years have been spliced together with this series from published sources, so that the resulting series matches the NESDB series for the year 1988. The exception is that the published data for municipal areas and sanitary districts have been aggregated to an 'urban' category using their respective population shares in the total for urban areas (the sum of the two) as weights. The data from 1962 to 1988 are summarized in Medhi (1993).
2. One *rai* is 0.4047 acres or 0.16 hectares. The range 5 to 19 *rai* thus corresponds to 2.02 to 7.69 acres, or 0.77 to 3.04 hectares.
3. For example, the study defines benefits in terms of the costs of activities making no allowance for differences in quality of delivery.
4. In each case, a linear equation was estimated, including an intercept term, which is not reported in the table.
5. The negative relationship between size of province and expenditure per person, observed for the total budget allocation, is concentrated in the 'Infrastructure' and 'Others' categories.
6. Some authors use the term 'anti-poor' to refer to expenditures that favor the rich. This term is avoided here because it implies that the poor are actually harmed by these expenditures and this is not necessarily true, except in a relative sense, compared with the rich. The poor are not necessarily harmed in absolute terms by the existence of these programs unless the absolute benefit they receive from these expenditures is smaller than the additional tax revenues they must pay to finance them.

REFERENCES

Chalongphob Sussangkarn and Direk Patmasitiwat (1999), 'Characteristics of the distribution of the Tax Burden and Expenditure Benefits: Thailand', Thailand Development Research Institute, Bangkok, preliminary report submitted to Fiscal Policy Office, Ministry of Finance, revised version, December (in Thai).

Chalongphob Sussangkarn, Pranee Tinakorn and Tienchai Chongpeerapien (1988), 'The tax structure in Thailand and its distributional implications', Thailand Development Research Institute, Bangkok, October.

Mehdi Krongkaew (1976), 'Tax and revenue burden and household income distribution, 1969', in N. Akrasanee and R. Thanapornpun (eds) *Love Thailand*, *(Rak Thai)* vol. 2, (in Thai) , Bangkok: Social Science Association of Thailand.

Mehdi Krongkaew (1993), 'Poverty and inequality', in Peter G. Warr (ed.), *The Thai Economy in Transition*, Cambridge: Cambridge University Press.

Mokoro Ltd (1999), 'Thailand: public expenditure review, 2 vols', Oxford, England, report prepared for the Bureau of the Budget, Government of Thailand, February.

Pichit Likitkijsomboon (1985), 'Taxation and income distribution in Thailand: a case study for 1981', MA Thesis, Faculty of Economics, Thammasat University, Bangkok.

6. Poverty targeting in the Philippines

Arsenio Balisacan and Rosemarie Edillon

INTRODUCTION

Economic growth has been the traditional prescription for poverty reduction in developing countries. Indeed, one regularity in cross-country studies is that the incomes of the poor move almost one-for-one with overall economic growth (Dollar and Kraay, 2001; Bhalla, 2002). Yet a closer examination of recent individual country experiences suggests that while growth is good for the poor (as well as the non-poor), it is often not good enough, suggesting that other factors apart from growth matter as well. That is, an effective program for poverty reduction has also to include mechanisms for directly improving the institutional and economic environment facing the poor so that they are able to participate more actively in the growth process and its consequent benefits.[1] Indeed, addressing current poverty has the added benefit of raising subsequent growth rates, that is moving the country to a higher growth path.

For the Philippines, the absence of a comparatively high and enduring economic growth has been the single biggest constraint to the pace of poverty reduction (Balisacan, 2003). But even during periods when growth was considerable, the incremental response of the incomes of the poor to overall income changes was quite muted compared with the country's neighbors, especially Indonesia and Vietnam. For instance, the elasticity of the income of the poor – defined to be those in the bottom 20 per cent of the population – with respect to overall average income is 0.54 for the Philippines (Balisacan and Pernia, 2003), while the comparable figures for Indonesia (Balisacan et al., 2003a) and Vietnam (Balisacan et al., 2003b) are 0.72 and 1.37, respectively.

It is not, of course, surprising to find considerable differences in the response of households to economic growth, both within and across countries. This is because socio-economic conditions and circumstances of households in society vary considerably. There are usually some groups who are unable to benefit – either partially or fully – during episodes of growth, or who in fact may be hurt by public decisions chosen to move the economy to a higher growth path. These groups may include: (i) individuals who do not have the assets, particularly skills, necessary to take advantage of opportunities offered by growth; (ii) households located in geographic areas bypassed by growth, that is geographic poverty traps; (iii) households whose entitlements are shrunk by public actions chosen to bring the economy to a higher growth path; and (iv) households falling into poverty traps owing to the reinforcing effects of adverse shocks and imperfect capital markets, the latter leading to a failure to smooth consumption.

Policy and institutional responses to the poverty problem thus require more than growth-mediated long-run poverty reduction initiatives. They should involve direct intervention to meet short-run poverty reduction objectives, including avoidance of transient poverty, as well as provision of the conditions for some groups to escape poverty traps.

While the roots of the Philippines' economic malaise during the past 30 years have been well articulated (that is weak governance, low investment in basic infrastructure, political and macroeconomic instability, and a highly unequal distribution of productive assets such as land), that is not quite the case for programs intended to efficiently deliver assistance to the poor, especially in the event of adverse shocks such as during a macroeconomic crisis or natural calamities. In short, how must programs intended for the poor be designed so as to achieve the desired objective? What lessons have been gleaned from recent experience to serve as an input to this design?

Efficiency in the use of funds for poverty reduction underlies the principle of targeting, in which benefits are channeled to the high priority group that a program aims to serve. Targeting requires the identification of the poor as distinct from the non-poor, as well as the monitoring of program benefit flows to intended beneficiaries. As such, it is a potentially costly activity, both in terms of time and administrative outlay.

This chapter examines the Philippines' recent experiences in poverty reduction efforts. It begins with an overview of the country's poverty profile. A brief review of government spending on sectors strongly linked to poverty is then provided. It then discusses the features of poverty targeting in the Philippines and some simulation results illustrating the impacts of different spending patterns on growth and poverty.

POVERTY IN THE PHILIPPINES – AN OVERVIEW

The past quarter century has seen the Philippines lagging behind most of the major East Asian countries in practically all aspects of economic and social development. The chapters in Balisacan and Hill (2003) discuss in detail broad development issues and concerns in the Philippines. The country's average economic growth was only slightly higher than its population growth, which was, and continues to be, comparatively high by most Asian standards. Further blunting the impact on poverty of whatever growth that occurred has been its persistently high level of economic inequality. Indeed, not a few observers characterize the country's social structure, especially with reference to land distribution, as a largely Latin American rather than an East Asian feature (see, for example, Hayami, 2001 and Ranis and Stewart, 1993). The co-existence of huge plantations and industrial enclaves owned by a few families and of several million semi-subsistence small farmers and vast colonies of urban poor depicts a highly inequitable Latin American-like society that is quite uncommon elsewhere in East Asia.

An almost regular pattern of boom and bust has characterized the Philippine economy during the period from 1960 to 2002 (see Figure 6.1). Bust and stagnation soon followed each episode of boom, fueled largely by massive foreign borrowing and capital-intensive import-substituting industrialization. The period also saw heavy government regulation of the market economy, as well as political instability, natural disasters, and major shocks in global trade and finance. However, notwithstanding the interruption in the late-1990s owing to the combined impact of the Asian economic crisis and the El Niño phenomenon, the growth episodes since the second half of the 1980s appear to have a fundamentally different character from previous ones. Economic growth, albeit meager compared with that in any of the country's South East Asian neighbors, has taken place in an environment of political stability, economic deregulation and institutional reform. While domestic political squabbling and policy coordination problems persisted, it could not be denied that the Philippines at the beginning of the new millennium was closer to a market economy than it had ever been in the past. One could ask: how have the poor benefited from the growth process?

Table 6.1 provides estimates of three dimensions of poverty – incidence, depth and severity – from 1985 to 2000.[2] All the poverty indices show significant reductions during periods of relatively rapid growth of mean expenditure (1985–88 and 1994–97). The highest three-year poverty reduction was achieved during the 'economic boom' of 1994–97, when real per capita expenditure rose by 21 per cent. But poverty also fell when the growth of mean expenditure was negative (1991–94). Surprisingly too poverty depth and severity increased even when the growth of mean expenditure was positive (1988–91), though at a comparatively low rate. It thus appears that the observed poverty changes are related to the growth (and stagnation) of real mean consumption, while obviously also influenced by other factors. Indeed, as Table 6.1 indicates, another 'proximate' cause for poverty changes may well be the evolution in expenditure distribution.

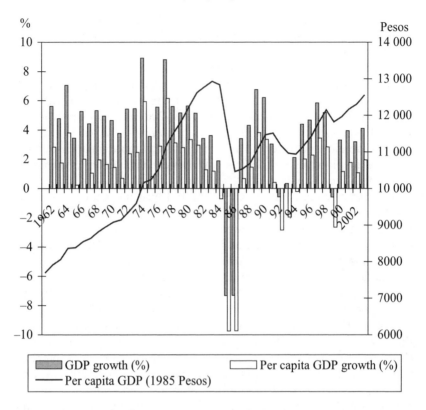

Figure 6.1   Growth of Gross Domestic Product, 1960–2002

After falling slightly to 0.40 in 1988 from 0.41 in 1985, the expenditure Gini coefficient rose to 0.43 in 1991. It fell back to its 1988 level in 1994, only to rise to 0.43 in 1997 and 0.45 in 2000. The same pattern emerged for two other simple inequality indicators – the share of the richest 10 per cent and poorest 20 per cent of the population in total expenditures. While these changes are not spectacular, they had a considerable impact on aggregate poverty, as shown in Balisacan (2003).

The evolution of poverty, inequality and average welfare (given by average per capita expenditure) in the 1980s and 1990s may well be related also to movements in price levels. Inflation averaged 25 per cent in 1983–85. The rate dropped from 18 per cent in 1985 to 9 per cent in 1988, possibly benefiting the majority of the poor, who tended to be fixed-income earners or self-employed workers in rural areas. Inflation surged once more to an average of 15 per cent per year at the end of the decade. This was accompanied by an increase in inequality. Inflation decelerated to only 7.9 per cent per year during 1992–94, 7.7 per cent during 1995–97, and 6.9 per cent during 1998–2000. As shown elsewhere (Balisacan, 1995), high inflation during a period of low growth increases aggregate poverty. Particularly vulnerable to commodity (particularly food) price increases are the numerically large small-scale agricultural producers and landless workers who are net buyers of food.

In an earlier study (Balisacan, 2003), it was shown that the national poverty profile was quite robust for periods of relatively high mean consumption growth, such as for 1985–88, 1994–97, and 1997–2000, regardless of the choice of poverty indicator or of aggregation procedure. The same thing, however, cannot be said for periods of low or negative mean consumption growth. Moreover, the same study showed that for the entire 1985–2000 period, the increase in inequality reduced the impact of growth on poverty, but this effect was proportionately small relative to the reduction of poverty attributable to consumption growth. It is thus the changes in real mean consumption, rather than changes in its distribution, that have mainly contributed to the observed changes in poverty in recent years. This result runs counter to the common claim in policy dialogue in the Philippines that recent episodes of growth have not benefited the poor.

Table 6.1   Poverty and inequality, 1985–2000

	1985	1988	1991	1994	1997	2000
Average per capita expenditure[1] (at 1997 prices)	17197	18926	20049	19600	23694	22865
Dimension of poverty						
Incidence[a] (%)	40.9	34.4	34.3	32.1	25.0	27.5
Depth[b] (%)	13.2	10.1	10.6	8.7	6.4	7.2
Severity[c] (%)	5.8	4.2	4.5	3.4	2.3	2.7
Inequality						
Gini	0.412	0.400	0.428	0.397	0.427	0.450
Share of richest 10%	26.2	24.2	26.9	24.9	28.4	28.2
Share of poorest 20%	8.6	9.1	8.4	9.7	8.8	8.8

Notes:
[1] Adjusted for provincial cost-of-living differences. Reference province is Metro Manila.
[a] Incidence is the headcount ratio.
[b] Depth is the poverty gap.
[c] Severity is the squared poverty gap.

Source: Balisacan (2003), based on Family Income and Expenditure Survey data.

Table 6.2 shows poverty and inequality estimates for both the urban and the rural sector.[3] A high mean consumption disparity between urban and rural areas is apparent. Mean consumption in urban areas was nearly twice that in rural areas, rising significantly during the high-growth periods of 1985–88 and 1994–97 for both sectors. Correspondingly, all poverty indices declined significantly during both periods. The direction of inequality for both sectors also generally followed the overall pattern reported in Table 6.1. Clearly, poverty reduction during high-growth periods was quite broadly based – that is, taking place in both urban and rural areas.

Table 6.2   Poverty and inequality in urban and rural areas, 1985–2000 (%)[a]

	1985	1988	1991	1994	1997	2000
Urban						
Incidence	21.7	16.0	20.1	18.6	11.9	13.2
Depth	5.9	3.8	5.7	4.4	2.6	3.0
Gini	0.41	0.39	0.42	0.39	0.43	0.41
Share of richest 10%	26.9	24.5	28.0	25.7	31.1	30.7
Share of poorest 20%	7.5	8.0	7.0	8.2	6.7	7.0
Rural						
Incidence	53.1	45.7	48.6	45.4	36.9	41.3
Depth	17.8	14.0	15.6	13.0	9.8	11.3
Gini	0.35	0.35	0.36	0.34	0.35	0.41
Share of richest 10%	23.2	23.1	23.9	23.1	24.3	24.3
Share of poorest 20%	9.6	9.7	9.8	10.7	10.3	10.7

Note: [a] Poverty and inequality estimates are based on per capita consumption expenditure adjusted for provincial cost-of-living differences. Poverty lines employed to calculate poverty indices are fixed in terms of living standards.

Source: Balisacan (2003).

Table 6.3 provides poverty estimates across regions of the country from 1985 to 2000, as well as the importance of each region to national poverty. While considerable variation exists, Metro Manila consistently had the lowest poverty, and Bicol, Western Mindanao and the Visayas the highest. In 2000, poverty incidence in Bicol was nine times higher than in Metro Manila. Some significant re-rankings also occurred, such as Central Mindanao becoming the fourth poorest region in 2000 when it was only the ninth poorest in 1985. Even more significant is the differential evolution of poverty over time. In two regions, Central and Western Mindanao, poverty – in all three dimensions – was higher in 2000 than in 1985. Toward the close of the 1990s, these two regions, particularly Western Mindanao, were at the center of violent confrontations between the military and armed dissidents.

Not a few observers contend that income disparity between urban and rural areas, across regions and between economic sectors, is at the core of the poverty problem. Mean income in urban areas was at least twice that in rural areas during the 1980s and 1990s. Metro Manila, which accounted for about 14 per cent of the population, had the highest mean income. In 2000, its mean income was more than twice the national average or about three to four times the mean income for Bicol and Eastern Visayas. Except for Bicol and Cagayan, mean income for the Luzon regions was higher than for most of the regions in Visayas and Mindanao.

In the 1990s, average income in agriculture, where the large majority of the poor are located and where about 40 per cent of the labor force are employed, was much less than one-half of those in virtually all other sectors (except construction). It is thus claimed that the key to winning the war against poverty is to focus development priorities on agriculture, so as to raise incomes in that sector vis-à-vis those in other sectors of the economy.

If indeed spatial and sectoral income disparities are at the core of the poverty problem in the Philippines, then policy reforms aimed at reducing these disparities have to be central elements of the country's poverty reduction program. This may also promote efficiency goals: important dynamic externalities can arise from targeting by area or according to sector-specific characteristics (Bardhan, 1996; Ravallion and Jalan, 1996). Investment in physical infrastructure (such as roads, communications and irrigation) in backward areas, or in the rural sector in general, may improve the productivity of private investment, influence fertility through its effect on labor allocation and educational investment decisions, promote the development of intangible 'social capital' (in the form of social networks, peer group effects, role models, and so on), and mitigate erosion in the quality of life in urban areas through its effect on rural–urban migration decisions.

However, if disparity in incomes and human achievement within each of the regions or areas of the country were itself the major problem, a different approach to poverty reduction would have to be found. It is possible, for example, that systematic differences in levels of human capital between low- and high-income groups within a geographic area translate into considerable differences in earning opportunities between these groups within each area. In this case, the policy prescription to reduce overall income inequality and poverty would have to involve expanding the access of low-income groups to basic social services, technology and infrastructure, regardless of their location.

Table 6.3   Poverty incidence by region, 1985–2000 (%)[a]

	1985	1988	1991	1994	1997	2000	Contribution to total poverty, 2000
National Capital	11.6	9.5	5.9	5.6	3.5	5.5	2.9
Ilocos	33.1	27.6	27.3	26.5	21.0	19.4	4.6
Cagayan Valley	44.9	39.7	42.2	39.8	29.5	29.7	4.4
C. Luzon	19.1	15.3	15.4	24.3	13.2	16.1	5.8
S. Luzon	35.4	31.7	22.9	28.6	19.6	19.5	10.3
Bicol	67.0	60.9	62.2	50.2	45.6	53.3	14.4
W. Visayas	49.4	34.4	31.6	34.5	21.8	28.1	8.1
C. Visayas	66.5	55.2	53.2	42.8	35.2	39.4	10.2
E. Visayas	59.3	53.7	54.4	51.5	50.6	46.8	8.0
W. Mindanao	52.5	43.8	44.0	53.7	44.6	56.0	10.5
N. Mindanao	52.6	41.4	54.2	37.9	29.9	30.1	6.2
S. Mindanao	51.8	43.7	53.9	30.7	27.8	25.8	7.0
C. Mindanao	35.8	30.1	42.3	39.8	32.9	39.9	7.6

Note: [a] The regional classification of provinces and cities is kept fixed to that existing in 1985.

Source: Balisacan (2003).

A parametric procedure, such as that suggested in Fields (2002), might be useful for exploring systematically the relative contribution of location- and household-specific attributes to the observed variation in household income. Specifically, one can estimate a standard set of income-generating functions and use the parameter estimates to calculate the relative contribution of each factor to differences in household income. Table 6.4 summarizes the results of such an exercise for the six survey data covering the 1985–2000 period, giving the proportions in the total variance of (log) income accounted for by location- and household-specific attributes. Together all variables included in the regression explain 55–58 per cent of the variance of log-incomes for the six survey years (Balisacan and Piza, 2003).

Household composition and the household head's attributes, most especially educational attainment, accounted for one-third of the total variance of (the log of) income. Educational attainment contributed about a fifth of the observed variation in income. After controlling for the effects of other factors, location (regional and urban location) contributed only about 15 per cent of the observed variation in income. Economic attributes (sector of employment and class of worker) represented only a small amount, roughly 10 per cent, of the total variance. This suggests that, by and large, it is the differences in income levels within a sector or location, rather than differences in mean income levels between sectors or locations, that account for a significant proportion of the variation in household income nationally, and this weakens the case for the type of location targeting discussed below. This conclusion holds for each of the survey years.

Table 6.4   Relative contribution of factor in total variance of (log) income (%)

	1985	1988	1991	1994	1997	2000
Household attributes	34.4	33.6	33.1	33.4	34.8	33.6
Family size	10.2	9.5	9.5	9.5	8.9	8.3
Household type	1.5	1.1	1.3	1.2	1.3	1.5
Child dependency ratio	1.3	1.5	1.5	1.8	1.6	1.4
Employment ratio	−0.3	0.0	0.0	0.2	0.2	0.0
Spouse employed	0.2	0.4	0.5	0.5	0.8	0.6
Experience	0.5	0.7	0.6	0.3	0.5	0.4
Gender	0.0	0.1	0.1	0.1	0.1	0.1
Marital status	0.6	0.8	0.7	0.5	0.6	0.7
Education	20.4	19.5	18.9	19.3	20.8	20.6
Economic sector	5.4	7.6	8.7	9.6	9.9	10.1
Class of worker	4.1	4.5	5.4	5.5	6.2	5.4
Sector of employment	1.3	3.1	3.3	4.1	3.7	4.7
Location	15.8	14.1	15.8	15.5	13.1	14.3
Urban	3.1	3.6	2.7	2.8	3.9	4.4
Region	12.7	10.5	13.1	12.7	9.2	9.9
Residual	44.4	44.7	42.4	41.5	42.2	42.0
Total	100.0	100.0	100.0	100.0	100.0	100.0

Source: Estimates of income-generating functions based on unit record data from the Family Income and Expenditures Survey (various years) of the National Statistics Office; see Balisacan and Piza (2003).

TARGETING IN THE PHILIPPINES

The literature distinguishes between two types of targeting – broad and narrow targeting. Broad targeting specifies the intervention. The effectiveness of the strategy lies in the comparative propensity of the poor to utilize the intervention more intensively than the non-poor. Meanwhile, narrow targeting stipulates inclusion and exclusion criteria to distinguish qualified beneficiaries (the poor) from the non-beneficiaries (the non-poor). Broad targeting may probably result in substantial leakages, but narrow targeting may entail significant administrative costs. In practice, the design of anti-poverty projects employs both types of targeting.

Poverty reduction has always been a central element of the development effort of the government, as articulated in its development plans and official policy statements. By and large, only the emphasis and the strategy to achieve these goals have changed over recent decades.

The development program of the Aquino administration (1986–92) primarily stressed the alleviation of poverty, the generation of more productive employment opportunities, and the promotion of equity and social justice. Unlike previous programs, which had emphasized import-substituting development, the new program called for the removal of policy biases against agriculture and the rural sector, with agrarian reform serving as the program's key focus. The centerpiece of the administration's poverty reduction strategy was the *Tulong sa Tao* program, of which provision of subsidized credit was a key element.

The Ramos administration (1992–98) focused on accelerating the pace of economic growth, by building the international competitiveness of domestic industries, reforming regulation in services and industry, and investing in basic infrastructure. It also had a Social Reform Agenda for achieving its human development targets. A package of government interventions organized around 'flagship programs' for the country's 20 poorest provinces, the Social Reform Agenda is considered to be the first effort of the Philippine public administrative system to organize the various sectors of government toward securing so-called minimum basic needs before attending to other demands of priority sectors._

The Comprehensive and Integrated Delivery of Social Services (CIDSS) was the flagship anti-poverty project of the Ramos administration. The basic strategy of the CIDSS was to 'break down the culture of poverty'. It was based on the concept of empowerment. Previous programs were ineffective either due to underutilization of funds, or if utilization was high, impacts were not sustained, and the thinking was that this was because they did not coincide with the needs of the target beneficiaries, who had no sense of ownership of the anti-poverty projects involved. Under the CIDSS, beneficiary communities were organized with the help of full-time community workers, and were taught to identify their problems, prepare a work program, mobilize additional funding resources as necessary and implement projects themselves. Civil society groups were also included in all the project stages.

The CIDSS employed a minimum basic needs approach in project prioritization. The approach used a set of 33 indicators, spanning the different basic needs for survival (food and nutrition, health, water and sanitation and clothing), security (shelter, peace and order, income and employment), and an enabling environment (basic education and literacy, people's participation, family care and psycho-social needs). Priority projects were those corresponding to the top unmet 'needs'. In practice the most common projects were day care centers, water supply systems, sanitary toilet facilities, shelter assistance and credit provision. Others included were skills training programs and school facilities. The innovative contribution of the CIDSS was the mobilization of the community to participate in all project stages. In implementation within provinces priority was given to the poorer municipalities and within these to poorer districts (*barangays*).

The Estrada administration (1998–2001) came to power with a lavish pro-poor agenda. It recognized the imperative of broad-based rural development to win the war against poverty. Its Medium-term Philippine Development Plan for 1999–2004 identified the main elements of the development strategies required to spur growth and achieve sustainable development in rural areas. The plan envisioned, for example, an aggressive delivery of basic social development services, removal of policy and regulatory distortions, sustained development of rural infrastructure, improvement in governance, and macroeconomic stability. The administration's flagship program for poverty alleviation was the Care for Poor (*Lingap Para sa Mahihirap*) program, which involved the identification in each province and city of the 100 poorest families, who would be provided with a package of assistance, including livelihood development, price support for staple foods, medical assistance, socialized housing, and a rural waterworks system. Several modalities were employed in the selection of families, but in principle the aim was to use data on unmet minimum basic needs. If there were no data available, local social workers were consulted to identify the poorest families.

The ascension to power of the Macapagal-Arroyo administration (2001–2004) gave birth to a new program of direct poverty alleviation dubbed KALAHI (*Kapit-Bisig Laban sa Kahirapan*) which covers asset reform, provision of human development services, creation of employment and livelihood opportunities, participation of so-called basic sectors in governance, and social protection and security against violence. Interventions are delivered using the administrative apparatus of national government agencies and local government units, but the emphasis as in earlier programs is on local community empowerment.

The KALAHI has been combined with the earlier Comprehensive and Integrated Delivery of Social Services (CIDSS) program in the KALAHI-CIDSS. The principal development activity is small-scale infrastructure work. These projects should provide needed physical infrastructure and thereby benefit the local community, and at the same time serve as pilot projects for the *barangay* governing bodies, in terms of developing better planning, implementation, operation, and management techniques which will result in more self-sufficient organizations. Project choices are determined by communities themselves. The project employs multi-stage targeting. At the first stage, provinces are ranked on the basis of poverty incidence and the top 40 (roughly the poorest one-half) are selected. At the second stage, only the poorest quarter of municipalities are selected. The selection is based on a poverty map developed by Balisacan et al. (2002). The poverty map uses an aggregation methodology applied to proxy indicators of poverty. All *barangays* in the beneficiary municipality are included in the project to access grants. A major modification from the old CIDSS is the formation of an organization within the community that operates in parallel with the local *barangay* council. This has resulted in conflicts in some *barangays*, since it is the community organization that identifies a project, prepares the program of work, and monitors implementation, although the local *barangay* council is called upon to provide the counterpart funds.

Cutting across all of these initiatives has been the operation of the National Food Authority (NFA), which implements a number of subsidy schemes, the most important of which is that for rice. Given the importance of rice for the poor as both a consumer and producer good, the operations of the NFA potentially have strong poverty implications.[4] The authority aims to meet potentially conflicting objectives of maintaining a floor price for producers and a ceiling price for consumers of rice. NFA buys the grains from the farmers during times of bumper harvest, when the buying price is higher than the market price. The program essentially provides a subsidy to the farmers, so that they are assured of a stable income, independent of the supply situation in the market. NFA procures grains only from 'bona fide' farmers. Verification is done through the use of a passbook that is issued only to farmers. However, in practice in recent years the NFA has been able to procure only less than 5 per cent of total rice production, so it has only a very marginal impact on average producer rice prices.

On the consumer side subsidies are provided for sales of supported goods in selected retail outlets and NFA rolling stores. The main objective of the program is to protect consumers against large increases in the price of basic commodities, not just rice but also sugar, cooking oil and more recently common drugs. NFA has a monopoly control over rice imports and its import quota has combined with relatively high import tariffs on rice to keep domestic consumer prices well above world prices (Roumasset, 1999). Targeting is essentially through self-selection as there is no filter mechanism to exclude non-bona fide customers. Sales are made as long as the customer is willing to buy from the NFA retail stores and outlets, which in principle should be in depressed urban areas.

Government expenditure on poverty alleviation

Estimates of the total expenditure on the types of narrowly targeted interventions discussed above suggest that they have been only a very modest share of government expenditure. More recent figures are not available but data for the late 1990s show poverty-related measures at no more than 0.60 per cent of central government expenditure. When the cost of the NFA operations are added the figure comes to about 1.5 per cent. Expenditure by local government on poverty programs at this time was tiny at only 60 centavos per capita compared with Pesos 37 per capita by the central government (Manasan, 2001).

In terms of the broad targeting expenditure categories a recent review suggests that real public expenditure per capita on key activities has been in decline in recent years. Total social services spending per capita in real terms has declined from Pesos 2487 in 1997 to Pesos 2016 in 2003. In particular, education expenditures per capita fell from Pesos 1790 to Pesos 1455 between 1997 and 2003 (Manasan, 2003; Igaya, 2001).

Impact of Narrow Targeting Programs

Relatively few detailed independent evaluations are available for the narrow targeting schemes discussed above. The subsidized credit component of the *Tulong sa Tao* program was examined to see how far the aim that beneficiaries should come from low-income groups in rural areas was met. It appears that in practice detailed inclusion and exclusion criteria were not enumerated and therefore there was no effort to screen prospective beneficiaries. Estimates suggest that only about one-third of beneficiaries were really from the low-income groups. Also there was no mechanism to disqualify borrowers who were no longer poor. On the contrary, the project allowed individual micro-entrepreneurs a higher ceiling on the second loan, and an even higher ceiling for the third and each subsequent loan (Balisacan et al., 2000).

The official impact evaluation of the CIDSS was favorable, although vague. It stated that 'unmet basic needs were reduced by an average of 57 per cent'. An external evaluation of the project (Bautista, 1999) revealed that the incidence of poor families in the sample of households covered by CIDSS actually increased, although in the non-CIDSS communities, the incidence also increased and by more than the increase in the CIDSS sample. A more rigorous evaluation was conducted using data from the 1997 and 2000 Family Income and Expenditure Survey. Here the real per capita incomes in the original set of priority provinces benefiting from the CIDSS were compared against an equivalent set of provinces.[5] The analysis shows that real per capita incomes decreased, but in comparison with the change in the control group, this reduction is not statistically significant. Poverty incidence also increased between 1997 and 2000, but again, in comparison with the control, this negative impact is not statistically different from that in the other provinces. This simple evaluation suggests that the CIDSS did not result in a significant improvement in incomes or in poverty reduction, at the provincial level. The alternative interpretation is that it will take some time for community empowerment to translate into poverty reduction.

To compare alternative poverty targeting measures Balisacan et al. (2000) simulated several experiments on geographical targeting. Given a fixed program cost of Pesos 10 billion, they simulated ten experiments, and for each, the rates of leakage and undercoverage were computed. The assumed objective was reduction of national poverty incidence, thus effectiveness is measured as the impact on national poverty incidence for a given cost. Of note is the fact that the strategy of the *Lingap para sa Mahihirap* (Care for the Poor) program of the Estrada administration, which involved directing assistance at an equal number of poorest households in each province and city (regardless of differences in regional income), is by far the least effective. The authors test for the influence of administrative or screening costs of targeting and find that once these are introduced, the preferred ranking of alternatives changes. Once the administrative cost per applicant rises to a modest Pesos 135 then a simple form of geographic targeting, allocating funds only to the poorest provinces, comes to dominate the 'perfect targeting' solution where each province and city receives the same funding but to be distributed only among the genuinely poor. They use this as evidence that if the screening cost is substantial it pays to implement geographical targeting.

National Food Authority (NFA)

The NFA operations and particularly its rice subsidy have been the subject of a number of studies. Subbarao et al. (1996) reported that in 1991 and 1992, it cost NFA 2 to 3 pesos to transfer a peso of benefit to the consumer. The net cost of the NFA rice subsidy is the gross cost, consisting of its palay procurement price, milling cost, debt service, and other costs, less its sales receipts. In 1991 and 1992, this cost amounted to Pesos 6097 and Pesos 5691 per metric ton, respectively, or two to three times the income transfer to consumers (defined as the annual average retail price minus the weighted average NFA sales price of rice to consumers). More recent data show that this inefficiency persists. Roumasset (1999) found that in 1997 and 1998, NFA's subsidy to consumers amounted to Pesos 1.87 billion and Pesos 4.89 billion, respectively. Thus, it cost the agency an average of Pesos 1.68 to deliver one peso of benefit to the consumer. Manasan (2001) noted that economic costs from NFA importations (losses in tariff revenue, and consumer and producer surplus) were not accounted for in these estimates.

As the program is of the general food subsidy type, non-poor families also benefit from it. Citing similar schemes in other countries where leakage ranged from 50–70 per cent, Subbarao et al. (1996) and Manasan (2001) assumed a 50 per cent leakage for the Philippines. With this assumption in 1991 and 1992, the cost of the income equivalent transfer of one peso to the poor was Pesos 4.30 and Pesos 5.98, respectively. In 1997 it was Pesos 4.19, declining to Pesos 2.54 in 1998.

Subbarao et al. (1996) noted that the 50 per cent leakage assumption is reasonable given the 'large regional mistargeting' of the program. Of the total NFA subsidized rice in 1991–1993, the National Capital Region and Cagayan Valley received 35 per cent even though they accounted for only 3 per cent of total food poverty in the Philippines; the poorer regions of Southern Tagalog, Bicol, Central Visayas, Northern Mindanao, and Southern Mindanao obtained 29 per cent even though they accounted for about 62 per cent of total food poverty. Similarly in 1998, the share of NFA rice in total rice consumption in the Autonomous Region of Muslim Mindanao, Cordillera Administrative Region, and Western Visayas was well below the 22 per cent national average, although poverty incidence in these regions was relatively higher than average (Manasan, 2001).

Several other studies also show that the NFA has not been effective in achieving one of its other objectives as NFA's operations tend to destabilize, rather than stabilize, domestic prices. Untimely importation (if a decision to import is made) and grain procurement and releases have aggravated palay and rice price fluctuations (David, 1999; Roumasset, 1999). It has been estimated that consumers pay 35 per cent to 100 per cent higher rice prices than would be possible under unrestricted trade. Also it is argued that NFA policy offers potentially very lucrative profits for well-connected rice traders and political insiders (Roumasset, 1999).

Some Broad Targeting Experiments

Given the very modest sums of money attached to direct anti-poverty programs and given the apparently weak poverty impact, an important question is how far broad targeting based on general categories of public expenditure can meet the goal of poverty reduction. To address this question we apply a simulation exercise looking at the poverty and growth impact of different expenditure packages. The calculations are based on parameters from a regression model developed by one of the authors (Balisacan and Pernia, 2003).

Balisacan and Pernia (2003) compiled longitudinal provincial data for the 1980s and 1990s to examine empirically the link between the average expenditure of the various population quintiles, on the one hand, and overall income growth and other factors on the other. The dependent variable is average per capita expenditure in each quintile. The impact of overall provincial income growth on poverty reduction is distinguished from the direct impact of certain economic and institutional factors.

The explanatory variables are categorized into two groups, namely initial condition variables and time-varying variables. Included in the first group are province-specific human capital endowment, farm and land characteristics, social capital, geographic attributes, and political economy characteristics. The proxy for initial human capital endowment is the (three-year lagged) average years of schooling of household heads. Two alternative variables representing farm characteristics are average farm size and irrigation. The latter, expressed as the ratio of irrigated land to total farm area, is a proxy for the quality of agricultural land. Geographic attributes are an indication of spatial isolation or high transport cost (given by a dummy variable indicating whether a province is landlocked or not) and the average frequency of typhoons hitting the province. These variables are intended to capture geographic poverty traps. Meanwhile, the initial political economy variables aim to reflect the quality of local governance and access to fiscal resources. One variable is 'local political dynasty', defined as the proportion of local officials – related to each other by blood or affinity – out of the total number of elective positions. This variable is meant to capture the extent of collusion or competition in local politics. The other political economy variable pertains to the political party affiliation of the provincial chief executive. This is represented by a dummy variable indicating whether the provincial governor belongs to the national President's political party.

The time-varying variables include relative price incentives, road access and electricity, agrarian reform, and overall average per capita income. The price incentives variable is given by the agricultural terms-of-trade, defined as the ratio of the price of agricultural to non-agricultural products. The time-varying infrastructure variables pertain to road access and electricity. The roads variable, representing access to markets, off-farm employment, and social services, is defined as quality-adjusted road length per square kilometer of land area. Electricity is used as a proxy for access to technology, or simply the ability to use modern equipment. It is defined as the proportion of households with access to electricity. The agrarian reform variable, defined as the proportion of the cumulative completed agrarian reform area to total potential land reform area, serves as a proxy for households' ability to smooth consumption in response to shocks, given imperfections in credit markets.

Certain variables may have strong complementarities, so the impact of one variable on the living standards of the poor may be conditioned by the values of the other variables. To allow for this possibility, interaction terms on certain variables are introduced; in particular, schooling and roads, and schooling and electricity.

The econometric estimation takes into account the possibility of a reverse causation in the poverty–growth relationship, so overall mean income may systematically respond to changes in the average living standards of the poor. The regression results for each of the quintiles are reproduced in Table 6.5.

In general, the results for the second quintile closely resemble those for the first quintile. This is significant considering that estimates of poverty in the Philippines vary widely – from 20 per cent to 40 per cent – depending on, among other things, the poverty norm employed. The official estimate roughly corresponds to the bottom 40 per cent of the population.

Other observations are also worth noting:

- The growth elasticity of poverty tends to increase monotonically with income quintile. This confirms what has been noted above, that the benefits of growth are unevenly spread throughout the various income groups.
- The roads variable is significant, but has a negative sign for the first three quintiles, suggesting that roads per se directly reduce the welfare of the poor, unless complementary factors like schooling are present. In contrast, this variable is significant and has a positive sign for the top quintile, indicating that roads raise directly the average welfare of the richest group in society, as expected.
- Apart from its impact through other channels, overall schooling does not seem to have a direct, significant effect on average welfare for all quintiles. However, as noted above, when interacted with roads, schooling tends to raise the average income and welfare in the first three quintiles. This suggests that complementarity matters for other quintiles as well.[6]
- Other things being equal, agrarian reform raises the average welfare of all quintiles, except the top one. Note that those in the top 20 per cent do not normally depend on agriculture for employment and income.
- Irrigation tends to have a pro-poor bias. Farm size does not have significant effects on the average welfare of all but the richest group,

implying that it is the quality of the land, not farm size per se, that favorably affects the welfare of the lower-income groups.

Investment Simulations

We simulate the above model and determine which of a range of investment options yields the greatest overall benefit, the least leakage, and the least cost. In simulating each option, the values of the other exogenous variables are set at their mean values. In each case, both the direct (redistribution) effect and the indirect (growth) effect are taken into account.

The base data set is the 1997 Family Income and Expenditure Survey. In this exercise, a person is deemed poor if their standard of living, represented by per capita consumption, falls below the absolute poverty line constructed for that person's province of residence. We use a social discount rate of 15 per cent to reduce streams of future benefits and costs to present terms. Although high as a real discount rate, this is the rate set by the National Economic and Development Authority on aid projects.

The cost of investment is assumed to be incurred in the first year. Meanwhile, benefits are received starting year 2 (except those for education whose stream of benefits begin in year 3) and remain constant over the assumed economic life of the investment. The operating cost is assumed to be fully recovered by charges to users. Assumptions on the cost of maintenance vary by type of investment. Total benefits, as well as benefits to the poor specifically, are calculated. The benefit–cost ratios for different expenditure packages are then computed and ranked. We discuss each package briefly.

Electricity

Presently, the proportion of households with no electricity is 30 per cent. These are in the remote and poor *barangays*. Recently, the Department of Energy has embarked on an electrification project that seeks to 'energize' every *barangay* in the country. The source of energy need not be electricity. In the far-flung *barangays*, especially those in the islands, the strategy is to promote alternative energy sources, such as solar power, and small hydro-powered generators.[7]

In this experiment we assume that the present power-generating capacity is sufficient to provide electricity to every household. This is a reasonable assumption given the current situation of excess capacity and the fact that the poor households are likely to be small consumers of electricity. The simulated project is such that in provinces where less than 90 per cent of households have access to electricity, the intervention will result in access for exactly 90 per cent of households. Meanwhile, in provinces

Table 6.5 Determinants of average living standards (per capita expenditure) by income quintile

Explanatory Variable	1st Quintile (Poorest)	2nd Quintile	3rd Quintile	4th Quintile	5th Quintile (Richest)
Initial conditions					
Schooling	-0.010	0.080	0.107	0.075	-0.139
Local dynasty	-0.104 ***	-0.069 ***	-0.055 **	-0.029	0.041
Political party	0.029 **	0.013	0.022 *	0.022 *	0.030 **
Landlocked	-0.067 ***	-0.077 ***	-0.070 ***	-0.061 ***	0.041 **
Typhoon	-0.064 ***	-0.055 ***	-0.046 ***	-0.048 **	0.059 ***
Irrigation	0.233 ***	0.157 ***	0.093 ***	0.008	-0.115 **
Farm size	0.010	-0.012	-0.011	0.010	0.072 ***
Time-varying variables					
Per capita income	0.544 ***	0.621 ***	0.676 ***	0.798 ***	1.045 ***
Terms of trade	0.140 ***	0.149 ***	0.135 ***	0.119 ***	-0.051
Roads	-0.212 **	-0.264 ***	-0.215 **	-0.051	0.478 ***
Electricity (×100)	0.049	0.098	0.162 **	0.143 **	-0.006
Agrarian reform	0.041 **	0.033 **	0.029 **	0.026 *	-0.009
Interactions					
Schooling*Roads	0.110 **	0.133 ***	0.102 ***	0.015	-0.251 ***
Schooling*Electricity (×100)	0.007	0.019	0.009	0.002	0.002
Intercept	3.324 ***	2.760 ***	2.418 ***	1.625 ***	0.491
R-squared	0.758, 0.385	0.833, 0.498	0.864, 0.576	0.879, 0.610	0.854, 0.686

Notes:
Estimation is by three-stage least squares.
Instruments are actual values of schooling, roads, electricity, political-economy and geographic variables, terms of trade, and lagged values of the other variables, including land Gini; tenancy and twice-lagged value of average income growth.
Data are for provincial panel covering the 1980s and 1990s.
The R-squared values apply to the level and the difference form of the estimated log (per capita expenditure) function.
***, ** and * denote significance at the 1%, 5% and 10% level, respectively.

Source: Balisacan and Pernia (2003).

where the proportion of households with electricity is at least 90 per cent, no intervention is provided. The simulated intervention results in 92 per cent of households in total having access to electricity.

The development cost is estimated to be roughly Pesos 175 000 per linear kilometer plus an average connection cost of Pesos 5000 per household.[8] The total cost of the project is Pesos 561 million for public electricity utilities plus Pesos 16 billion for households. The infrastructure is expected to last for 15 years. An annual operating and maintenance cost of 5 per cent of the total cost is assumed. Total incremental benefit in terms of net income change is Pesos 19.6 billion, but only Pesos 2.6 billion accrues to the poor. This is equivalent to a leakage of 87 per cent. Poverty incidence is reduced by 1.39 percentage points. The simulated project results in a benefit–cost ratio of 5.35.

Roads

Outside the highly urbanized cities, the road system in the country is generally poor. Considering only the concrete roads, regarded as superior in quality to gravel, paved or asphalted roads, the average road density is 0.72 km per square km. Some provinces, especially those that have large mountainous areas (such as Ifugao), have very few concrete roads.

The simulated intervention increases the road density to 1 km per square km, but only in provinces where the current road density is less than 1 km. The simulated road project will increase the average road density to 1.58 km per square km. Assuming a cost of Pesos 1 million per km of concrete road, the total project cost is Pesos 280 billion. We also assume annual maintenance costs of 5 per cent of total project cost, and an economic life of 15 years.[9]

Overall benefit is estimated to be Pesos 170 billion, but total benefit to the poor is negative. Note that in the model, the direct impact of roads on the four poorest quintiles is negative. However, due to the indirect effects through economic growth created by road investment, poverty incidence is still estimated to decrease by 0.03 percentage points. The benefit–cost ratio is equal to 2.7.

Agrarian reform

The most aggressive land redistribution program in the Philippines began in 1987 with the enactment of the Comprehensive Agrarian Reform Program (CARP). Changing ownership of land is seen as an important wealth redistribution program and a means of effecting social justice. Average accomplishment is 57 per cent as of 1997 using as a base the revised reform coverage of 8 million hectares.[10]

In the simulation the land reform project is taken to imply the full accomplishment of the CARP in each province. The cost of the project is based only on the cost of land acquisition. For prime lands, the average cost is taken to be Pesos 350 000 per hectare, while for non-prime lands, it is taken to be Pesos 10 000 per hectare. The total cost of land acquisition is Pesos 202 billion. Assuming an economic life of 30 years the total benefit is estimated to be Pesos 3.3 billion, and roughly half a billion of this accrues to the poor. The leakage rate is estimated to be 82 per cent and there will be a reduction of poverty incidence by approximately 0.30 percentage points. CARP accomplishment is beneficial to the poorest four quintiles, but detrimental to the richest quintile. However the net benefit–cost ratio is surprisingly low at only 0.11, due to the low coefficients on the agrarian reform variable in the original model (see Table 6.5).

Irrigation
David (2003) describes the poor state of irrigation development in the country. As of 1999, less than 30 per cent of potential irrigable land is served by an irrigation system. Worse, the present systems are very inefficient and in urgent need of repair and rehabilitation. In the simulation, the level of irrigation development is increased to the level of irrigable land estimated for the region, if the current profile is less than the potential level. This brings the irrigated area to about 25 per cent of the total agricultural area.[11]

In computing the cost of the simulated project, the mix and cost estimates suggested by David (2003) are adopted.[12] As before, we impute full cost recovery of maintenance and operating expenses. Different economic lives are assumed for different elements of the mix. The marginal effect of the irrigation package can be considered small and the inefficiencies of the current irrigation system are captured by the model. Overall benefit is estimated to be Pesos 1.6 million, but benefits to the poor are almost Pesos 3 million, as the richest quintile is affected negatively. However, these gains to the poor are small and are not sufficient to pull anyone above the poverty line. The benefit–cost ratio is estimated to be very small, at 0.0008.

Education
It is often said that the main asset of the poor is labor and that anti-poverty projects should always include a component that improves the quality of labor. Among the poor, the highest educational attainment of the household head is only Grade 5 on average.[13] In the regression model, the impact of education is only significant when interacted with roads. This latter proxies access to technology and access to markets. In effect, the model implies that the positive benefits of education will be realized only if there is access to

technology (so that skills can be honed) and access to markets (to encourage skilled labor to produce marketable surplus).

In the simulation every head of household undergoes an additional two years of education. This results in more than 9 years of schooling on average. The cost of the education package includes the operating cost for public school facilities, as well as the out-of-pocket expenses of households.[14] We assume that the stream of benefits will be for 16 years, roughly equal to the difference between retirement age (65 years) and the average age of household heads (47 years) adjusted for the duration of project implementation (2 years).

Allowing for the mean value of road expenditure the total benefit of the simulated education project is more than Pesos 50 billion per year. Of this the benefit to the poor equals Pesos 2.4 billion, giving a leakage rate of 95 per cent. Poverty incidence goes down by 1.35 percentage points as a result of the education package. The benefit–cost ratio is 0.96, but if out-of-pocket expenses are not considered, the ratio increases to 3.92.

Summary of simulation results

The above results can be summarized in Table 6.6 and Figure 6.2. On the vertical axis of Figure 6.2, we plot the overall benefit–cost ratio. Higher up the axis, the project is bound to have substantial political support, especially from the non-poor. On the horizontal axis, we plot the poor's share in total benefits from the investment.[15]

The above simulations can only be approximations of actual projects, as they take as the measure of benefit the impact derived from a regression model rather than from a detailed assessment of specific markets. Furthermore in most cases benefits are assumed to arise immediately and to be constant

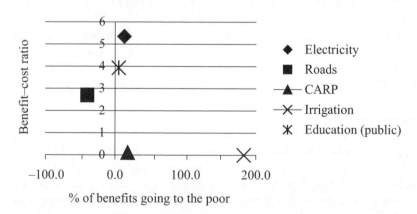

Figure 6.2   Benefit–cost ratios vs. benefit coverage for the poor

Table 6.6 *Summary of simulation results*

	Electricity	Roads	CARP	Irrigation	Education	(public only)[a]
PV[b] of total benefits ('000 pesos)	97 388 761	845 350 736	18 708 734	6 639	218 938 576	218 938 576
PV of benefits to the poor ('000 pesos)	12 748 961	(338 171 186)	3 345 476	12 145	10 358 596	10 358 596
PV of total costs ('000)	18 203 094	313 456 728	175 474 402	14 780 201	227 578 718	55 819 572
Share of non-poor in benefits (%)	87	140	82	−83	95	95
Share of poor in benefits (%)	13	−40	18	183	5	5
Overall benefit/cost ratio	5.35	2.70	0.11	0.0008	0.96	3.92

Notes:
[a] Excludes private out-of-pocket expenses met by families themselves.
[b] PV is present value.

241

over time. Efficiency requires a benefit–cost ratio exceeding unity and from this perspective the irrigation and agrarian reform packages appear highly inefficient. Even the education package has measurable benefits below the full costs involved. However, the electricity and road packages are found to have high returns, with rural electrification having the highest benefit–cost ratio and the largest effect on the poor. It is also expected to have political support, given the high overall benefits.

However, the simulations emphasize the need to undertake complementary measures to increase the returns to investments. Quite expectedly, the model captures the substandard performance of current infrastructure. For irrigation investments, the model assumes the same poor state of current irrigation systems. For agrarian reform, the lesson here is that land distribution alone will not result in desired income gains for the poor. It has to be coupled with aggressive provision of support services. In addition, the simulations show that some broad categories of expenditure, in this case principally electrification, can have strong growth and poverty reduction effects.

CONCLUSIONS

Economic growth sustained over a long period is the key to the poverty problem in the Philippines. This growth mediates the development of human capabilities for meeting basic needs. Indeed, where chronic poverty is pervasive owing mainly to the failure of the economy to generate productive employment opportunities, it is hard to imagine a more enduring solution to the poverty problem than one requiring policy and institutional reforms aimed at enhancing the economy's capacity to grow and generate these opportunities.

However, while growth is necessary, it is not a sufficient response to the poverty problem. The reason is quite simple: socio-economic conditions and circumstances of households in society vary considerably. Indeed, the response of the income of low-income groups to growth has been quite weak in the Philippines compared with that in major East Asian countries. Policies and institutions thus need to be made pro-poor as well. Improved access of the poor to basic services, particularly education and health, is a fundamental element of such reform. This necessarily involves difficult choices owing to the country's fiscal constraint and tightly competing uses of government funds.

The poverty alleviation programs examined in this chapter provide examples of targeting schemes. However, the funding they have received has been modest and the limited evaluations available suggest that their impact has been modest also. The simulation exercise conducted here has shown that gains to the poor can occur through packages of activities of a general (that is non-targeted) nature. In an environment of weak governance and poor delivery of services to the poor this simple lesson needs to be borne in mind.

NOTES

1. See the evidence for Thailand, Indonesia, Vietnam and the Philippines in Pernia and Deolalikar (2003).
2. In this chapter, the incidence, depth and severity dimensions of poverty are characterized by the headcount index, poverty gap index, and the squared poverty gap, respectively. The headcount index is simply the proportionate number of the population deemed poor. The poverty gap index is defined by the mean distance below the poverty line as a proportion of that line (where the non-poor are counted as having a zero poverty gap). The distribution-sensitive measure is the mean of the squared proportionate poverty gaps. This index incorporates a society's 'moderate' aversion to poverty (see Foster et al., 1984). The estimation employs per capita consumption expenditures as indicator of living standard, and consistency-conforming provincial poverty lines given in Balisacan (2001). Data sources are mainly the various Family Income and Expenditure Survey rounds from 1985 to 2000.
3. Rural poverty indicators constructed from the Family Income and Expenditure Survey for the 1980s are not comparable with those for the 1990s owing to the urban–rural reclassification problem. The classification into urban or rural areas is based on population density and the presence and quantity of public infrastructure facilities and establishments. As the population grows and economic activity expands, an initially rural area will be classified as urban, sooner or later. While this may not be problematic for purposes of measuring, say, urbanization trends, it tends to create a systematic upward (downward) bias to urban (rural) performance indicators. Substantial reclassification of villages occurred between the 1980 and 1990 population censuses, though not between the 1990 and 1995 censuses. Thus, when disaggregating by urban area, the only strictly comparable years are 1985 with 1988, 1991 with 1994, and 1997 with 2000, since, for each pair, the classification (that is the sampling frame used) is based on the same census.
4. Cororaton (2004) finds that the net effect of the rice import quota operated by the NFA is poverty-reducing; in other words the poor are net rice producers and gain more from higher producer prices than they lose from higher consumer prices due to the operations of the quota.
5. The latter set was constituted by first ranking the provinces according to the poverty incidence in 1997. The lowest poverty incidence observed for the original priority provinces became the cutoff. This set was later subdivided into 'treatment' and 'control'. Since there were more provinces in the 'control' group, the 'excess' provinces were randomly sampled out.
6. The other infrastructure variable, electricity, was found to be insignificant for the bottom two quintiles and for all quintiles when interacted with schooling. It is possible that this variable is a poor proxy for access to technology.
7. Another assessment of the social and economic benefits of rural electrification in the Philippines found substantial gains from increased and cheaper electricity (Barnes and DomDom, 2002).
8. Inclusive of electric posts, wires and cables and distribution transformers. Cost estimate is courtesy of GENMAR Power and Energy Systems, Inc.
9. REECS and Meganomics (2003) provide estimates of benefits from rural roads financed as part of the First Agrarian Reform Communities Development Project.

10. When the CARP started the target scope was 11 million hectares. Reyes (2002) uses panel data from 1500 farm households to estimate benefits from land reform.
11. David (2003) describes the poor state of irrigation in the Philippines. Edillon and Velarde (2004) present an analysis of the Agrarian Reform Communities Strategy that highlights potential gains from irrigation.
12. He recommends that new systems should consist of 28 per cent shallow tube wells, 10 per cent small water impounding projects, 36 per cent national irrigation systems and 26 per cent communal irrigation systems.
13. Edillon and Velarde (2004) demonstrate high returns to education for the poor in the Philippines.
14. Costs are based on Tan et al. (2000), whose estimated out-of-pocket expenses were inflated to reflect 1997 prices.
15. The preferable approach is to report the benefits and costs to the poor, specifically, alongside the overall benefit–cost ratios. However, the interventions considered are highly non-excludable, making it difficult to extract the cost of providing the good or service to the poor and to the non-poor.

REFERENCES

Balisacan, A.M. (1995), 'Anatomy of poverty during adjustment: the case of the Philippines', *Economic Development and Cultural Change*, vol. 44, pp. 33–62.

Balisacan, A.M. (2001), 'Rural development in the 21st century: monitoring and assessing performance in rural poverty reduction', in D.B. Canlas and S. Fujisaki, (eds), *The Philippine Economy: Alternatives for the 21st Century*, Manila: University of the Philippines Press.

Balisacan, A.M. (2003), 'Poverty and inequality', in A.M. Balisacan and H. Hill (eds), *The Philippine Economy: Development, Policies, and Challenges*, New York: Oxford University Press.

Balisacan, A.M. and H. Hill (eds) (2003), *The Philippine Economy: Development, Policies, and Challenges*, New York: Oxford University Press.

Balisacan, A.M. and E.M. Pernia (2003), 'Poverty, inequality and growth in the Philippines', in E.M. Pernia and A.B. Deolalikar (eds), *Poverty, Growth and Institutions in Developing Asia*, Hampshire, England: Palgrave Macmillan.

Balisacan, A.M. and S.A. Piza (2003), 'Nature and causes of income inequality in the Philippines', paper presented at the Conference on Comparative Analyses of East Asian Income Inequalities, Bangkok, 27–28 January.

Balisacan, A.M., R. Edillon and G. Ducanes (2002), 'Poverty mapping and targeting for KALAHI-CIDSS', final report prepared for the Department of Social Work and Development.

Balisacan, A.M., E.M. Pernia and A. Asra (2003a), 'Revisiting growth and poverty reduction in Indonesia: what do subnational data show?', *Bulletin of Indonesian Economic Studies*, **39** (3), 331–53.

Balisacan, A.M., E.M. Pernia and G.E.B. Estrada (2003b), 'Economic growth and poverty reduction in Vietnam', in E.M. Pernia and A.B. Deolalikar (eds), *Poverty, Growth and Institutions in Developing Asia*, Hampshire, England: Palgrave Macmillan.

Balisacan, A.M., R.G. Edillon, A.B. Brillantes and D.B. Canlas (2000), *Approaches to Targeting the Poor*, Manila: United Nations Development Program and National Economic and Development Authority.

Bardhan, P. (1996), 'Efficiency, equity and poverty alleviation: policy issues in less developed countries', *Economic Journal*, vol. 106, pp. 344–56.

Barnes, D. and A. DomDom (2002), *Rural Electrification and Development in the Philippines: Measuring the Social and Economic Benefits*, Washington, DC: World Bank.

Bautista, V.A. (1999), *Combating Poverty through the Comprehensive and Integrated Delivery of Social Services*, Quezon City: National College of Public Administration and Governance, University of the Philippines.

Bhalla, S. (2002), *Imagine There's No Country: Poverty, Inequality, and Growth in the Era of Globalization*, Washington, DC: Institute for International Economics.

Cororaton, C. (2004), 'Rice refoms and poverty in the Philippines: a CGE analysis', ADB Institute Discussion Paper No. 8, available at www.adbi.org.

David, C.C. (1999), 'Constraints to food security: the Philippine case', Discussion Paper Series No. 99–31, Makati City: Philippine Institute for Development Studies.

David, W.P. (2003), *Averting the Water Crisis in Agriculture: Policy and Program Framework for Irrigation Development in the Philippines*, Quezon City: University of the Philippines Press and Asia Pacific Policy Center.

Dollar, D. and A. Kraay (2001), 'Growth is good for the poor', World Bank Policy Research Paper No. 2587, Washington DC: World Bank.

Edillon, R.G. and R.B. Velarde (2004), 'Pathways to poverty reduction: assessing the impact of agrarian reform and the ARC strategy on poverty using census, national housing surveys, and ARC data', final report prepared for the Food and Agriculture Organization.

Fields, G.S. (2002), 'Accounting for income inequality and its change: a new method, with application to the distribution of earnings in the United States', unpublished paper, Cornell University, Ithaca, NY.

Foster, J., J. Greer and E. Thorbecke (1984), 'A class of decomposable poverty measures', *Econometrica*, vol. 52, pp. 761–5.

Hayami, Y. (2001), 'Ecology, history, and development: a perspective from rural Southeast Asia', *World Bank Research Observer*, vol. 16, pp. 169–98.

Igaya, G.A. (2001), 'Implementing and monitoring the 20/20 initiative in the Philippines', DP Series No. 2001–01, Manila: Presidential Task Force on the 20/20 Initiative.

Manasan, R.G. (2001), 'Social safety nets in the Philippines: analysis and prospects', in 'Strengthening policies and programmes on social safety nets: issues, recommendations and selected studies', Economic and Social Commission for Asia and the Pacific (ESCAP) Social Policy Paper No. 8, New York: United Nations.

Manasan, R.G. (2003), 'Analysis of the President's budget for 2004: looking for the complete (fiscal) picture', Discussion Paper Series No. 2003–17, Makati City: Philippine Institute for Development Studies.

Pernia, E.M. and A.B. Deolalikar (eds) (2003), *Poverty, Growth and Institutions in Developing Asia*, Basingstoke, UK: Palgrave Macmillan.

Ranis, G., and F. Stewart (1993), 'Rural nonagricultural activities in development: theory and experience', *Journal of Development Economics*, vol. 40, pp. 75–101.

Ravallion, M. and J. Jalan (1996), 'Growth divergence due to spatial externalities', *Economics Letters*, vol. 53, pp. 227–32.

Resources, Environment and Economics Center for Studies, Inc. (REECS) and Meganomics Specialists International, Inc (2003), 'Impact assessment project of the Agrarian Reform Communities Development Project', final report prepared for the ARCDP, Department of Agrarian Reform.

Reyes, C.M. (2002), 'Impact of agrarian reform on poverty', Discussion Paper Series No. 2002–02, Makati: Philippine Institute for Development Studies.

Roumasset, J. (1999), 'Market-friendly food security: alternatives for restructuring NFA', unpublished paper, Department of Economics, University of Hawaii, Honolulu.

Subbarao, K., A.U. Ahmed and T. Teklu (1996), 'Selected social safety net programs in the Philippines: targeting, cost-effectiveness and options for reforms', World Bank Discussion Paper No. 317, World Bank, Washington, DC.

Tan, E., R. Borromeo and C. Castel (2000), 'Efficiency and effectiveness', in M.D. Valino (ed.), *The Reform and Development of Higher Education in the Philippines*, Manila: UNESCO Philippines.

7.   Micro-finance and poverty reduction in Asia

John Weiss, Heather Montgomery and Elvira Kurmanalieva

INTRODUCTION

The micro-finance revolution has changed attitudes towards helping the poor in many countries and in some has provided substantial flows of credit, often to very low-income groups or households, who would normally be excluded by conventional financial institutions. Bangladesh is the starkest example of a very poor country, where currently roughly one quarter of rural households are direct beneficiaries of these programs (Khandker, 2003). Much has been written on the range of institutional arrangements pursued in different organizations and countries and in turn a vast number of studies have attempted to assess the outreach and poverty impact of such schemes. However, amongst the academic development community there is a recognition that perhaps we know much less about the impact of these programs than might be expected given the enthusiasm for these activities in donor and policy-making circles. To quote a recent authoritative volume on micro-finance:

> MFI field operations have far surpassed the research capacity to analyze them, so excitement about the use of micro-finance for poverty alleviation is not backed up with sound facts derived from rigorous research. Given the current state of knowledge, it is difficult to allocate confidently public resources to micro-finance development. (Zeller and Meyer, 2002)

This is a very strong statement of doubt and in part reflects lack of accurate data, but also in part methodological difficulties associated with assessing exactly what proportion of income and other effects on the beneficiaries of micro-credit can actually be attributed to the programs themselves. In recognition of this uncertainty this chapter aims to bring together some of the recent evidence that has been accumulating on the impact of micro-finance activities on poverty reduction. In particular we ask what the evidence is on three specific issues:

- the extent to which micro-finance initiatives have made a lasting difference in pulling households out of poverty on a permanent basis;
- the extent to which micro-finance programs reach only the better-off amongst the poor, leaving the 'core poor' unaffected;
- how far micro-finance is a cost-effective means of transferring income to the poor.

These are very basic questions and the fact that they can still be posed reflects the extent of uncertainty in the literature.

The chapter is organized in four sections. The first provides a brief overview of some of the features of micro-finance activities in Asia, which is our region of focus. The second discusses a few concepts from the poverty literature and links these with micro-finance programs. The third surveys the evidence from recent research studies on the first two of the three questions posed above. The fourth section addresses the third question. Since a number of other surveys are also available we give most attention to evidence produced in the last three or four years.[1] Finally we draw some brief conclusions.

SOME FEATURES OF MICRO-FINANCE IN ASIA

'Asia is the most developed continent in the world in terms of volume of MFI (micro finance institution) activities'. This conclusion, drawn by Lapenu and Zeller (2001: 27), is based on analysis of over 1500 institutions from 85 developing countries. Comparing MFIs in Asia with those in Africa and Latin America, the study found that in the 1990s Asia accounted for the majority of MFIs, whilst Asian MFIs had the highest volume of savings and credit, and served more members than any other continent.

This generalization of course covers up some wide disparities within the region. East Asia is particularly well served by MFIs. The sheer number of members served and the largest distribution of loans and mobilization of savings in terms of GNP is found in Bangladesh, Indonesia, Thailand and Vietnam. In contrast, the two most populated countries in Asia, India and the PRC, have very low outreach, despite a high concentration of the region's poor. Countries such as Afghanistan, Myanmar and Pakistan also have low outreach due to a variety of factors.

Despite these disparities within the region, overall it is said that MFIs have flourished in Asia and that compared to other regions they exhibit good outreach and high repayment rates.[2] Table 7.1 presents data from the *Microbanking Bulletin*, which reports only data on the limited number of MFIs who choose to supply the Bulletin. Those reporting to the Bulletin are thought to be amongst the best and are therefore unlikely to be representative (Meyer, 2002: 14). Nonetheless amongst these, by various measures, Asian MFIs demonstrate relatively good outreach. Asian MFIs account for the largest number of borrowers (70 per cent of whom are women) and are second to African MFIs in terms of number of voluntary savers. In terms of impact, size of loans and deposits are often taken as a simple indicator of impact on the poor. By this criterion Asian MFIs have among the lowest Loan and Savings Balance per Borrower, even after adjusting for GNP per capita, suggesting that they are effectively reaching the poor.

Table 7.1   Outreach indicators by region

	Average loan balance per borrower (US$)	Average saving balance per saver (US$)
Africa	228	105
Asia	195	39
Eastern Europe/ Central Asia	590	n.a.
Latin America	581	741
Middle East/ North Africa	286	n.a.

Source: *Microbanking Bulletin*, Issue no. 9, July 2003.

The institutions that provide micro-finance and the method used to deliver micro-finance products take a variety of forms and we see almost all of these varieties within Asia, whether cooperatives, village banks, and lending to solidarity groups or individuals.

As there can be a variety of lending approaches, a range of institutional models are also found for MFIs. These include unregulated NGOs, credit unions or cooperatives (which are often regulated), registered banking institutions (either banks or non-bank financial institutions) and government organizations. In some cases the institutional forms blur into one another, with government banks operating micro-finance services in collaboration with NGOs or credit cooperatives.

In recent years there has been a significant shift in both thinking and practice in the micro-finance sector with MFIs coming to be seen as providing a range of financial services to the poor, including savings facilities, not just micro-credit. The intellectual argument for this comes from the insight that the poor have a strong need to manage their very limited resources and that various forms of savings play an important role in household budgeting by the poor (Rutherford, 2000). The practical demonstration of this is the shift from the original Grameen model of micro-credit for productive purposes to Grameen Mark II with its emphasis on a range of flexible financial products, including loans of varying repayment periods for consumption as well as investment and a range of short- and longer-term savings accounts (Rutherford, 2003).

In parallel with this reappraisal of micro-finance within the NGO sector has gone a move towards the transformation of NGOs into regulated financial institutions with a view to allowing them to tap non-donor sources of funding and to allow them to offer a wider range of financial services. This trend, which has seen 39 important NGOs (15 in Asia) transformed over the period 1992–2003, places micro-finance squarely within the conventional financial sector and raises important issues of governance and regulation in connection with the new instititions (Fernando, 2003). Given that the failure of commercial financial institutions to reach the poor provided the initial impetus for MFIs, this new trend is paradoxical and raises questions as to whether the initial poverty reduction objectives of the transformed NGOs will be subjugated to commerical criteria (so-called 'mission drift'), although Fernando (2003) argues that as yet there is little evidence of this.

POVERTY AND MICRO-FINANCE

Here we define poverty as an income (or more broadly welfare) level below a socially acceptable minimum, and micro-finance as one of a range of innovative financial arrangements designed to attract the poor as either borrowers or savers. In terms of understanding poverty a simple distinction can be drawn within the group 'the poor' between the long-term or 'chronic poor' and those who temporarily fall into poverty as a result of adverse shocks, the 'transitory poor'. Within the chronic poor one can further distinguish between those who are either so physically or socially disadvantaged that without welfare support they will always remain in poverty (the 'destitute') and the larger group who are poor because of their lack of assets and opportunities. Furthermore within the non-destitute category one may distinguish by the depth of poverty (that is how far households are below the poverty line), with those significantly below it representing the 'core poor', sometimes categorized by the irregularity of their income.

In principle, micro-finance can relate to the chronic (non-destitute) poor and to the transitory poor in different ways. The condition of poverty has been interpreted conventionally as one of lack of access by poor households to the assets necessary for a higher standard of income or welfare, whether assets are thought of as human (access to education), natural (access to land), physical (access to infrastructure), social (access to networks of obligations) or financial (access to credit) (World Bank, 2000: 34). Lack of access to credit is readily understandable in terms of the absence of collateral that the poor can offer conventional financial institutions, in addition to the various complexities and high costs involved in dealing with large numbers of small, often illiterate, borrowers. The poor have thus to rely on loans from either money-lenders at high interest rates or friends and family, whose supply of funds will be limited. Micro-finance institutions attempt to overcome these barriers through innovative measures such as group lending and regular savings schemes, as well as the establishment of close links between poor clients and staff of the institutions concerned. As noted above, the range of possible relationships and the mechanisms employed is very wide.

The case for micro-finance as a mechanism for poverty reduction is simple. If access to credit can be improved, it is argued, the poor can finance productive activities that will allow income growth, provided there are no other binding constraints. This is a route out of poverty for the non-destitute chronic poor. For the transitory poor, who are vulnerable to fluctuations in income that bring them close to or below the poverty line, micro-finance provides the possibility of credit at times of need and in some schemes the opportunity of regular savings by a household itself that can be drawn on. The avoidance of sharp declines in family expenditures by drawing on such credit or savings allows 'consumption smoothing'. In practice this distinction between the needs of the chronic and transitory poor for credit for 'promotional' (that is income creating) and 'protectional' (consumption smoothing) purposes, respectively, is over-simplified since the chronic poor will also have short-term needs that have to be met, whether it is due to income shortfalls or unexpected expenditures like medical bills or social events like weddings or funerals. In fact, it is one of the most interesting generalizations to emerge from the micro-finance and poverty literature that the poorest of the chronic poor (the core poor) will borrow essentially for protectional purposes, given both the low and irregular nature of their income. This group it is suggested will be too risk averse to borrow for promotional measures (that is for investment in the future) and will therefore be only a very limited beneficiary of micro-finance schemes (Hulme and Mosley, 1996: 132).[3]

The view that it is the less badly-off poor who benefit principally from micro-finance has become highly influential and, for example, was repeated in the World Development Report on poverty (World Bank, 2000: 75). Apart from the risk-aversion argument noted above, a number of other explanations for this outcome have been put forward. A related issue refers to the interest rates charged to poor borrowers. Most micro-finance schemes charge close to market-clearing interest rates (although these will often not be enough to ensure full cost-recovery given the high cost per loan of small-scale lending). It may be that, even setting aside the risk-aversion argument, such high rates are unaffordable to the core poor given their lack of complementary inputs; in other words, despite having a smaller amount of capital, marginal returns to the core poor may be lower than for the better-off poor. If the core poor cannot afford high interest rates they will either not take up the service or take it up and get into financial difficulties. Also where group lending is used, the very poor may be excluded by other members of the group, because they are seen as a bad credit risk, jeopardizing the position of the group as a whole. Alternatively, where professional staff operate as loan officers, they may exclude the very poor from borrowing, again on grounds of repayment risk. In combination these factors, it is felt by many, explain the weakness of micro-finance in reaching the core poor.[4]

Even where micro-finance does reach the core poor, when (as in many instances) donor or government funds are required to subsidize the micro-finance institutions involved, it is not inevitably the case that this is an efficient strategy. As funds are fungible within households the use of the loan is not the issue and what matters is the cost of transferring the funds through a micro-credit institution per dollar received by the target group, as compared with the benefit–cost ratio for alternative schemes for reaching the core poor, such as food subsidies, workfare, integrated regional development initiatives and so forth. Such comparisons must take account of not just the administrative costs involved, but also the leakage rate (that is the benefits to the non-poor).

Given the new trends in the sector and their possible effect in diluting the original poverty focus of MFIs the question of their impact on the poor (and particularly the core poor) is clearly of great policy interest. It might be thought that if such instititions are designed to serve only poor clients and if repayment rates are high, no further detailed analysis is needed. Such a view is misleading for a number of reasons. First, there is no guarantee that only the poor will be served unless strong eligibility criteria (like land ownership) are enforced. Often the aim is to dissuade the non-poor by the inconvenience of frequent meetings or the stigma of being a member of a credit group of the poor. Such disincentives may not work, and eligibility criteria where they exist may not be enforced. Second, high repayment rates may be due to social pressure within a group or family and may not reflect the capacity to repay (if for example loans from moneylenders have to be taken out to repay the micro-credit). Third, even if the poor are genuinely served by MFIs as long as public funds are required to finance the MFI there is the issue of how cost-effective this means of reaching the poor is, compared with alternatives. Hence for these sorts of reasons there is a strong case for attempting to assess the impact of such loans on the welfare of the target group.

Nonetheless assessing the true relationship between micro-finance services and poverty reduction is not straightforward. It is not simply a case of looking at a group of borrowers, observing their income change after they took out micro-credits and establishing who has risen above the poverty line. Accurate assessment requires a rigorous test of the counterfactual – that is how income (or whatever measure is used) with micro-credit compares with what it would be without it, with the only difference in both cases being the availability of credit. This requires empirically a control group identical in characteristics to the recipients of credit and engaged in the same productive activities, who have not received credit, and whose income (or other measure) can be traced through time to compare with that of the credit recipients.[5] Furthermore, to allow for changes over time, in principle assessments should allow for the possibility of reversals, with households slipping back below the poverty line if the productive activities financed by the credits are unsustainable. Studies based on a rigorous counterfactual find much smaller gains from micro-finance than simple unadjusted before-and-after type comparisons, which erroneously attribute all gains to micro-credit.

Here we examine some of the recent rigorous studies on the impact of MFIs based on various survey data. We do not report the results of work based on more qualitative or participatory approaches.[6] Table 7.2 summarizes the results of the studies surveyed here.

POVERTY IMPACT

One of the early and most widely cited of the poverty impact studies is Hulme and Mosley (1996). This employed a control group approach looking at the changes in income for households in villages with micro-finance programs and changes for similar households in non-program areas.

Table 7.2 *Micro-finance impact studies*

Study	Coverage (in Asia only)	Methodology	Results
Hulme and Mosley (1996)	Indonesia (BKK, KURK, BRI), India (Regional Rural Banks), Bangladesh (Grameen, BRAC, TRDEP), Sri Lanka (PTCCS)	Borrowers and control samples, before and after.	Growth of incomes of borrowers always exceeds that of control group. Increase in borrowers' income larger for better-off borrowers.
MkNelly et al. (1996)	Thailand (village banks – Credit with Education)	Non-participants in non-program villages used as controls	Positive benefits, but no statistical tests for differences reported.
Khandker (1998)	Bangladesh (Grameen, BRAC)	Double difference comparison between eligible and ineligible households and between program and non-program villages	5 per cent of participant households removed from poverty annually. Additional consumption of 18 taka for every 100 taka of loan taken out by women.
Pitt and Khandker (1998)	Bangladesh (BRAC, BRDB, Grameen Bank)	Double difference estimation between eligible and ineligible households with and without micro-finance programs. Estimations are conducted separately for male and female borrowing.	Positive impact of program participation on total weekly expenditure per capita, women's non-land assets and women's labor supply. Strong effect of female participation in Grameen Bank on schooling of girls. Credit programs can change village attitudes and other village characteristics.
Coleman (1999)	Thailand (village banks)	Double difference comparison between participant and non-participant households and between villages in which program introduced and villages where not yet introduced	No evidence of program impact. Village bank membership no impact on asset or income variables.

Study	Context	Method	Findings
Chen and Snodgrass (2001)	India (SEWA bank)	Control group from same geographic area	Average income increase rose for bank's clients in comparison with control group. Little overall change in incidence of poverty, but substantial movement above and below poverty line.
Coleman (2004)	Thailand (village banks)	Double difference estimation between participants and non-participants and villages with and without micro-finance program	Programs are not reaching the poor as much as they reach relatively wealthy people. Impact is larger on richer committee members rather than on rank-and-file members.
Park and Ren (2001)	China (NGOs, government programs, mixed NGO–government programs)	(i) Probit estimation of participation and eligibility for each type of program; (ii) ordinary least squares and instrumental variable estimation of impact of micro-credit on household income	In NGO and mixed programs the better-off even if eligible (for mixed programs) are excluded from participation. In the government program the better-off are both eligible and more likely to participate. Impact estimation finds evidence of positive impact of micro-credit on income.
Duong and Izumida (2002)	Vietnam (VBA 84 per cent of total lending), VBP, PCFs, commercial banks, public funds)	Tobit estimation of (i) participation in rural credit market; (ii) behavior of lender toward credit-constrained household and (iii) weighted least square estimation for impact on output supply.	Poor have difficulties in accessing credit facilities: livestock and farming land are determinants of household participation; reputation and amount of credit applied for are determinants of credit rationing by lenders. Impact estimation shows positive correlation between credit and output
Kaboski and Townsend (2002)	Thailand (production credit groups, rice banks, women's groups, buffalo banks)	Two-staged least squares test of micro-finance impact on asset growth, probability of reduction in consumption in bad years, probability of becoming moneylender, probability of starting business and probability of changing job. Separate estimation according to type and policies of MFI	Production credit groups and women's groups combined with training and savings have positive impact on asset growth, although rice banks and buffalo banks have negative impacts. Emergency services, training and savings help to smooth responses to income shock. Women's groups help to reduce reliance on moneylenders.

Table 7.2 (continued)

Study	Coverage (in Asia only)	Methodology	Results
Amin et al. (2003)	Bangladesh (Grameen Bank, BRAC, ASA)	1) Non-parametric test of stochastic dominance of average monthly consumption of members and non-members 2) Maximum likelihood test of micro-credit membership on vulnerability, consumption and household characteristics.	Members are poorer than non-members. Programs are more successful at reaching poor, but less successful at reaching vulnerable. Poor vulnerable are effectively excluded from membership.
Gertler et al. (2003)	Indonesia (Bank Rakyat Indonesia, Bank Kredit Desa, commercial banks)	1) Basic consumption-smoothing test on household's ability to perform daily living activities 2) State dependence tests of basic regression (relative male–female earning, physical job, savings) 3) Test of geographical proximity to financial institutions on consumption smoothing	Significantly positive correlation between household's consumption and measure of health. Wealthier households are better insured against illness. Households that live far from financial institutions suffer more from sudden reduction in consumption.

Khandker (2003)	Bangladesh (Grameen Bank, BRAC, BRDB)	1) Fixed effect Tobit estimation of borrowing dependent on land and education endowments of households. 2) Panel data fixed effects, instrumental variable estimation to define long-term impact of micro-finance borrowing on expenditure, non-land assets and moderate and extreme poverty	Households who are poor in landholding and formal education tend to participate more. Micro-finance helps to reduce extreme poverty much more than moderate poverty (18 percentage points as compared with 8.5 percentage points over 7 years). Welfare impact is also positive for all households, including non-participants, as there are spillover effects.
Pitt et al. (2003)	Bangladesh (BRAC, BRDB, Grameen Bank)	Maximum likelihood estimation controlling for endogeneity of individual participation and of the placement of micro-finance programs. Impact variables are health of boys and girls (arm circumference, body mass index and height-for-age)	Significantly positive effect of female credit on height-for-age and arm circumference of both boys and girls. Borrowing by men has either negative or non-significant impact on health of children.

Programs in a number of countries are considered, including the Grameen Bank in Bangladesh and the Bank Rakyat Indonesia (BRI). In general a positive impact is found on borrower incomes of the poor (1988–92) with on average an increase over the control groups ranging from 10–12 per cent in Indonesia, to around 30 per cent in Bangladesh and India (Hulme and Mosley, 1996, Table 8.1). Gains are larger for non-poor borrowers, however, and within the group the poor gains are negatively correlated with income. Despite the breadth of the study and its use of control group techniques, it has been criticized for possible 'placement' bias, whereby micro-finance programs may be drawn to better placed villages, so that part of the advantage relative to the control group may be due to this more favorable location. Further, the quality and accuracy of some of the data, particularly in relation to the representative nature of the control groups, has been questioned (Morduch, 1999: 1600).

Another major early initiative that has provided some of the firmest empirical work involved the surveys conducted in the 1990s by the Bangladesh Institute of Development Studies (BIDS) and the World Bank; these provided the data for several major analyses, such as Pitt and Khandker (1998). Khandker (1998) summarizes a number of different studies conducted in Bangladesh using the 1991/92 survey and focuses on three major micro-finance programs, including the Grameen Bank and the Bangladesh Rural Advancement Committee (BRAC). Methodologically impact is assessed using a double-difference approach between eligible and ineligible households (with holdings of land of more than half an acre making households ineligible) and between program and non-program villages. After controlling for other factors, such as various household characteristics, any remaining difference was attributed to the micro-finance programs. The study draws a number of conclusions, but the main one is that the programs had a positive effect on household consumption, which was significantly greater for female borrowers. On average a loan of 100 taka to a female borrower, after it is repaid, allows a net consumption increase of 18 taka. In terms of poverty impact it is estimated that 5 per cent of participant households are pulled above the poverty line annually.

Khandker (2003) follows up this earlier work by employing panel data. He uses the BIDS–World Bank survey conducted in 1998–99 that traced the same households from the 1991–92 survey.[7] He finds apparently strong and positive results. Whilst borrowing by males appears to have no significant impact on consumption, that by females, who are the dominant client group, does have a positive impact. From this analysis a 100 taka loan to a female client leads to a 10.5 taka increase in consumption (compared with 18 taka in the earlier analysis). Allowing for the impact of higher consumption on poverty gives estimates of poverty impact. It is estimated that due to participation in micro-finance programs, moderate poverty among program participants decreased 8.5 percentage points over the period of seven years, and extreme poverty dropped about 18 points over the same period.[8] He also finds evidence of positive spillovers on non-program participants in the program villages with the impact greater for those in extreme poverty. Poverty for non-participants is found to decline by 1 percentage point due to the programs whilst extreme poverty declines by nearly 5 percentage points. This impact is due solely to female borrowing.

The same data set has also been used to identify health impacts as opposed to income changes. Pitt et al. (2003) find that credit going to females has a large and significant impact in two out of three health measures for children. Male borrowing has no such effect. For example, a 10 per cent increase in credit to females increases the arm circumference of daughters by 6.3 per cent. A 10 per cent increase in female credit on average increases the height of girls by 0.36 cm annually and of boys by 0.50 cm. The relations are stronger for daughters than sons. Hence in Bangladesh micro-credit and improved family health appear to be related.

These results from Bangladesh are strong and positive and probably are the clearest evidence there is that micro-finance is working in the way intended to bring sustained relief from poverty. However, a couple of caveats are in order. First, the accuracy of the original results as presented in Pitt and Khandker (1998) has been disputed on the grounds that the eligibility criteria of low land holdings was not strictly enforced in practice. In a reworking of the results focusing on what are claimed to be more directly comparable households no impact on consumption from participation in a program is found (Morduch, 1999: 1605).[9] Second, in the BIDS–World Bank survey data the 'ultra poor' (defined as those with less than 0.2 acres of land) form nearly 60 per cent of participants and the likelihood of participation is strongly and negatively associated with level of land holding. Nonetheless, how much is borrowed depends principally on the entrepreneurship of households, so that the charge that the risk-averse very poor will benefit proportionately less has not been totally dispelled. Furthermore, the panel data reveal a relatively high drop-out rate of around 30 per cent, indicating that there were problems for many households.

There are examples of many other studies that are either inconclusive or provide less convincing results. Coleman (1999) and MkNelly et al. (1996) both focus on experiences with village banking in Thailand. Coleman (1999) utilizes data on villages that had participated in village bank micro-finance schemes and those control villages that were designated as participants, but had not yet participated. This allows a double difference approach that compares the difference between income for participants and non-participants in program villages with the same difference in the control villages, where the programs were introduced later. From the results here the poverty impact of the schemes appears highly dubious. Months of village bank membership have no impact on any asset or income variables and there is no evidence that village bank loans were directed to productive purposes. The small size of loans implies that they were largely used for consumption, but one of the reasons there is a weak poverty impact is that there was a tendency for wealthier households to choose to join village banks.

Coleman (2004) uses the same survey data but reconsiders the estimation strategy to control for this participation by richer households, who tend to dominate village bank committees. The results of Coleman (2004) indicate that there is substantial difference between ordinary members and committee members of village banks. The impact of micro-credits on ordinary members' well-being is either insignificantly different from zero or negative. On the other hand, the impact of micro-finance programs on committee members' income and wealth is positive, implying a form of program capture by the better-off in the village, even though this group may not be well-off by national standards. A similar result in terms of rationing micro-credit in favor of better-off groups or village bank members is found in Duong and Izumida (2002) in a study of six villages in Vietnam. There household economic position and prestige in a village, plus the amount of credit applied for, are the main determinants of how credit is allocated.

MkNelly et al. (1996) evaluated the Freedom from Hunger credit with education program in Thailand operated through village banks. The results show positive benefits; however although non-participants in non-program villages are used as controls, there are problems in accepting the results. No statistical tests are reported, so one cannot judge whether differences between participants and non-participants are significant. There is also a potential measurement bias since the staff responsible for the program also did the interviewing.

Chen and Snodgrass (2001) examine the operations of the Self Employed Women's Association (SEWA) bank in India providing low-income female clients in the informal sector with both saving and loan services. The study tests for the impact of these services by comparing the bank's clients against a randomly selected control group in a similar geographic area. The two surveys were conducted two years apart. Average incomes rose over time for all groups – borrowers, savers and the control, although the increase was less for the latter. In terms of poverty incidence there was little overall change, although there was substantial 'churning', in that amongst the clients of SEWA there was quite a lot of movement above and below the poverty line. In interpreting these results, Meyer (2002) argues that the evidence on the counterfactual – that is what would have happened to the clients in the absence of the services of SEWA – is not sufficiently strongly established to draw any firm conclusions on poverty impact.

The smoothing of consumption over time to protect the poor against adverse shocks is one of the principal objectives of micro-credit. Using data again for Bangladesh, Amin et al. (2003) compute several measures of vulnerability.[10] They find that the micro-credit participants in the two villages covered are more likely to be below the poverty line than if they had been selected at random, so that the programs have reached the poor. However, the vulnerable are more likely to join a micro-credit program in only one of the two villages. Further, for the vulnerable below the poverty line in one village there is no evidence that they are more likely to be members of a program, and in the other village there is evidence that they have either chosen not to join or are actively excluded, presumably on the grounds that they are a poor credit risk. Hence the very poor and vulnerable do not appear to be reached.

More positive conclusions in terms of the ability of micro-finance to reduce vulnerability are found for Indonesia by Gertler et al. (2003) who find that access to micro-finance helps households smooth consumption in the face of declines in health of adult family members. Having established an empirical relationship between health condition and consumption, the authors test for a relation between access to a financial institution and consumption shortfalls associated with ill health. Using geographic distance as a measure of access they find that for households in an area with a BRI branch, health shocks have no effect on consumption.[11] The study does not differentiate within the group of the poor.

FORMS OF MICRO-CREDIT INTERVENTIONS AND COST-EFFECTIVENESS

It is clear that experimentation and local variation are likely to be important aspects of successful MFIs. A few studies have looked in detail at the impact and cost effectiveness of different forms of intervention. For example, Park and Ren (2001) look at the Chinese experience, drawing on household survey data for 1997. They are able to compare three types of program based on ownership characteristics – NGO-based, mixed programs and government ownership. Whether in terms of conventional financial criteria like repayment rates, or measures of initial impact like targeting effectiveness, the NGO programs appear to function best, with the government-run programs the least successful.

Detailed mechanisms for micro-lending are examined for Thailand by Kaboski and Townsend (2002) who look at different institutional variants such as production credit groups, women's groups, rice banks and buffalo banks, as well as a variety of services including training and various savings facilities. Of the forms of institution, allowing for a range of other factors, women's groups appear to have the largest positive impact on their members. Of the services offered, training in conjunction with credit appears to work well and the availability of savings facilities appears to be associated with asset growth amongst households. Of the savings services regular 'pledged savings' have the largest positive impact on numbers. This is likely to be due to the use of savings as collateral for further loans either from the institution itself or from other sources. However, since the poorest may not be in a position to offer regular savings this also provides an explanation for why they may benefit relatively less from MFIs.[12]

Most studies of the impact of different forms of micro-finance do not conduct a full cost-effectiveness analysis in order to judge both the effectiveness of different alternatives and how micro-finance interventions compare in efficiency terms with other ways of reaching the poor. However, there is often a general expectation that MFIs are an effective and efficient means of reaching the poor. For example, Wright (2000) argues that 'microfinance has a particular advantage over almost (and probably) all other interventions' in providing cost-effective and sustainable services to the poor.

The early work by Khandker (1998) attempts to assess the cost-effectiveness of micro-credit in Bangladesh (that is costs per taka of consumption for the poor) as compared with more formal financial institutions and other poverty-targeted interventions. His data are summarized in Table 7.3. They appear to be based on the assumption of a zero leakage rate to the non-poor. The interesting result that emerges is that the Grameen Bank is considerably more effective than BRAC and that, as expected, loans to female borrowers are considerably more cost-effective than loans to males. Further, subsidies to Grameen (but not to BRAC) appear to be a more cost-effective means of reaching the poor than various food-for-work programs. However a food-for-education scheme appeared very cost-effective relative to the food-for-work programs and to BRAC.[13] Formal financial institutions are less cost-effective than Grameen for both female and male borrowers and less cost-effective than BRAC in some, but not all, cases examined (Khandker, 1998: 134–9). The high figure for BRAC is in part due to the range of services, such as training, offered in addition to micro-credit (see note 4), but nonetheless if such services are essential to the success of micro-credit, the inclusion of their cost in a cost–benefit assessment of micro-credit is legitimate.

It is interesting to note that Khandker does not conclude from this that all subsidies to other poverty interventions should be withdrawn and reallocated to micro-finance. Rather he points out that because participants in micro-credit borrowing self-select (that is they judge that micro-credit suits their particular needs, often for self-employed work) others amongst the poor may not be able to benefit. For this latter group other forms of targeting will still be required.

Table 7.3   Cost effectiveness ratios:[a] Bangladesh early 1990s

Intervention	Female	Male	All borrowers
Grameen Bank	0.91	1.48	
BRAC	3.53	2.59	
Agricultural Development Bank (BKB)[b]			4.88
Agricultural Development Bank (RAKUB)[c]			3.26
Vulnerable Group Development			1.54
Food-for-work (CARE)[d]			2.62
Food-for-work (World Food program)			1.71
Food-for-education[e]			0.94 (1.79)

Notes:
[a]   Ratio of costs to income gains to the poor.
[b]   Bangladesh Krishi Bank.
[c]   Rajshahi Krishi Unnayan Bank.
[d]   Run by CARE on behalf of USAID.
[e]   Source for this data is Wodon (1998); figure in brackets is the cost-effectiveness ratio for the very poor.

Source: Khandker (1998), Tables 7.2 and 7.3 and Wodon (1998).

The above data provide ambiguous support for the idea that micro-finance is a cost-effective means of generating income for the poor. The figures for Grameen support this view, whilst those for BRAC do not. More recently a couple of other estimates are available. Burgess and Pande (2003) examine whether the pattern of commercial bank expansion in India, into rural areas previously not served by banks, has impacted on rural poverty, and their work allows a simple comparison with micro-finance. Their estimates suggest that it costs Rs 2.72 to generate an additional rupee of income for the poor via social banking programs. Compared with the data in Table 7.3 this ratio is higher than the cost-effectiveness ratio for Grameen, but lower than that for BRAC.[14]

A further look at the effectiveness of Grameen is provided by Schreiner (2003), who calculates the subsidy–lending ratio at 0.22 over the period 1983–97. This is not directly equivalent to the ratios in Table 7.3, but assuming the same return to borrowing as in Khandker (1998) these figures can be converted into a broadly equivalent ratio of cost to gains to the poor of 1.15. This is consistent with the figures in Table 7.3 which would need to be averaged to give an overall return to male and female borrowing combined. The result confirms Grameen as a relatively cost-effective form of poverty intervention, although it says nothing about how the benefits from its activities are distributed between the poor, the very poor and those above the poverty line.

CONCLUSIONS

Despite the extensive spread of micro-finance, research studies on the actual impact of MFIs are often more ambivalent about their impact than is the aid community. In part this reflects the methodological problems of establishing appropriate statistical controls and in part no doubt also the range of variation found in practice in the way in which micro-finance operates. Our view is that, despite the difficulties, more good poverty impact studies that address adequately problems of bias in comparisons of borrowers are important to sharpen understanding of its role as an anti-poverty tool, to assess its impact in different environments and to shape the debate on ways forward for MFIs.

Amongst practitioners there is widespread acceptance of the view that it is necessary to both diversify the products of micro-finance and adapt them to local circumstances. Any simple replication of formulae successful elsewhere is rightly treated with suspicion. The evidence surveyed here suggests that the conclusion from the early literature, that whilst micro-finance clearly may have had positive impacts on poverty it is unlikely to be a simple panacea for reaching the core poor, remains broadly valid. Reaching the core poor is difficult and some of the reasons that made them difficult to reach with conventional financial instruments mean that they may also be high risk and therefore unattractive micro-finance clients.

There has been an extensive debate that we do not touch on here, on the financial sustainability of MFIs. We would simply make the point that just because an institution needs a subsidy to cover its costs, this in itself is no reason for not supporting the institution. The issue would be what benefits in terms of income gains for the poor can be achieved with the subsidy and how the ratio of subsidy to benefits compares with that for other interventions. Detailed cost-effectiveness studies are rare, and those that are available show both high and low scores for MFIs in the same country. Hence there is a need to continually improve design and outreach and to see MFIs as part of the package for targeting the poor, rather than the whole solution.

Our view is that despite the difficulties, poverty impact studies of MFIs can provide important information and that continued efforts should be made to sharpen understanding of the impacts of different forms of MFI activity on the poor, including their cost effectiveness.

NOTES

1. An earlier helpful survey is Meyer (2002). This draws out some of the methodological problems in assessing impact, and surveys a number of important studies available at the time of writing (around 2001). Morduch (1999) is an extremely authoritative earlier survey focusing on both conceptual and empirical questions.
2. Lapenu and Zeller (2001: 28) Table 16.
3. Morduch (2003) points out that, although this argument may be true, the data in Hulme and Mosley's book cannot be used to infer this since the arithmetic basis for their comparison of income changes for different categories of borrowers biases their results in favor of their conclusion.
4. An important attempt to address this problem has been the Income Generation for Vulnerable Group Development (IGVGD) program run by BRAC in Bangladesh, which combines measures of livelihood protection (food aid) with measures of livelihood promotion (skills training and micro-credit). Hence micro-credit is provided as part of a package approach. Matin and Hulme (2003) survey the evidence on how far the benefits of this program actually reach the core poor and conclude that although the program was more successful than more conventional micro-credit schemes, none the less many target households were still missed.
5. Coleman (2001) has a useful non-technical explanation of the difficulties of applying this approach and eliminating 'selection' and 'placement' bias in micro-credit studies.
6. See Hulme (1999) for a discussion of different approaches to impact. He points out that despite their cost in funds and time, such rigorous studies involving detailed sample surveys are the most common approach where the aim is to establish impact for policy or investment purposes.
7. Technically the study is rigorous in employing a two-stage instrumental variable approach along with a household fixed-effects method to control for possible endogeneity bias, particularly the fixed unobserved characteristics of households (that is the more entrepreneurial amongst the poor are those who borrow, and these may do better anyway).
8. Poverty is based on a calorie intake of 2112 and extreme poverty on one of 1739.
9. This debate, which in part centers around details of econometric estimation, has not been resolved. An unpublished paper by Pitt reworks the original analysis to address the concerns of Morduch and is said to confirm the original results (Khandker, 2003, footnote 1).
10. Unlike the Khandker studies this data picks up households before they joined a micro-credit scheme. Their vulnerability measure is broader than simply fluctuations in consumption.
11. Patten et al. (2001) find evidence that the micro-finance side of the Indonesian banking system performed much more robustly during the macro crises of the late 1990s than did the commercial banking sector.
12. Fujita (2000) makes this point in the context of Bangladesh.
13. The study on this scheme by Wodon (1998) appears considerably more sophisticated than the other studies and compares costs with the future stream of estimated benefits to the poor in terms of gains from education. The ratio for this activity may not be directly comparable with the other figures in the table.

14. It should be noted that the benefits from Grameen lending found in Khandker (2003), which are almost half of those found in his earlier study, imply considerably higher cost-effectiveness ratios than those reported in Table 7.3, unless there has been a corresponding rise in the efficiency of operations.

BIBLIOGRAPHY

Amin S., A.S. Rai and G. Ropa (2003), 'Does microcredit reach the poor and vulnerable? Evidence from Northern Bangladesh', *Journal of Development Economics*, vol. 70, pp. 59–82.

Burgess, R. and R. Pande (2003), 'Do rural banks matter? Evidence from the Indian social banking experiment', The Suntory Centre, Suntory and Toyota International Centres for Economics and Related Disciplines, Discussion Paper No. DEDPS/40, London School of Economics and Political Science.

Chen, M.A. and D. Snodgrass (2001), *Managing Resources, Activities, and Risk in Urban India: The Impact of SEWA Bank*, Washington DC: AIMS.

Coleman, B.E. (1999), 'The impact of group lending in Northeast Thailand', *Journal of Development Economics*, vol. 60, pp. 105–41.

Coleman, B.E. (2001), 'Measuring impact of microfinance programs', *Finance for the Poor*, Asian Development Bank, December 2001, 2 (4), 5–7.

Coleman, B.E. (2004), 'Microfinance in Northeast Thailand: who benefits and how much?', *World Development* (forthcoming).

Duong, Ph.B. and Y. Izumida (2002), 'Rural development finance in Vietnam: a microeconometric analysis of household surveys', *World Development*, **30** (2), 319–35.

Fernando, N. (2003), 'Transformation of NGOs into Regulated Financial Institutions: expectations fulfilled?', paper presented at ADBI Annual Conference, *Microfinance in Asia: poverty impact and outreach to the poor*, 5 December 2003, Tokyo.

Fujita, K. (2000), 'Credit flowing from the poor to the rich: the financial market and the role of Grameen Bank in rural Bangladesh', *The Developing Economies*, vol. 38, pp. 343–73.

Gertler, P., D.I. Levine and E. Moreti (2003), 'Do microfinance programs help families insure consumption against illness?', University of California, Berkeley, Center for International Development Economics Research (CIDER), Working Paper.

Hulme, D. (1999), 'Impact asssessment methodologies for microfinance: theory, experience and better practice', Finance and Development Research Program, Working Paper no. 1, IDPM, University of Manchester.

Hulme, D. and P. Mosley (1996), *Finance Against Poverty*, Volumes 1 and 2, London: Routledge.

Kaboski, J. and R. Townsend (2002), 'Policies and impact: an analysis of village-level microfinance institutions', mimeo, University of Chicago.

Khandker, S. (1998), *Fighting Poverty with Microcredit: Experience from Bangladesh*, New York: Oxford University Press for the World Bank.

Khandker, S. (2003), 'Micro-finance and poverty: evidence using panel data from Bangladesh', World Bank Policy Research Paper 2945, World Bank, Washington.

Lapenu, C. and M. Zeller (2001), 'Distribution, growth and performance of microfinance institutions in Africa, Asia and Latin America', Food Consumption and Nutrition Division Discussion Paper no. 114, International Food Policy Research Institute, June.

Matin, I. and D. Hulme (2003), 'Programs for the poorest: learning from the IGVGD program in Bangladesh', *World Development*, **31** (3), 647–65.

Meyer, R.L. (2002), 'Track record of financial institutions in assisting the poor in Asia', Asian Development Bank Institute Research Paper 49, ADB Institute, December.

MkNelly, B., C. Watetip, C.A. Lassen and C. Dunford (1996), 'Preliminary evidence that integrated financial and educational services can be effective against hunger and malnutrition', Freedom From Hunger Research Paper no. 2, April.

Morduch, J. (1999), 'The microfinance promise', *Journal of Economic Literature*, vol. XXXVII, December, pp. 1569–614.

Morduch, J. (2003), 'Can the poor pay more? Microfinance and returns to capital in Indonesia', mimeo.

Park, A. and C. Ren (2001), 'Microfinance with Chinese characteristics', *World Development*, **29** (1), 39–62.

Patten, R.H., J.K. Rosengard and D.E. Johnson (2001), 'Microfinance success amidst macro economic failure: the experience of Bank Rakyat Indonesia during the East Asian Crisis', *World Development*, **29** (6), 1057–69.

Pitt, M.M. and S. Khandker (1998), 'The impact of group-based credit programs on poor households in Bangladesh: does the gender of participants matter?', *Journal of Political Economy*, **2**, 958–77.

Pitt, M.M., S.R. Khandker, O.H. Chowdhury and D.L. Millimet (2003), 'Credit programs for the poor and the health status of children in rural Bangladesh', *International Economic Review*, **44** (1), 87–118.

Rutherford, S. (2000), 'Money talks: conversations with poor households in Bangladesh about managing money', at IDPM website www.man.ac.uk/idpm.

Rutherford, S. (2003), 'Microfinance's evolving ideals: how they were formed and why they're changing', paper presented at ADBI Annual Conference, *Microfinance in Asia: poverty impact and outreach to the poor*, 5 December 2003, Tokyo.

Schreiner, M. (2003), 'A cost-effectiveness analysis of the Grameen Bank of Bangladesh', *Development Policy Review*, **21** (3), 357–82.

Wodon, Q.T. (1998), 'Cost–benefit analysis of Food for Education in Bangladesh', background paper for the poverty assessment of Bangladesh at the World Bank, mimeo, World Bank, April.

World Bank (2000), *World Development Report 2000/01: Attacking Poverty*, Washington: World Bank.

Wright, G.A.N. (2000), *Microfinance Systems. Designing Quality Financial Services for the Poor*, Dhaka, Bangladesh: The University Press Limited.

Zeller, M. and R.L. Meyer (eds) (2002), *The Triangle of Microfinance: Financial Sustainability, Outreach and Impact*, Baltimore: Johns Hopkins for the International Food Policy Research Institute.

Index